PORTRAITS
AND
MINIATURES

Discover books by Roy Jenkins published by
Bloomsbury Reader at
www.bloomsbury.com/RoyJenkins

Baldwin
Dilke
European Diary, 1977–1981
Mr. Balfour's Poodle
Portraits & Miniatures
Truman

PORTRAITS
AND
MINIATURES

ROY JENKINS

BLOOMSBURY READER
LONDON · NEW DELHI · NEW YORK · SYDNEY

This edition published in 2012 by Bloomsbury Reader

Bloomsbury Reader is a division of Bloomsbury Publishing Plc,

50 Bedford Square, London WC1B 3DP

First published 1993 by Macmillan London Limited

ISBN: 978 1 4482 0321 5
eISBN: 978 1 4482 0288 1

Visit www.bloomsburyreader.com to find out more about our authors and their books
You will find extracts, author interviews, author events and you can sign up for
newsletters to be the first to hear about our latest releases and special offers

Contents

Introduction

The core of this book is formed by the six medium-length portraits, three British and three foreign, with which it opens. They were conceived as a sequel to a somewhat larger and longer group of profiles which I wrote twenty years ago for three-part publication in *The Times* and which subsequently constituted a 1974 book entitled *Nine Men of Power*.

The nine I chose then were Ernest Bevin, Maynard Keynes, Stafford Cripps, Edward Halifax, Hugh Gaitskell, Léon Blum, Adlai Stevenson, Robert Kennedy, and Senator (Joe the bad rather than Eugene the good) McCarthy. McCarthy was the black joker in the pack, for he was the only one of the nine for whom I did not have considerable respect and/or sympathy. For him I had none, but I did not think that this mattered in the case of one limited length essay, although I would regard it as depressing, almost corrupting, to spend several years of one's life writing a full book about someone for whom it was possible to feel no empathy.

This time there is no black joker. The three British politicians I chose as front-rank figures about whom I had never written anything substantial before. From Bevan I had been divided during the last ten years of his life by Labour Party tribal disputes, but in retrospect wished that I had known him better and felt that I ought now to be able to look at him free of these old prejudices. In Macleod's case too my judgement of him at the end of his life, although not I think earlier or subsequently, had been clouded by the fact that he was my 'shadow' when I was Chancellor of the Exchequer, and one who was made unusually partisan by a combination of pain and impatience, feeling that office was the only worthwhile experience in politics and that time was running out for him. There was no comparable difficulty with Butler. I had always liked and been amused by him since 1949 when I first came to know him. I might have doubted whether he had the cold steel which is mostly necessary to become Prime Minister, but I found it easy to sympathize with this deficiency.

Adenauer and de Gaulle were obviously the two dominant leaders of continental Europe in the twenty years after the war. The question was whether they were not exhausted seams to mine. In the case of Adenauer in particular, however, any such hesitations soon disappeared. Except for German specialists the history of the early years of the Federal Republic has become unfamiliar to a British audience, and this applies still more strongly to Adenauer's Weimar Republic activities and wartime experiences. Even with de Gaulle there is a considerable fog of forgetfulness over anything before the beginning of the Fifth Republic in 1959 and much opportunity, particularly following the English publication of Lacouture's biography, for reappraisal even after that. Acheson was sharp about Britain's post-imperial lack of direction (a deficiency we have hardly repaired thirty-five years after he made his 'not found a role' remark), but as first Under-Secretary and then Secretary of State under Truman he had done more than anyone else to make effective Ernest Bevin's central foreign policy aim for getting America firmly committed to European security and prosperity. He was also an interesting example of the species of East Coast pro-consular gentlemen, now nearly extinct, who ran American foreign policy in the plenitude of their country's power.

Next there are two essays which started life as full-length lectures. The first is on Cardinal John Henry Newman and his 1852 Dublin discourses which became a book under the title of *The Idea of a University*, one of the most resonant of all nineteenth-century titles. This was part of a series of six Oxford 1990 lectures to mark the centenary of Newman's death, and was delivered in the Examination Schools of the University with which he is indelibly associated despite the fact that he never saw it (except from the Birmingham to London train) between 1846 and 1877. My difficulty here was that all the other five lecturers were considerable Newman experts, whereas I started almost from scratch. Newman, however, was such a star, still more dazzling than pious in my view, that he easily drew me into an enthusiastic attempt to repair my deficiency.

The second of these lecture/essays, first prepared for the Institute of Contemporary History, was a comparison between the styles of government of four long-serving twentieth-century Prime Ministers, Asquith, Baldwin, Attlee and Lady Thatcher. Of the first three of this quartet I had, at roughly twenty-year intervals, written biographies.

The next section contains twelve pieces which are not about individuals. Two of these also began as lectures. *An Oxford View of Cambridge* for my 1988 Rede Lecture foray into the Cambridge Senate House. *Glasgow Amongst the Cities of the World*, an encomium prepared for that Scottish metropolis's 1990 year as European City of Culture. This however was well after I ceased to seek the franchise of its citizens and should therefore be interpreted as a true tribute rather than as vote-seeking flattery.

Amongst the others in this section are an introduction to the Trollope Society's 'edition of one of its eponym's late political novels, a historical review of *The Times*, its proprietors, editors and policies, written for its bi-centenary; a socio-architectural view of Pall Mall clubs based on anniversary speeches made at two of them; and a couple of frivolous pieces about wine and croquet. There is also a piece, first given as a speech at the Library of Congress in Washington, about the decline of historical knowledge amongst politicians, and an appraisal of whether this matters.

In the third section there are twenty-two 'miniatures', based mostly on *Observer* book reviews (although with a few from other stables) of recently published biographies or autobiographies. Seven of these are of more or less contemporary British politicians, and five of their dead predecessors. But there is also a clutch of reviews (done appropriately for *The European)* of Paris-published books, a category which is now little noticed in England – less so I think than sixty or so years ago – about dead or living Frenchmen: Guizot, Giscard, Mitterrand and J. J. Servan-Schreiber. Sakharov, G. M. Trevelyan, Garret FitzGerald and John Kenneth Galbraith (this an eightieth-birthday speech rather than a review) also appear, as do two sharply contrasting moulders of sharply contrasting newspapers, Beaverbrook and David Astor.

Apart from the six long opening essays, written as in 1971–4 for *The Times*, I cannot claim that there are great sinews of logic in the choice. What is consistent, however, is that all the subjects considerably interested me at the time I wrote about them, and continue so to do. And that this, while it is not a guarantee of interesting others, is at least a necessary qualification for hoping to do so.

Roy Jenkins

East Hendred
December 1992

R. A. Butler

Although miles away from being 'a great man' in the sense epitomized by the inner certainties of a General de Gaulle, Rab Butler was in many ways the most intriguing British political personality of those born since 1900. This stems from his ambiguity of character, from the paradoxes of his career and style, and from the fact that he was a richly comic figure, around whom anecdotes and aphorisms clustered, who was also capable of being extremely and intentionally funny himself.

He was most famous for not becoming Prime Minister. There have been other renowned 'near-misses' – Austen Chamberlain, George Nathaniel Curzon, even Hugh Gaitskell – but no one quite rivalled Rab in making a *métier* out of being pipped at the post. He is also credited (semi-apocryphally) with sustaining Anthony Eden, one of the seven heads of government under whom he served, with an unforgettable declaration of support: 'He is the best Prime Minister we have.' This phrase, which rang around the political world, neatly illustrated nearly all the attributes possessed by Butler and previously described. But it missed out one, which was his gift for quiet constructive statesmanship. By his Education Act of 1944, at once boldly conceived and

1

skilfully engineered, his deft tenure of the Exchequer in the early 1950s, and his frequent provision of the administrative cement which held disintegrating governments together, he showed himself a great public servant, with, for most of his career, some streaks of vision as well.

Amongst his paradoxes were his devotion to public life without the steel of ultimate ambition; his assuming the mantle of a deep-rooted Essex man, while representing in Conservative politics the antithesis of the values which have now come to be associated with that maligned county; and of becoming in some ways a grander grandee than Macmillan, because a less self-conscious one, without having a drop of non-bourgeois blood in his veins.

As a very young man Butler had been for a year a teaching fellow of Corpus Christi College, Cambridge, but from his resignation there following his marriage into Courtauld wealth in 1926 until his forty-year-later somewhat weary return to Cambridge, this time to the splendour of the Master's Lodge at Trinity, his attention never flickered away from the bright light of politics, and above all from the politics of office. He was in the House of Commons for thirty-six years and for no less than twenty-six of them in a government of one sort or another. He was the quintessential front bench insider politician. He once (in 1949) said to me with typically feline indiscretion: 'The trouble with Anthony [Eden] is that he has no intellectual interests.' Rab liked some non-political moorings such as his presidency of the Royal Society of Literature or the possession of his father-in-law's fine collection of French Impressionist paintings, but it never seriously occurred to him to make a life away from politics or even away from office. His career went through a lot of fluctuations, and he suffered many indignities at the hands of both Eden and Macmillan. But he never responded to them by deciding he had had enough, or even with the serious threat of resignation. It was always better to be in than out.

His marriage gave him not only his wealth but his Essex roots. Samuel Courtauld settled £5000 a year tax free upon him, which was a very considerable income in 1926. He also subsequently gave him Stanstead Hall, a substantial north Essex country mansion, into which he moved in 1934. On top of this he left him Gatcombe Park in Gloucestershire, which Butler eventually sold to the royal family as a residence for Princess Anne, as well as a life interest in the pictures, with the residue of his fortune going to Sydney Butler, Rab's first wife until her death in 1954 and Courtauld's only child. The nomination to the Saffron Walden Conservative candidature, which Rab secured at the age of twenty-four and which gave him a secure constituency for four decades, although its safeness never prevented him cultivating it with skill and assiduity, also came through the Courtauld connection. And when he married again in 1959, as the result of a fine middle-aged romance about which his widow has written with a moving vividness, it was to another Courtauld, this time by marriage, who lived in another, although smaller, Essex country house in which he eventually finished his days.

With Stanstead Hall, a substantial Westminster house in Smith Square and plenty of money to keep up both of them he lived in pre-war days on a scale that was lavish without being flamboyant. In 1935 he achieved the accolade of being host at Stanstead to a great Conservative fête with all the Essex MPs except for Churchill on the platform and Stanley Baldwin as the principal speaker and his guest for the weekend. Butler's cup was made more overflowing by the fact that Baldwin, whom he insisted to the end of his life was the one of his seven Prime

Ministers to whom he felt closest, assured him at the railway station on departure that his squirearchal way of life would underpin his political balance and future.

Rab's later grandeur, however, came to be based much more on his idiosyncratic indifference to appearance or discretion than to the affluence of his way of life. Mollie Butler (his second wife) described him as having an inherent distinction of appearance because he was *tiré à quatre épingles*. About the inherent distinction I agree, while regarding the use of that French phrase, which I think can best be translated as 'in band box condition', as clear evidence of the blindness of love. Rab could look a notable, even a superior figure with his cheeks half-shaven and with dandruff spilling on the shoulders of a shabby suit, but what he certainly could not do, for at least the last twenty years of his life, was win a competition for glossiness. He looked more like the Lord Derby of the 1870s, whom Sir Charles Dilke at first mistook for a tramp when he unexpectedly met him in a Surrey country lane, than like, shall we say, Lord (Cecil) Parkinson.

I find more convincing shafts of illumination in two anecdotes about Rab's year as Foreign Secretary, the last act of his twenty-six-year tour of half the departments of Whitehall. Sir Nicholas Henderson, his principal private secretary for this final phase, noticed on a foreign tour that Rab was wearing his none-too-spotless dinner-jacket trousers at breakfast, although with an ordinary coat above them. He hesitantly drew attention to this possible absent-mindedness but was assured by the Secretary of State that it was intentional and due to the downy wisdom he had acquired over many years. 'I generally find it a wise precaution,' he said. 'You never know abroad how much time you have to spare before dinner.'

The second relates to an attempt by Lyndon Johnson half to

bully and half to pour obloquy on Rab's head. The British Government were irritating Washington by permitting the sale of Leyland buses to Cuba. Butler, paying a pre-arranged White House visit, was harangued by Johnson, who thought he could strengthen his point by pulling out a wad of dollar bills, fingering them derisively as though he might be about to toss them at Rab, and suggesting needlingly that if Britain was too hard up to behave as a proper member of the Western Alliance she should none the less cancel the contract and send the bill for compensation to LBJ's Texas estate office. The culprit was intended to slink out in shame, with head bowed and his tail between his legs. No doubt Rab did leave with his head bowed, for that was its habitual posture. But so far from ingesting shame he regaled many a dinner party for months to come with accounts of the President's extraordinary mixture of menace, vulgarity and naïveté, chortling and gurgling with pleasure as he further embellished each attempt to make him feel humiliated.

Yet in this cultural clash, while Butler represented the forces of urbane civilized superiority and Johnson the raw brashness of the insecure *arriviste,* it was also the case that Rab was the natural servant of the state and LBJ the natural ruler. The Texan who clawed his way into the US Senate and then to the vice-presidency which became the presidency would never have let power slip three times through his hands in the way that Rab did.

Butler's provenance was half academic and half Indian public service. His father was in India for thirty-seven years, ending as Governor of the Central Provinces, before coming back first as Lieutenant-Governor of the Isle of Man and then as Master of Pembroke College, Cambridge. But his great-uncle, Henry Montagu Butler, had been a dominating headmaster of Harrow and then Master of Trinity (in both of which institutions he

5

ironically succeeded in flattening the intellectual enthusiasm of Rab's hero Stanley Baldwin) from 1859 to 1918. Rab's mother was a Miss Smith of Edinburgh, whose father had been editor of the Calcutta *Statesman* and one of whose brothers was Principal of Aberdeen University as well as a Moderator of the Church of Scotland, while another had been private secretary to the Viceroy. There was a hint of eighteenth-century Cornish parliamentary gentry in his father's family, but the aristocratic influence was minimal, although the top of the upper-middle-class status was assured and constant. Rab's father and three of his brothers became knights, although only the least academically regarded one made any money. Wealth was indeed a somewhat alien concept, and Sir Montagu Butler was distinctly shocked by the amount of money that Sam Courtauld settled on Rab. Although this separated him from the lifestyle of his parents and other forebears, making him at once broad-acred and more metropolitan, as well as less at home in the comfortable villas of the Cambridge academic clans, he remained a dutiful and affectionate son. I would guess he remained closer to similar parents than Maynard Keynes had done twenty years earlier.

As a young Member of Parliament Butler pursued a course of great party rectitude. Almost his first action to attract any public notice was a May 1930 anti-Harold Macmillan letter to *The Times,* of which he was the author, but for which he organized three other MP signatories as well as himself. Oswald Mosley had just resigned from the Labour Government and issued a manifesto of economic and constitutional innovation against the hidebound complacency which seemed to be the approach of both the main parties to unemployment and other evils. It was the beginning of the road that was to lead Mosley to the British Union of Fascists, but this was at first by no means the obvious direction, and many respectable people, from Harold Nicolson to Aneurin Bevan, were attracted by his ideas. So was Macmillan, who had written to *The Times* supporting Mosley's call for a change in the rules of politics. '… if these [existing] rules are to be permanently enforced, perhaps a good many of us will feel it is hardly worth bothering to play at all', Macmillan rather rashly wrote. The Butler-drafted reply was intended both as a put-down and as a warning off the grass, and from the point of view of party orthodoxy was neatly done: 'When a player starts complaining "that it is hardly worth bothering to play" the game at all it is usually the player, and not the game, who is at fault. It is then usually advisable for the player to seek a new field for his recreation and a pastime more suited to his talents.' Macmillan stood rebuked by the prefects, who no doubt hoped the head-master would be pleased, for lack of proper school spirit.

This was odd, for Butler had incomparably less of 'school spirit' about him than did Macmillan. He was too irreverent for that. He was no good at games (although quite a good shot) because of an arm permanently damaged in a childhood Indian riding accident, and he did not much like Marlborough, where he was sent after failing to get an Eton scholarship. He was born two years too late for the World War I army. He showed no particular affection for either of the two middle-grade Cambridge colleges (Pembroke and Corpus) of which he was a member, and although he warmed much more to Trinity in later life this was on the basis of a worldly old Master enjoying a success in a new field rather than of an enthusiastic college loyalist.

Macmillan, on the other hand, was full of *schwärmerei* for the institutions with which he was associated. He loved Summer Fields, Eton, Balliol and the Grenadier Guards. So this early Butler-Macmillan dispute was fought with each occupying paradoxical terrain. It may none the less have cast its shadow on to future relations.

It was, however, successful at commending Butler to the headmaster and the other beaks. In September 1931 on the formation of the National Government he became parliamentary private secretary to Samuel Hoare, the Secretary of State for India, and then, a year later and still under thirty, he was promoted to be parliamentary under-secretary and a full member of the Government. It was a considerable opportunity because it meant that for the next three years he was concerned with the preparation for and the steering through the House of Commons of the Government of India Act, which within the Conservative Party provided the central battlefront of politics throughout the period. Butler profited from Hoare's patronage and served him well. But he accumulated no affection for him, wrote many years later of his lack of humanity as a departmental chief, and treated his 1935 downfall as Foreign Secretary, first at the Quai d'Orsay in the wily hands of Pierre Laval and then on the ice in Switzerland, with the deadpan dismissiveness that became one of the characteristics of Rab's style.

While Butler was serving the unloved Hoare he clashed directly with the unreconstructed Churchill, who until 1935 devoted more effort to frustrating the India Bill than to denouncing the dictators. Not only did Rab have to refute a whole series of Churchill-inspired amendments, he also found himself trying to organize against Churchill's position in the press and in the constituency parties. He then compounded his sin by progressing via an uneasy nine months at the Ministry of Labour to becoming parliamentary under-secretary at the Foreign Office in February 1938, and as such the principal Commons spokesman for appeasement during the last eighteen months of the peace. When Eden and Cranborne (later Salisbury) resigned, Halifax became Foreign Secretary and Butler moved into Cranborne's junior job. But it was more important and more exposed than is that job now. First, he was the sole Foreign Office junior minister, as against today's five. Second, he had the Commons to himself, subject to a great deal of Chamberlain supervision. He had the advantages and disadvantages of becoming almost the Prime Minister's parliamentary adjutant, with one foot in the Foreign Office and the other across the road in 10 Downing Street.

In all these circumstances he built up remarkably little resentment in Churchill. His subsequent relations with him were obviously (in retrospect although by no means necessarily in advance) to turn out to be much more important than with Baldwin, for whom his affection was real and personal, or with Chamberlain whom he served so faithfully in the appeasement years, and to whom, in the company of Alec Home, Chips Channon and Jock Colville (whose presence as the future chronicler of the life of St Winston renders the occasion almost respectable), he drank a toast, *on May 10th* 1940, as 'the King [already just] over the water'. Churchill, who was by no means always magnanimous even in victory and very rarely so in defeat, had paid Rab a high tribute for his parliamentary skill at the end of the India Bill struggles in 1935, and had markedly failed to extend this to Hoare. And in 1940 he first kept him in the new coalition government with the elliptical tribute that he 'could go on with [his] delicate manner of answering parliamentary questions without giving anything away', and then refrained from sacking him when, at the time of the fall of France, Butler engaged in a highly indiscreet 'peace feeler' conversation with the head of the Swedish Legation in London.

9

This latter restraint may have been because no one knew better than Churchill, following the two days of War Cabinet discussion on 27 and 28 May 1940, that the under-secretary's desire for a negotiated peace was exceeded by that of his ministerial chief, and that to have got rid of Butler while leaving Halifax immune would have been a classic example of shooting the monkey rather than the organ grinder. But it probably owed at least as much to a somewhat mocking affection Churchill was developing for Rab. In *The Art of the Possible* Butler gives a memorable description of being bidden to 'dine and sleep' at Chequers in March 1943. At mid-morning the next day he was summoned to the bedroom where Churchill lay smoking a cigar and stroking a black cat, although working hard at the same time. Rab was asked to assent to the proposition that the cat did more for the war effort than did he (then Minister of Education), for it provided Churchill with a hot-water bottle and saved fuel and power. Rab delicately declined to agree but said that it was a very beautiful cat, which seemed to please Churchill.

There may have been more symbolism in the occasion than Rab realized. I think Churchill felt towards him rather as he did towards the cat. He was aware that Butler regarded him with detachment, but found Rab useful, up to a point elegant, capable both of being stroked and pushed off the bed when he was fed up with him, and in a sense easy because he was so utterly unlike himself. He appointed Butler President of the Board of Education (as it was then called) because he thought he deserved promotion (he had been a parliamentary under-secretary for nine years), wanted him out of the Foreign Office, and believed he would keep quiet a sector of the home front that bored Churchill. The last thing the Prime Minister wanted was a major and controversial measure of educational reform.

Rab's tactical skill was to see that he could make such a measure major only if he could also negotiate it out of controversy. To his ultimately successful progress to this end there were considerable setbacks. One was when the Cardinal Archbishop of Westminster wrote to *The Time* a letter which combined (a by no means impossible feat) a highly conservative approach with a skilful appeal to Labour sympathy. Churchill is alleged to have cut it out and sent it to Rab with the scribbled message: 'There you are, fixed, old cock.' The tone, bantering, friendly, half dismissive but without total assurance that the aim would be achieved, almost perfectly captured Churchill's attitude to Butler. Its authenticity is, however, in doubt for there was no record of it except in Rab's memory, and no one was more addicted than Rab to making up stories at least superficially hostile to himself, in which the punchline owed more to verisimilitude than to fact.

The important practical outcome, however, was that Butler got his Education Act, which was so well prepared that it lasted with credit for nearly half a century, was sufficient of a personal achievement for it rightly and unusually to be commonly referred to by his name, and that Churchill subsequently continued, half reluctantly, to give him great opportunities. This was so when he allowed him to reform Conservative Party policy after 1945 (which resulted in Butler and Lord Woolton, who was similarly engaged in reforming the Conservative Party machine, becoming mortal enemies), and it was still more strikingly so when he gave him the Chancellorship of the Exchequer in 1951. Churchill did not then say 'I want you to be Chancellor.' Instead he showed him a list with his name against the office, and when Rab expressed pleased surprise said, 'Anthony and I think it had better be you.' And then, lest there should be any gilt still clinging to the gingerbread, he gave him about the lowest rank in the Cabinet (number five below two peers and the Foreign and Home Secretaries) that it has recently been possible to allot to a Chancellor, more seriously tried to give him an overlord in the shape of the portentous Sir John Anderson, and in fact gave him an 'underlord' in the shape of Sir Arthur Salter whom he described as 'the best economist since Jesus Christ', but who happily from Rab's point of view proved totally ineffective as a minister.

None of this, however, could detract from the central reality that Churchill gave Rab the unmatched opportunity of the Treasury at a time of superficial difficulty but of great underlying potential, and that Rab at the age of forty-eight had the verve and the dexterity fully to seize it. The result was his golden period from 1952 to 1954 and the consequence that when, in the summer of 1953, there occurred the greatest vacuum ever known at the top of a British government he was at the plenitude of his powers. In June of that year, when Eden, the heir apparent, was in a New England clinic and incapacitated for six months, and Churchill, the seventy-eight-year-old Prime Minister, had a major stroke, Butler ran the government for three months, including presiding over sixteen successive Cabinet meetings. He was irreplaceable. Even Macmillan, not then a serious rival but soon to be one, retired to hospital for most of July. Although it was gently exercised, Rab's power was temporarily immense. He had no rival, and the swirl of opinion in his favour was considerable.

This was the moment when, more even than in 1957 when he was passed over for Macmillan or in 1963 when he accepted the same fate at the hands of the much less formidable Alec Home, had he possessed the steely will for power of a Lloyd George or a Mrs Thatcher, he would have insisted that he could no longer accept the responsibility of running the government without the perquisites of being Prime Minister. He would have met with resistance, both from those who hoped, against what at first seemed to be overwhelming odds, for a Churchill recovery and from those who wanted to keep the succession open for Eden. Salisbury and Woolton, a formidable alliance of Church and trade, would have been dedicated opponents. There was indeed some hatching of a constitutionally improper plot to make Salisbury an interim Prime Minister until Eden returned to his inheritance like Richard Cœur de Lion back from the Crusades.

None the less, had he had ruthlessness in him, Butler could have blown the charade away, for he had one deadly weapon. He merely had to refuse to be a party to the deceit of the British public involved in pretending that Churchill was much less ill than he was. Butler had two emperors without any clothes between him and the premiership: one in his pyjamas at Chartwell and the other in a surgical shift in Boston. He merely had to point out how relatively naked they each were for the position of both of them to become untenable. From a mixture of decency and weakness I doubt if he was within miles of doing so. But once he had omitted to do so he had become an intendant and not an animator. After 1953, the events of 1957 and 1963 were in the stars, particularly as Rab was never again as buoyant or powerful as he had been at the middle point of his Chancellorship.

In December 1954 his first wife died, having been fluctuatingly ill for more than a year. In 1955 he besmirched his brilliant Treasury record by introducing an electioneering budget in the spring (although there is no evidence that it was either necessary or effective from this point of view) and then retracting it in the autumn. The Eden Government, so disastrous for its chief, was also uncomfortable for Rab. But he and the Prime Minister did not even have the solace of being linked together like brothers. On the contrary, Eden took advantage of Rab's weakness after his humiliating autumn budget of 1955 to ease him out of the Treasury (in favour of Macmillan) without giving him the Foreign Office, where he wanted a junior and compliant incumbent in the shape of Selwyn Lloyd. Rab accepted the non-job of Leader of the House of Commons and, even more surprisingly, a compensating invitation to spend Christmas at Chequers. That feast having passed without recorded horrors, he retaliated with 'the best Prime Minister we have' in January and with a classic 'anxious to wound but afraid to strike' performance throughout the summer and autumn of the Suez imbroglio.

In fact Rab's Suez ambiguity did more harm to himself than to Eden (who needed no assistance in self-destruction at that stage), and even an affectionate admirer like myself cannot excuse his complete failure to stand up to Eden in his crucial one-to-one interview with him on 18 October, accompanied by his constant mutterings of semi-detachment. Butler's sins in that ghastly three months when every leading member of the British Government covered himself with discredit were less than those of Macmillan whose militancy (and misjudgement of Eisenhower) on the eve of the battle was only matched by his determination to run away as soon as the bombardment (of sterling) began. Yet Macmillan kept a constituency, whereas Butler, despite the competence, even the brilliance, of his clearing up of the mess once defeat was obvious and Eden had retired hurt to the West Indies, alienated almost everybody. The meeting of the 1922 Committee on 22 November at which he and Macmillan jointly appeared had about it an almost allegorical quality that should

14

be enshrined in a tapestry or painting in the room in which the meeting took place. Butler gave a pedestrian account of the hard work he had done in retreat from Eden's rashness. Macmillan, who was only there because Butler unwisely thought that maybe he should be accompanied, gave one of the great virtuoso performances of his life. Every stop was pulled out. The retreat was still the reality, but it was conducted under a thunderous barrage of patriotic braggadocio.

When Eden resigned seven weeks later Butler was still the favourite in the predictions of the press. But in the Cabinet, where the effective decision was made, and with Churchill, who was called in for consultation by the monarch, Macmillan was given the edge. Butler's support was varyingly estimated at between one and three of his Cabinet colleagues as against the *circa* fifteen who plumped for Macmillan. Whether he would have done better amongst the junior ministers and Tory back-benchers is uncertain. In any event they were not asked, and Rab began six and a quarter years of being Macmillan's facto-tum, a major-domo, even a chamberlain, rather than a butler, although eponymy made it inevitable that he was often cartooned as precisely that. He had an independent fame in the country and commanded considerable reserves of faintly amused affec-tion. He never attempted to modify his style to suit Macmillan's, or to echo his words, or to pretend to a warmth towards him that he did not feel. Butler was none the less Macmillan's deputy, depended upon to 'run the government' (his old Martha-like skill) during Macmillan's fairly long and frequent absences abroad.

Despite this dependence, Macmillan often treated Butler with a surprising lack of consideration. He refused to give him the Foreign Office at the beginning of the government, on the some-what specious ground that Selwyn Lloyd had to be kept there because a second head on a charger (the first being Eden's) would be too much of a repudiation of Suez. So Rab had to make do with the Home Office, where, however, he became considerably and constructively engrossed. To this was added the leadership of the House of Commons, in which post his capacity for elliptical and non-partisan ambiguity brought him great success, particularly with the Opposition. Two and a half years later, after the victorious election of 1959, Macmillan, rather like a cricket captain piling sweaters upon a patient umpire, added the chairman ship of the Conservative Party, which required too much enthusiasm and partisanship to be Rab's natural habitat. Then, in the summer of 1960, when he moved Selwyn Lloyd to the Treasury, he again passed over Rab's claims to the Foreign Office, preferring Alec Home despite his then being a peer, and making Rab the derisory counter-offer of succeeding Home as Commonwealth Secretary.

Even Rab could not accept that, and so he continued for another year with his three top-heavy home front jobs, until in the long recess of 1961 Macmillan simply stripped him of two of them in order to provide for Iain Macleod a route out of the Colonial Office where he was causing too much internal Conservative Party disruption. Then, after another six months, Macmillan persuaded Butler to accept responsibility for disman-tling the ill-fated Central African Federation, while retaining the Home Office across an uncomfortable gulf of 4000 miles. Finally, as a result of the disastrous day of the long knives of 12 July 1962, Rab lost the Home Office and was left for the last year of the Macmillan Government with a potentially poisoned chalice in Africa (out of which, however, he skilfully sucked most of the poison) and the meaningless title of First Secretary of State at home. It is difficult to contest Anthony Howard's conclusion that by 1962 Butler had become for Macmillan 'a trout that he could tickle and play with at will'.

In these circumstances Butler approached his third and last Prime Ministerial opportunity. He may have been a little *réchauffé*, but he was not old, only just over sixty, younger than Churchill, Attlee, Macmillan and Callaghan when they succeeded, and the same age, within a few months, as his vanquisher, Home. In some ways his position was stronger than in 1957, for in 1963 he had no Suez record of equivocation immediately behind him, he had much weaker opposition, and he had in the mean time acquired a splendid wife who had the buoyant determination which Rab himself lacked. 'I vowed privately never to speak to Harold Macmillan again,' she wrote simply and starkly after the 1963 débâcle. Moreover, she translated her private vow into public action. Débâcle it none the less was. I understand Rab's position perfectly. He could have blocked Alec Home and become the only possible Prime Minister. He would have had to force himself in. He did not want to do so. He did not have a vast vanity that demanded he should be acclaimed with trumpets and fanfares. But he did want to be freely accepted. That he could not achieve, so he preferred the course of submission with many regretful backward looks and much need for reassurance that he had behaved well.

From there the road led on to the Foreign Office, which might have excited him in 1955 but which merely wearied him in 1963, to the refusal of an earldom from Home in October 1964 and the acceptance of a life barony from Wilson in January 1965 (a very Rab touch this, half disdainful throwaway and half unfortunate cock-up), thirteen years of hesitant spring and glorious autumn as Master of Trinity, followed by three and a half years of declining health, death on Budget day 1982, and a memorial service in Westminster Abbey with the Government reeling at the beginning of the Falklands crisis. Even at the end Rab could not be far from the epicentre of politics. Maybe he was the best Prime Minister we never had. Certainly he was the most ambivalently fascinating of the nearly men.

Aneurin Bevan

When Bevan died in the summer of 1960, aged only sixty-two and after six months of cruel illness, he had already become something of a national hero. Conservatives who throughout his active career had portrayed him as a symbol of destructive evil, a compounded mixture of Tony Benn and Arthur Scargill at the height of their powers, members of the Labour right who had spent most of the previous decade in implacable battle with him, and even his own old allies and friends who had been dismayed and affronted by his 1957 endorsement of the British H-bomb, were united in their affection and respect.

This final wave of feeling has had the paradoxical affect of leaving an opaque film over his memory. Neither Ernest Bevin nor Stafford Cripps who had died a decade before him, the latter at almost exactly the same age, was mourned as Bevan was, but both have left a more sharply defined imprint upon the recollection of the informed public, Bevin for brutal but constructive working-class statesmanship, Cripps for an ascetic, almost Robespierrian moral authority.

Yet much more than either is Bevan enshrined in the small

pantheon of Labour heroes. Although the Labour Party has been less ruthless in disposing of its failing leaders than has the Conservative Party, it has also been more reluctant to award them posthumous honours. From Disraeli to Mrs Thatcher there is a clutch of former Conservatives whose names, appropriately dropped, should evince a cheer. Before a general Labour audience it would now be wise only to try Keir Hardie, Attlee and Bevan in this context. And of these only Attlee was leader and Prime Minister. Of the other three Labour Prime Ministers, Ramsay MacDonald, Harold Wilson and James Callaghan, the last might do the best, but even his ripple of applause might be embarrassingly faint.

Bevan, however, is a safe name to play with. 'As Nye said' is the Labour equivalent of Mrs Thatcher's over-familiar references to the 'Winston' she did not know and whose consensual style, in both his governments, she did not understand. But Bevan's posthumous clouds of glory have by no means swirled exclusively around the Labour Party. His cross-party reputation at the end of his life and in subsequent years was as high as it had at one time been abysmal. Both Churchill's 'squalid nuisance' of the war years and the Minister of Health who in 1948 had rather overdone his sanitary responsibility in referring to the Tories as 'lower than vermin' were forgotten. For a short time he was presented as almost all things to all men. He became at once the patriot who rose above petty politics and the keeper of the Labour Party's socialist conscience; the expression both of the provinces' revolt against London and of the welcoming tolerance of the metropolis, which made him as much at home in the Café Royal and the Savoy Grill as in the Tredegar Workmen's Institute (latterly perhaps more so); and the symbol of the generosity as well as the conflict of British politics. Such generalized

20

reverence is a helpful qualification for national sainthood. But it inevitably leaves a certain fuzziness of impression.

Is it now possible to remove the fuzz from Bevan? There have been two main biographies since his death. Michael Foot's two volumes of inspired hagiography came out in 1962 and 1973. They were hagiography not only because every account of Bevan's many disputes disparage his opponents with all the fervour of a contemporary polemic, but also because such a normally witty writer as Mr Foot never permits himself to make a joke at Bevan's expense. He is portrayed as unlaughable at as well as omniscient and impeccable.

The second biography was written by John Campbell and published in 1987. Campbell had previously written about Lloyd George (after his fall from power), F. E. Smith, and me, and is currently engaged on Edward Heath. So he can be regarded as an eclectic political biographer. His portrait of Smith, later Birkenhead, was not only his best book but achieved to a unique degree a combination of the enhancement of the reputation of the author and the destruction of that of the subject. In Bevan's case he set out to provide a corrective to Foot, and showed convincingly that Bevan's basic political idea, which was that socialism was essential for efficient production and was therefore in accordance with the tide of history, was about as false as it could have been, and that his only piece of sustained political writing, *In Place of Fear* (a better title than a text), was fairly flatulent.

Yet, in spite of this 'pricking of the bloated bladder of false-hood with the poniard of truth' (to use the opening of one of Bevan's most successful House of Commons speeches), I think Campbell, too young to have known him, fell under Bevan's spell while sceptically reading and writing about him. His

21

concluding words were: 'As well as a rare humanity and gaiety, intelligence, anger and wit, Bevan brought to the life of politics a passionate seriousness which no one who has come after him has begun to match. If to be irreplaceable is to be great, Bevan was a great man after all.' The tribute is perhaps the more impressive for the apparent reluctance with which it is paid.

I, unlike Campbell, observed Bevan and knew him, although never intimately, over many years. In my adolescent, Oxford and army years he sat in Parliament for the adjacent constituency to my father's. I was subsequently in the House of Commons with him for the last twelve years of his life. For the first three of them I admired him to the verge of extravagance. For the last nine I was separated almost completely from him by the bitter depth of the Gaitskellite/Bevanite divide in the Labour Party. Although the ideological gap between the two sections was narrower than that which convulsed the party in its lurch to the left in the early 1980s, the tribes were then more hermetically sealed.

There were a few MPs who managed to transcend this narrowness, but I was emphatically not one of them. Bevan could sometimes be generous across the floor of the House of Commons but amongst young Labour MPs he liked acolytes and not critics, and as a core Gaitskellite I was regarded as outside his pale. For five years or more I exchanged hardly a word with him. He would stalk past in a corridor with a scowling leonine disdain, unnodding and unspeaking. But he was an immanent presence in my early political life, and reactions to his echoing if often petulant and disruptive words and actions dominated a great part of my thoughts, conversations and tactical discussions.

Yet I do not think that this period of living in an opposing armed camp biases me against Bevan today. If anything, it does the reverse, for I am not proud of my narrowness of those years and regret having cut myself off from someone who, whether or not he was a great man, was certainly the second most striking personality of my early years in the House of Commons. During my immersion in Bevan books for the purpose of this essay I find that, like Campbell, I have half fallen under his spell, and wonder why I was so immune to it forty years ago. His phrases ring remarkably fresh down the decades, his arrogance (which was vast) appears fierce rather than ridiculous, and he makes nearly every present Cabinet minister, or his shadow, look tailor-made to be an under-secretary.

This does not, however, answer the question of whether he was a great man. Margot Asquith (whose judgements were far from infallible but who may have been right on this occasion) dismissed Kitchener as a great poster masquerading as a great man. Bevan was not that. Hand in hand with Barbara Castle, who was similarly linked on the other side to Hugh Gaitskell, he did get on to Labour billboards at the 1959 election, but in general he was regarded as too abrasive to be advertising mate-rial. A more typical visual image was a 1955 cartoon showing a reassuring Attlee mask covering the reality of a menacing Bevan which lay behind. But if he was not a great poster masquerading as a great man he may have been a great word-spinner, both in oratory and in conversation, whose judgement, self-discipline and achievement failed to live up to his verbal talent.

He was born in 1897 with few advantages beyond that of starting in the centre of the Labour heartland. He was a non-Welsh-speaking Welshman from Tredegar, a Monmouthshire mining community a couple of miles over a bare hillside from the steel town of Ebbw Vale and eight miles east of Merthyr Tydfil, the cradle of the South Wales industrial revolution where

Keir Hardie became the first independent Labour MP three years after Bevan's birth. The renowned but raw South Wales industrial community, which had erupted into the steep sylvan fortresses of Glamorgan and West Monmouthshire from about 1840 onwards, manifested the mixture of roughness and gentleness which was later to be a special characteristic of Bevan's oratory. Its class conflict was jagged, its strikes were visceral, but it respected education and learning. Its men, like Bevan's father, were often quiet and bookish, and its households, again like Bevan's, were often matriarchal. Essex man would not have been esteemed in Tredegar.

Bevan was none the less not a typical product of the South Wales political class. He did everything too quickly, some would have said too superficially, and once he had an avenue of escape he seized it as completely as did Lloyd George from the very different background of rural North Wales, or Gracie Fields from Rochdale, or Richard Burton from the same South Wales. From his early thirties onwards Tredegar and Ebbw Vale were for Bevan a base and an audience, but not a home or even a place of rest and recreation.

He was a miner for only nine years, although he started at thirteen, as was normal at the time. He was chairman of his lodge (or union branch) at nineteen. He went for two years to the Central Labour College in London soon after the 1918 armistice, but he was a lazy student. He never properly returned to the pits, although he remained in South Wales for eight subsequent years. He was a local councillor for six of them, and then an impatient county councillor for one. In the meantime he had played a central part in running the Tredegar Workmen's Institute, half a home university library and half a medical insurance scheme. At the time of the General Strike (still aged only twenty-eight) he had filled a vacuum and seized almost as much of a commissar's local role as on a national scale did his later enemy, Ernest Bevin. ('His own worst enemy? Not while I'm alive he ain't,' as Bevin was to say of Bevan.) In 1929 he superseded the little more than fifty-year-old local MP, an almost unprecedented event in the job-preserving Labour culture. The victim must, however, have been very lackadaisical, for there were plenty of non-Bevan supporters who were anxious to get rid of him. As a result Bevan entered the House of Commons at the age of thirty-one, which was equally unprecedented in the semi-gerontocracy of South Wales miners' parliamentary representation.

In that 1929 world-slump-buffeted Parliament, with its minority Labour government and misty MacDonald leadership, Bevan's early speeches were constituency-orientated and surprisingly loyalist. They nevertheless presaged something of the vivid spontaneity of his later philippics. His maiden speech, neither a failure nor memorable, appears to have been made on the spur of the moment. This habit of making even his most important speeches without detailed preparation, which he shared with Gladstone although most conspicuously not with Churchill, makes an enormous difference to the pattern of a politician's life. In Gladstone's case it enabled him to carry on his voluminous correspondence with bishops and deans, statesmen and professors, station-masters and booksellers in the morning while electrifying the House of Commons for several hours in the evenings.

In Bevan's case it enabled him, at least at this stage in his life, to be both lazy and noticed, often not getting up before noon, but making more impact than more diligent colleagues. It also introduced additional hazard into his speech-making. Although he was a gourmand of unusual words he did not have the defences of Gladstone's convoluted qualifications. Many of Bevan's most notorious phrases were probably uttered without premeditation.

His early loyalist phase did not last long, and justifiably so, for the Government was supine before unemployment, and its leading members were determinedly unadventurous. Bevan was drawn to those – on both sides of the House – who were more so. It was those with off-beat glamour as well as a capacity for intellectual innovation who most attracted him. His closest House of Commons associates became Oswald Mosley, John Strachey, Frank Owen (a Beaverbrook protégé and subsequent editor who was Liberal member for Hereford), Bob Boothby and Edward Marjoribanks, Quintin Hogg's half-brother who subsequently committed suicide.

His one close 'proletarian' parliamentary friend was Jennie Lee, then looking less forbiddingly partisan than in her middle period, a Fifeshire miner's daughter but a graduate of Edinburgh University, who had become a Scottish MP at the same time as Bevan had become a Welsh one. There was little romantic attachment between them in that Parliament for her attentions were engaged with Frank Wise, also a Labour MP and a faintly sinister figure of the period, who was twenty years their senior but who died young, aged fifty-eight, in 1933. Miss Lee then married Bevan in 1934. Already by the election of 1931, however, Bevan was sufficiently involved to spend almost the whole time in her constituency of North Lanark, the bleakest part of the Clydeside industrial area, in a vain attempt to save her seat. Amazingly, in that Labour holocaust of an election, he was unopposed in Ebbw Vale.

Bevan's career in the 1930s did not advance as much as it

ought to have done. A Labour parliamentary party of little more than fifty until 1935, and only 150, no more than two or three of whom were aged under forty, after the general election of that year, created one of the great vacuums of political history. In 1931–5 the only surviving trio of ex-ministers, Attlee, Lansbury and Cripps, expanded beyond any previous appreciation of their size to fill it. Then in 1935–40 subsequently reviled governments lived through a series of parliamentary dramas, mostly provoked by stations on the road to Britain's nadir after a quinquennium of retreat before the Axis.

Bevan remained no more than a fringe politician during this period. He was elected neither to the Shadow Cabinet (by the parliamentary party) nor to the National Executive of the Labour Party (first by the whole conference and then by the constituency parties alone after 1937), but he could always be recruited for a Trafalgar Square or Marble Arch demonstration which the official Labour Party regarded as on the edge of respectability. He was much better known at them than in the House of Commons. He supported Cripps's call for a United Front with the Communists, and then for a Popular Front across a broader spectrum of politics 'from Churchill to Pollitt'. For the latter he got himself briefly expelled from the Labour Party but, unlike Cripps, came back a little humiliatingly as soon as he could. His most seminal activity was to be involved in the foundation of *Tribune* in 1937. In the great post-Norway debate of 7/8 May 1940 he did not speak (probably he tried and was not called), but he did not even pass Disraeli's test that the important thing was that it should be asked why one was not speaking. At the age of forty-two and after eleven years in the House of Commons his absence was not noticed in the greatest set-piece debate of the century. Everyone spoke their lines like characters in a

Shakespeare depiction of a Plantagenet council. But not Bevan.

Yet the consequences that flowed from that debate, and his reaction to them, determined the path of the second half of Bevan's career more than any participation of his in it could possibly have done. The debate destroyed the Chamberlain Government and the normal pattern of politics, which had made Bevan no more than a noisy irritant, a fly thrashing at a window pane in a vain attempt to get through it. Subsequent high-level party manoeuvres put in its place an all-party coalition, with a rumbustious but revered leader, underpinned by a desperate national situation and a political consensus that comprised almost the whole of the House of Commons except for one right-wing Conservative who was imprisoned and one Communist who was against the war until Hitler attacked Russia a year later. The Labour Party put its first eleven into the Government while its second eleven occupied the Opposition front bench with a determined loyalty, at least until 1943 when the tide had turned and post-war politics began to loom, which gratified Churchill and Attlee but made the House of Commons little more than a simulacrum of the parliamentary democracy which was supposed to be one of the causes for which the war was being fought.

Bevan saw the gap and devoted the next five years to trying to fill it. Primarily this meant attacking Churchill, which he did with a mixture of courage, verve and irresponsibility. His skill was that, although he talked a lot of presumptuous nonsense shot through with shafts of good sense, he never appeared defeatist. Some of his criticisms were ideological; Churchill was too much the prisoner of his class, whose 'ear is too sensitively attuned to the bugle notes of Blenheim for him to hear the whisperings in the streets'; but others were strategic and appealed more to

28

disgruntled Tories than to loyal Labour members. Probably he never wanted to bring Churchill down. He had no serious candidate to put in his place, for he discounted Attlee and clashed with Bevin and Morrison as violently as he did with Churchill himself. He may have played with the idea of Cripps or Beaverbrook, but then went off each of them in turn. It was more that he genuinely believed that Churchill would be a better war leader if he had more criticism and less adulation (a recipe Bevan singularly failed to apply to himself when he established his own court in the 1950s); and that he had the daring to build up his own reputation by going for the biggest target on the field as Disraeli had done with Peel a hundred years before, as Lloyd George had done with Joseph Chamberlain fifty years later, and as Iain Macleod was to do with Bevan himself ten years into the future.

Bevan's high point was a censure debate in July 1942, just before the global strategic balance was changed by the German defeat in front of Stalingrad and Britain's morale was transformed by Montgomery's victory over Rommel at Alamein. On the first day of the censure motion Wardlaw-Milne, the dissident Tory mover, produced bathos by his suggestion that the Duke of Gloucester be appointed Commander-in-Chief. Bevan, opening on the second day, had to retrieve the position. He did so with deadliness. 'The Prime Minister', he said, 'wins debate after debate and loses battle after battle.' It was probably the most damaging remark, six months after Singapore and four months before Alamein, made against Churchill during the whole course of the war. The Prime Minister defeated the censure motion by 475 to 25, but as Rab Butler with typical ambiguous felineness subsequently remarked, 'Churchill had had his day … but Aneurin Bevan had made his mark.'

Bevan's imagery was sometimes unforgettable. Churchill had described Italy as 'the soft under-belly of the Axis'. As the Allies endeavoured painfully to fight their way up the peninsula over the switchback of the Apennines in 1943–4, Bevan dismissed the strategy as nonsense. 'Is this the soft under-belly of the Axis? We are climbing up his backbone.' On another occasion he compared Churchill's slow approach to a Second Front in France with the approach of an old husband to a young bride: 'fascinated, apprehensive, sluggish'.

Yet it would be a mistake to allow his lapidary phrases to obscure the foolish recklessness of many of his ideas. He was totally starry-eyed about Russia in 1941–4 and looked to Moscow not merely for a stubborn national defence but for the libertarian leadership of the world. This led him to advocate a Second Front for 1941; even 1942 or 1943, he held, would be dilatory. Had his advice been taken, he would have been a butcher on a scale that dwarfed Field Marshal Haig. He never bought the idea of the Duke of Gloucester as Commander-in-Chief but in 1941 he wanted the British Army put temporarily under the command of émigré Czech, Polish or French generals, and in 1942 he wanted the Soviet Marshal Timoshenko to command British troops in an immediate assault on Fortress Europe. In 1944–5 he began to be disenchanted with Stalin, and being always suspicious and reserved in his attitude to America he played with an 'organic confederation' in Western Europe comprising all the obvious countries, plus 'a sane Germany and Austria' with 'an enlightened Britain' graciously accepting leadership. But as soon as such a European union began to become a practical proposition in the 1950s Bevan shied violently away from it.

Whatever his extravagances and inconsistencies, however, he

emerged from the war as a colourful and famous figure, even if on the whole an unpopular one. Any elected office in the Labour Party continued to elude him, and in 1944 he had been very close to his second expulsion from it. He was obviously anathema to 'patriotic' opinion, and although he burnished his steel on Churchill this did not arouse any feelings of chivalrous courtesy in the latter. 'As great a curse to his country in time of peace as he was a squalid nuisance in time of war,' which were Churchill's phrases in December 1945, well after victories had ceased to be elusive, was not the way in which one saluted a knightly opponent.

Why, then, did Attlee make Bevan the youngest and most controversial of his Cabinet appointments after the Labour landslide? Of those who were in a position to influence Attlee, his claims could hardly have been urged by Bevin or Morrison, who were even more antipathetic to Bevan than they were to each other, or by Dalton, who had recently written of him as being 'more than usually hysterical and abrasive'. Nor was there any obvious affinity between Attlee himself, 'reek[ing] of the suburban middle-class values which Bevan detested' as Michael Foot put it, and Bevan's flamboyant bohemianism. (Bevan's style was not suburban, whatever else it was. In 1944 he and Jennie Lee had removed themselves from the Berkshire countryside near Newbury to a fine house (cheap at the time) in Cliveden Place, between Eaton and Sloane Squares, as fashionable a London address as it is possible to imagine.)

Attlee liked balancing between the different factions of the Labour Party and was careful never to commit himself to tribal loyalties. But he also liked the quick despatch of Cabinet business and neat administration. He must have regarded Bevan's intoxication with words as the enemy of speed and at best a risky bet for neatness. And he increased the hazard by giving him a department with one of the heaviest administrative burdens in Whitehall. The Ministry of Health to which Bevan was appointed in 1945 was essentially the same partly misnamed ministry that Neville Chamberlain had preferred to the Exchequer in 1924. It embraced housing, local government and the Poor Law, as well as such limited responsibility as the state took before 1948 for hospitals and doctors.

It was therefore a crucial department for the Labour Government's impact upon the condition of the people. But it was also a 'safe' one in the sense which first Charles de Gaulle in the late 1940s and then François Mitterrand in the 1980s turned into a term of art when they were the only two French heads of state to accept Communists in their governments. Communist ministers were necessary but they must not be allowed to get their hands on foreign affairs, defence, finance, or the interior (police). No one (other than perhaps Senator McCarthy) ever thought Bevan was a Communist, but Attlee never let Bevan get near any of these four departments, even when in 1950–1 two of them became vacant in quick succession. The paradoxes of Attlee's attitude to Bevan were compounded by the fact that while Attlee destabilized his government by never giving him one of these great offices of state, there is quite a lot of evidence that, if Bevan could ever have brought himself to behave calmly for even a couple of years, Attlee would have preferred him, certainly to Morrison and maybe to Gaitskell, as his successor.

That was all in the future. The reality was that in 1945 Bevan was given an opportunity far beyond his or anyone else's expectations and advanced upon it with the eagerness of an enthusiastic schoolboy. Attlee bestowed it upon him with more of the bracing admonition of an old-style schoolmaster than of the comradely confidence of a fellow socialist campaigner. 'You are starting with me with a clean sheet … Now it is up to you. The more you can learn the better.'

Surprisingly, Bevan did not seem to resent this patronizing pat on the head (the size of the tip that accompanied it was no doubt a factor) and got down to the five and three-quarter years (five and a half of them at the Ministry of Health) that were his sole experience of office and his sole claim to constructive achievement as opposed to the magical deployment of words. During this period he built a moderate quantity of high-quality council houses and launched the National Health Service in a hybrid, pragmatic and original form which has broadly since persisted. He then flounced out of the government in April 1951, taking with him as a hardly noticed adjutant a future Prime Minister in the shape of Harold Wilson. It was the most seminal resignation since Joseph Chamberlain left the Balfour Government in 1903. In the late 1950s the Thorneycroft resignations were merely 'a little local difficulty'. In the 1960s George Brown's was just a banging of a door in the wind. In the 1980s Heseltine, Lawson and Howe achieved a cumulative effect, but Bevan's stood on its own and reverberated down the next decade.

The main question is how great was his 1945–50 achievement. Did it justify the Labour Party myth into which, quite a long time later, it became elevated? In the 1950s it was famously excoriated by Macleod, subjected to a rather loose bombardment by Churchill and Macmillan, and privately undermined (although under great provocation) by Dalton, Morrison and Gaitskell. 'Nye left a lot of loose ends. But what could you expect with someone with such an untidy mind who was in any event nearly always in the smoking room of the House of Commons from 5.30 p.m. onwards.' This was the sort of comment that became widespread. Did Bevan's administrative record deserve it?

His housing performance, for some time at least, bore an uncomfortable resemblance to his 1942 strictures of Churchill. He won debate after debate but was bereft of victories on the building sites. During this period he embellished his replies to House of Commons debates, and largely got away with, a series of remarkable animadversions on the aesthetics of housing policy. He denounced 'the fretful fronts stretching along the great roads out of London' of 1930s building and proclaimed that he was not going to have the landscape desecrated by 'ugly houses poking their stupid noses into the air because they are too high for their width'. Up to the end of 1946 there was not much danger of many new houses poking their noses anywhere, for only 60,000 had been completed in the eighteen months since the end of the war. In the third full year, as is the habit with production programmes, there was a movement into relative spate, and well over 200,000 were completed in 1948. By then he was in trouble with successive Chancellors for commanding too large a timber share of scarce dollar imports and had his programme cut back for several years to come. In the infinitely complicated game of bandying housing statistics he ended up with a defensible record in numbers and a good one for the quality of houses built. Harold Macmillan subsequently upstaged him on numbers although he achieved this partly by reducing the size and quality of the units.

The creation of the National Health Service was a less ephemeral battleground than was provided by the exchange of housing statistics. Bevan of course did not create it out of nothing. Two successive Tory ministers had been working on the issue since

1943, and the late 1940s would have seen the creation of some form of National Health Service whoever had been Minister of Health and even had Labour not won in 1945. Nevertheless, Bevan deserves the credit that belongs to those who are in the right place at the right time and who do not fumble the opportunity with which they are presented. Furthermore, he deployed his forces with great strategic skill, advancing from one to another battle that he could win, and never engaging in those that he could not, except occasionally to fight a drawn diversionary action the noise from which helped his more central purposes. His adversaries were not so much the Conservatives, who were throughout more embarrassed than aggressive, although obligingly voting against both the second and third readings of the bill. They were the doctors, a traditionally noisy profession, who had the advantage of being mostly popular with their patients, but the disadvantage of being fissiparous; and the local authorities, strongly represented in the Cabinet by Morrison, the 1930s leader of the London County Council, the most powerful and efficient of them, which wanted to keep control of their own hospitals.

The doctors, and particularly the grand ones associated with the voluntary teaching hospitals, wished at all costs to be free of the local authorities. However, their great hospitals, while trailing clouds of glory, had little prospect of financing themselves satisfactorily in the post-war world. Bevan, helped by his best officials whom he captivated almost as much as Napoleon did his marshals, saw the gap and drove through it with adventurous skill. He proposed to unify the hospital service (two-thirds local authority with whiffs of the Poor Law about it, and one-third voluntary with whiffs of Lady Bountiful) and run it nominally as a nationalized service, but with a great

35

deal of consultant control.

To do this he had to defeat Morrison in Cabinet, which he did in October 1945, but once he had done so he had the Royal Colleges on his side, particularly as he further sweetened the consultants by allowing them pay beds and the continuation of private practice alongside their public responsibilities. This left the British Medical Association, essentially representing the general practitioners, as an army whose commanders had defected. In compensation Charles Hill, their deputy secretary, widely known as the Radio Doctor and later to be a Conservative MP and minister, put on a great performance as a ranker general, and they also had the advantage, as general practitioners, of being close to the ground. Bevan was accused (by R. A. Butler, for example, who contrasted Bevan's behaviour with his own mollifying treatment of the teachers in 1944) of handling them truculently. It probably suited him to do so. First, the Lloyd George experience at the beginning of National Insurance in 1912–13 suggested that doctors always capitulated at the end. Second, Bevan needed some 'noises off' in order to distract attention from how far away his NHS was from the models which the Socialist Medical Association had previously promulgated. Doctors remained unsalaried, there were no local health centres, preventive medicine was discounted, and the split between the general practitioners and the hospitals became greater than ever before. But he got his bill on the statute book by the end of 1946, and, perhaps more difficult, the NHS in operation by 5 July 1948.

Bevan must therefore be accounted a considerable success as a departmental minister. He had the essential qualities of being able to command and enthuse his civil servants, of fixing his strategic objectives, and of getting his way in Cabinet. However, as is often the way with upwardly mobile ministers, three years was enough for him in one ministry, and in 1948/9 he was ripe for a move. Attlee did not give him one. Why not is a much greater mystery than why he put Bevan at Health in the first place. It was almost his only major failure in deft Cabinet management. The new job did not have to be close to the core. Even the Colonies, then an absorbing department, would have done. Instead he left Bevan to vegetate, powerfully but vainly defending his housing programme against the facts of Britain's overstrained resources, being accused of letting his health estimates run out of control, but probably doing so no more than anyone else introducing a new and thirsty service would have done.

Somewhere around 1951, however, Bevan began to acquire a messianic complex, exacerbated by the view, which by no means necessarily goes with being a messiah, that his rivals were pygmies. He had long been an irreverent critic, an impudent boy with a catapult aiming his stones, without much discrimination between his party opponents and his nominal friends, at the top hats of the great and the good. To do that required a self-confident courage, but was quite different from believing that he was surrounded by colleagues who were not only adversaries, but adversaries with whom it was an insult to have to soil his hands.

The transition from the boy David to Gulliver in Lilliput was an abrupt one, which it is difficult to feel did not stem substantially from his double passing over for both the Exchequer and the Foreign Office, although it was no doubt exacerbated by policy resentment that first his housing programme and then his health service were under attack from within the government. It showed itself not only in his bad-tempered resignation of April

1951, but also in a series of contemptuous denunciations. Of Gaitskell he had exploded to John Strachey in 1950: 'But he's nothing, nothing, nothing.' Five years later he was thought to have called him 'a desiccated calculating machine', but in fact it was Attlee whom Bevan then had in his sights.

For Gaitskell, however, he never had any real respect or liking, even when they were thrown into alliance by Bevan's 1957 denunciation of unilateralism and the need for both of them to win the 1959 election if either was ever again to hold office. At best Bevan regarded him as an honest but unimaginative bureaucrat who had too pedestrian a mind – and life – ever to be a real leader. The nearest he could get to friendliness was to be patronizing.

About Attlee his feelings were more mixed. He put him several notches above Morrison, whom he regarded as a squalid party boss, and with some reason. Attlee, after all, apart from the qualities that have given him such a vast posthumous reputation, had been the indispensable agent for Bevan's success at the Ministry of Health, both by appointing him and by decisive support in Cabinet. But indebtedness is not always the basis for respect, and Attlee's bourgeois primness grated on Bevan's flamboyance. It was by two acts of gross public discourtesy to Attlee in 1954 that he had his last brush with expulsion from the Labour Party.

When reproved for this behaviour by the Shadow Cabinet Bevan said that his nerves could not stand the strain of such 'impudent' attacks, and it was in much the same mood that he told Crossman a few months later that he was by no means sure that he wanted to be leader if he had to behave circumspectly in order to become it. 'I'm not a proletarian or an intellectual,' he inconsequentially added. 'I am an aristocrat with a real distaste for that kind of politics.'

There is a danger of seeing the Bevan of the 1950s too much through the prism of Crossman's voluminous *Diaries*. Crossman did not really either like or admire Bevan, although he followed him for nearly five years, but mainly because he could never win Attlee's approval and found it difficult to reconcile himself to Gaitskell whom he thought of as a much inferior Wykehamist to himself. Nevertheless, it is impossible not to cite Crossman once more because of the ironic memorability of his (mostly) benign description of Bevan's behaviour on their infamous trip to the Italian Socialist Party Conference in Venice in February 1957. 'Bland, ebullient, impeccably dressed in his beautiful new suit, fresh white linen with his handkerchief falling out of his breast pocket, pretentiously discussing the qualities of Italian wine, pretending to knowledge of Venetian architecture, laying down the law about Italian politics with vitality and charm, and occasionally with the wildest irresponsibility.'

The trip was infamous because, consequent upon it, Bevan put on one of the two really discreditable performances of his life. The first was in 1955 when he tried as a desperate last-minute manoeuvre to offer Morrison, whom he despised, an uncontested election to the leadership of the Labour Party in order to block Gaitskell, who was the strong majority choice.

The second was in the action against the *Spectator* following the Venice visit, when Bevan, Crossman and Morgan Phillips (the general secretary of the Labour Party) sued on an almost unbelievably mild libel ('they puzzled the Italians by their capacity to fill themselves like tanks with whisky and coffee ... Although the Italians were never sure if the British delegation was sober, they always attributed to them an immense political acumen') and sailed to victory on the unfortunate combination of Lord Chief

Justice Goddard's prejudice against the anti-hanging and generally libertarian *Spectator* of those days and the perjury of the plaintiffs, subsequently exposed in Crossman's endlessly revealing diaries.

The fact of the matter was that Phillips was a near-alcoholic, that Bevan was a heavy drinker with a good head, often 'tanked-up' ('tanks' was indeed a *mot juste)*, habitually in my observation drinking three times as much as he claimed in the witness box he had done in Venice, but never appearing drunk as opposed to flushed and didactic, and that even Crossman, the most abstemious of the three, had an intake that would have terrified most Italian livers. None of this would have mattered had they not falsely claimed the reverse.

All of the last quinquennium of Bevan's life was not therefore glorious. But much of it was. Maybe he lost the Labour Party the 1955 election, although my guess is that they would have lost it in any case. In 1959 he probably helped rather than hindered. By then he was becoming something of a paradox. He was a hero who was also an anachronism. He and Churchill were the last great politicians never to adapt to television. Both were in their different ways orators who needed audiences. Macmillan, and after him Wilson, would have made them both look flailing and florid on the box. Indeed the effects of great audiences, physically present, vibrant and adulatory, were a drug that did Bevan far more harm than alcohol or his inherent faults of temper. And the fault was compounded by the utter safeness of Ebbw Vale insulating him from the realities of marginal constituency life.

In addition, long before the manifest exposure of his central belief that ultimate victory must belong to socialist planning because of its productive efficiency, his subsidiary doctrine of a triumphant Labour Party based on proletarian solidarity (which was always violently contradicted both by his own lifestyle and by the fact that his acolytes were almost uniformly middle-class and even fashionable) began to fray badly at the edges. His last election – Macmillan's 'you've never had it so good' consumer durables triumph of 1959 – was the first to be strongly influenced by middle-class aspirations amongst the traditional working class.

Less than a year after that election Bevan was dead, having been incapacitated for six months. Two and a half years after that Gaitskell, nearly ten years his junior, was dead too. But I somehow doubt if Bevan, had he survived, would have been elected on Gaitskell's death. I think Wilson would have slipped in ahead of him. So Bevan would have been alive and almost sixty-seven when the first Wilson Government came in. What would have been done with him? He could hardly have been given a nostalgic appointment like Jim Griffiths becoming Secretary of State for Wales. But he would have been a difficult morsel to swallow. Indeed Wilson found it difficult enough to handle his widow, Jennie Lee, to whom he gave nominally only junior status but a privileged position in charge of the arts. I think a surviving Nye Bevan might have paralysed the whole government, a considerable but not a constructive feat.

Perhaps, in spite of his first three years at the Ministry of Health, that gives the key to his whole life: a considerable but not a constructive statesman. What he indisputably was, however, was a star. Amongst those born around the turn of the eighteenth into the nineteenth century there were four or five incontestable stars, Gladstone, Newman, Tennyson, Dickens, Darwin, maybe Carlyle. They were not always sensible, but anything they touched was infused with excitement. Amongst

41

those born around a hundred years later it is difficult to find a comparable list. Who are the possible candidates: Waugh, and Green, Henry Moore, Dylan Thomas, maybe Graham Sutherland? Bevan certainly deserves the politician's place on that polymathic list and the knowledge that this was so would, I suspect, have more than compensated him for the thought that, also of his generation, Macmillan, Eden and Home were Prime Minister and he was not.

Iain Macleod

Iain Macleod was a very professional politician in both the good and the bad senses of the word. Although he had a darting crossword-puzzle mind, fortified by a phenomenal memory, he was not an intellectual. But as he had a touch of magic about him, he was able to inspire a considerable range of people who were intellectually more gifted and more interested in ideas than he was himself.

I am not convinced that he was a particularly nice man, but he had insight and insolence, which latter quality put him in the tradition of Disraeli, Joseph Chamberlain and F. E. Smith, and sharply contrasted him with Austen Chamberlain, R. A. Butler and James Callaghan, three politicians who in their differing ways were notably deficient in daring unorthodox thrusts. But the political figure in British history to whom, across a gap of 150 years, Macleod bore an almost uncanny resemblance was George Canning. They both lived for within a few months of fifty-seven years. They were both financially insecure, socially a little indeterminate and had rakish aspects to their lives. They were both compact men with a riveting eye, who stood for a popular (not populist) but sometimes unpredictable Toryism.

They were both good at banking their treasure in the hearts of their friends and followers, so that their resonance has been somewhat greater than their achievements. Canning attained higher office than did Macleod (after two periods as Foreign Secretary he had been Prime Minister for six months when he died) and he also accomplished the feat, unique I think for a politician as opposed to a poet, although Gladstone, Disraeli and Churchill might come close, of putting four phrases into the English language.

So Macleod ought to be pleased with the comparison. He contributed no comparable hand of phrases (indeed the most remembered one associated with him was Salisbury's discreditable claim that he was 'too clever by half') but he was a very considerable orator, inspirational at a party conference, often with a mordant deadliness of phrase in the House of Commons, to whom many would give third place in the pantheon of British speakers of the past fifty years, after only Churchill and Bevan. I am torn in deciding whether he ought to be there. On the one hand I can think of no challenger to topple his oratory off its bronze medal plinth. On the other, I engaged in many parliamentary jousts with him and did not feel intimidated as I certainly would have done with either of the other two.

I did not find him an amiable 'shadow'. Quintin Hailsham, Reggie Maudling, Peter Thorneycroft and James Prior, who at one time or another also occupied this position in relation to me, were all much easier to get on with. Macleod had been friendly enough to me before I went to the Treasury, which he had already been shadowing for a couple of years, at the end of 1967. Then for the next two and a half years he became increasingly sour, partisan and withdrawn. He made a tremendous fuss about small change parliamentary procedure issues in relation to the

44

Finance Bill, rather embarrassing his backbenchers by forcing them to walk out of the Committee at one stage. When I followed his advice in 1968 and introduced a National Lottery, subject to a free vote of the House of Commons, he turned round like a squirrel in a cage and successfully voted against it, claiming that the times had become too grave for such frivolity. When I eventually got him to lunch alone at 11 Downing Street (probably a mistaken venue) he sulked throughout the meal, declining both conversational gambits (which was occasionally his habit) and alcoholic refreshment (which was not). No doubt he was in pain from the crippled back and neck which began with a war injury. Perhaps he also had a premonition that time was running out for him. He desperately wanted to be Chancellor, and it was a tragedy for himself, the Heath Government and the country that he occupied the post for only one month. Although he resented me as Chancellor in a way that inevitably diminished the warmth of my feelings for him at the time, this did not kill my longer-term admiration for many of his political qualities. Nor, I hope, does it now make it impossible for me to see and appraise him in perspective.

Macleod came of Hebridean stock on both sides, but I doubt if, apart from going to school in the ruggedly conformist atmosphere of Fettes in Edinburgh and enjoying holidays of fishing and rough shooting on the Isle of Lewis, Scotland meant a great deal to him. He was born at Skipton in the Yorkshire Dales, where his father was a family doctor, and brought up in a quiet middle middle-class way. He went to Gonville and Caius College, Cambridge, where he was an undistinguished undergraduate, save for his high skill at bridge and his liking for betting at Newmarket. Apart from an unsuccessful year's apprenticeship in the De la Rue banknote and playing-card company he did no job between coming down from Cambridge in 1935 and the outbreak of the war. He earned a substantial but insecure living from playing bridge, but used it to support a life which was more purposeless than gilded.

He enlisted early and was an officer in time to spend a few weeks in France before the collapse. He was quite badly wounded in a leg and thigh and sent home via St Nazaire before the retreat to Dunkirk. He then had a rather mixed army career. He ended a major on a divisional staff but as the division was in the forefront of the 1944 invasion this brought him no red-tabbed safety. He was back in France on D-day. His degree of promotion was about average for someone of his background and age (he was thirty-two when the war ended). He was not like one of those civilian (that is, non-regular army) brigadiers who were to be his companions on the Conservative benches in the House of Commons – Selwyn Lloyd, Enoch Powell, John Foster, Toby Low (Lord Aldington) – who had risen inexorably. Indeed, accounts of this phase of his life give the impression that he was a feckless, doubtfully disciplined officer. But his four months at the Staff College at the end of 1943 engaged him intellectually in a way that Cambridge never had. He discovered that he was remarkably good at solving the finite problems with copybook answers, and this gave him a new self-confidence which expressed itself in political ambition.

In 1945, because he happened to be on leave at his father's holiday house there, he more or less adopted himself as a sort of makeshift Conservative candidate for the Western Isles, and ran third to both the sitting Labour member and the Liberal challenger. Within two months of finally getting out of the army at the beginning of 1946 he had – together with Enoch Powell and Reggie Maudling – been taken on by the Conservative Research

Department as part of the parliamentary secretariat. The director thought Macleod was intellectually the least good of the
three, but ten years later he decided that Macleod balanced this
by being the most formidable politician amongst them. By either
criterion it was a distinguished trio amongst whom to compete.

After another couple of months he was adopted as candidate
for Enfield. With a Labour majority of 12,000 it was not an
obvious plum of a seat, but a redistribution before the next election (which could be foreseen at least as easily as the run of the
cards in a bridge game) gave Macleod only the much more
favourable western half of the borough to fight, a comfortable
majority in 1950, and no real constituency worries throughout
the six subsequent elections that he fought there.

For his first thirteen years in Enfield he lived there. In 1941 he
had married a war widow of striking good looks who had been
born Evelyn Blois, a descendant of Essex baronets on her father's
side and of a Disraeli-created peer on her mother's, and who is
now Lady Macleod of Borve, longer-lived but no less dependent
upon courage to overcome pain than was her husband. By the
end of the war they had two children and had settled in a moder-
ate-sized 1920s house on a sylvan suburban ridgeway. Perhaps
surprisingly the Macleods seemed to like suburban living, for
although they moved to an SW1 flat when he was Colonial
Secretary and then Leader of the House of Commons they were
back in Potter's Bar, just over the Hertfordshire county bound-
ary from Enfield, for much of the 1960s.

Macleod, more than any other politician I can think of, made
both his career and his reputation with a single highly effective
House of Commons intervention. F. E. Smith in 1906 sprang at
least as much into the public eye with a coruscating maiden
speech. But it did not directly make his career, for he was in

opposition for the next nine years and on the back benches for the first six of them. Aneurin Bevan achieved his first fame from the impact of his iconoclastic wartime attacks upon Churchill, but it was a cumulative effect rather than a single speech that produced the result. And, amongst Macleod's own contemporaries, Enoch Powell's 1959 speech on the Hola Camp massacre in Kenya remains in the minds of those who heard it at least as strongly as does Macleod's 1952 oration. But, as with Smith, it had no direct career impact, partly because it was a further attack on a government from which Powell had recently resigned and partly because its primary appeal was to a swath of cross-party opinion which he was subsequently bitterly to affront.

Macleod's speech, on the other hand, was manna to the ears of his party leaders and admirably attuned (although not necessarily calculatingly so) to bring its reward. Following on his Research Department experience he thought of himself as a health specialist. He had made his maiden speech on the subject with unspectacular success. Two years later his speciality gave him the opportunity to engage in and win a joust with Bevan. Bevan's debating reputation was at its height and he regarded the National Health Service as almost a personal political fief, although, brooding increasingly on wider issues, he had in fact become somewhat rusty on the subject. The Speaker had intended Macleod to precede Bevan, but he changed his mind and put in a maiden speaker so that Macleod immediately followed the great gladiator. Because he had the verve to exploit his opportunity it was a greater piece of luck than he had ever experienced at a gaming table. He began with an unusually phrased and riskily provocative sentence of invective: 'I want to deal closely and with relish with the vulgar, crude and intemperate speech to which the House of Commons has just listened.'

Churchill had come in to listen to Bevan and rose to depart as Macleod said these words. Hearing them he sat down again and stayed. Macleod, benefiting from his phenomenal factual memory, his quickness of reaction and the deadly beam of his delivery, fully justified his opening statement of intention. Early on Churchill turned to his Chief Whip and asked who Macleod was. Then he turned again and said 'Ministerial material?' Six weeks later he made Macleod Minister of Health. The post was not then in the Cabinet, but it none the less meant that Macleod at thirty-eight had moved ahead of his contemporaries and leap-frogged over the frustrations of junior office into a department of his own.

The circumstances of his appointment to that department were, however, more dramatic than his tenure of it. He stayed there three and a half years, identified well with the Health Service ethos and always looked at home in photographs with nurses or doctors. But he innovated little and achieved little extra money for a demanding service. Ironically, having used anti-Bevanism as a launching pad, he became a defender of the structure that Bevan had bequeathed as well as a mild friend and modified admirer of Bevan himself. This illustrated two points about Macleod's attitudes. The first was that, although he was always an overt campaigner for the centre ground, he preferred those on the other side who did not compete with him for it. He did not like Gaitskell any more than he liked me, and much preferred Bevan and maybe Foot and Crossman too. The second was that he regarded invective as a politician's stock-in-trade rather than as an expression of genuine indignation. He cared deeply about some mostly worthy causes, but his strictures on the moral turpitudes of his opponents had a certain calculated coldness about them. He frequently said that opposition was sterile and unimportant. It was office that counted, and there was almost an indifferent frivolity about his attacks on those who stood in his way of getting it. This was paradoxical, for it is at least arguable that he was better as a destructive critic than he ever was in any ministerial office.

After Health came promotion to the Cabinet in a major reshuffle at the end of 1955 and nearly four years, one under Eden (who had at last succeeded Churchill in April 1955) and three under Macmillan, as Minister of Labour. To that department of conciliation Macleod brought a more abrasive style than his predecessor, the famously emollient Walter Monckton. Was this a difference only of style or of substance as well? Mostly of style, I think. His main confrontation was with the London busmen under the new and truculent leadership of Frank Cousins. But it took place only after he had secured his flank by a compromise settlement of a more important and more dangerous dispute with the railwaymen, and only too after the Cabinet had forced him into a more intransigent (and arguably duplicitous) handling of Cousins than he might himself have chosen.

Macleod compensated, as was often his way, with a viciously successful House of Commons speech. Also typically, he muted his criticism of Alf Robens, who had moved a motion of censure upon him, and turned the blast of his invective against Gaitskell, the bigger target and never Macleod's favourite: 'I cannot conceal my scorn and contempt for the part that the Leader of the Opposition has played in this … We are having the debate because the Leader of the Opposition, in a parliamentary scene on Monday, could not control himself. Because of his refusal on Friday to say a single word that would uphold the authority of an arbitration award; because of his mischievous speech over the weekend; because of his lack of authority on Monday. If we are

50

to vote then let the censure of the House be on the right honourable gentleman tonight and from the country tomorrow.'

Most people would now think there was a good deal more mischief, and indeed irresponsibility, in Macleod than in Gaitskell, but it was high-order jugular debating. In fact Macleod beat the busmen and improved his own and the government's standing as a result, but it is none the less the case that throughout nearly his whole career he scored more triumphs with words than with deeds.

The exception was his period in his next office. Just as he had been eager to leave the Ministry of Health in 1955 so he looked for a move from the Ministry of Labour in 1959. They were perfectly reasonable desires in both cases. He had served more than adequate stints in both offices. In 1959 he was looking for a change rather than for a great promotion, and the office on which he had fixed his sights was the Colonial secretaryship. This office, which was historically the third of the secretaryships of state, had reached its apogee under Joseph Chamberlain, who chose it when he was the second man in the Salisbury Government in terms of power and the first in terms of public impact. For the Colonial Office it had mostly been gently downhill after that, and the path was to be far more precipitately so after Macleod, although this was because of the success and not the failure of his policies. The department was abolished in 1967.

In 1959–61, however, the job had plenty of political content. It was the period of the 'wind of change' in Africa, the affairs of the dark continent stood near the centre of the Westminster stage, and there was both risk and opportunity in being involved with them. Even so Macmillan was surprised that Macleod wanted the department, although it at first suited the Prime Minister very well that he did. In offering it Macmillan talked

51

about 'the poisoned chalice', but his surprise probably came at least as much from the fact that it was so far from the previous bent of Macleod's interests. The new Colonial Secretary had never made a significant speech on the subject, had cultivated no contacts with African or Caribbean leaders, and had never set foot in a colony. For the last deficiency there were plenty of near precedents in British imperial history. Gladstone's commitment to Irish Home Rule was not made less intense by the fact that only once in his life did he cross the sixty-five miles of St George's Channel. Baldwin showed more courage on India than on any other issue, but never even contemplated visiting the sub-continent. Macleod had plenty of colonial travel during his two years in the responsible office, but his previous abstinence did illustrate a certain insularity. Although he was politically a staunch pro-European throughout the 1960s, he was never much of a traveller across the Channel. He had seen more of France as a soldier than he was to do in any other way. His favourite European destination was a frequently revisited hotel on the Costa Brava. The capitals in which he seemed most at home were Washington and New York in the Kennedy/Johnson era.

Despite this lack of preparation or previous interest, Macleod did not approach the Colonial secretaryship as a routine 'stage in a career' appointment. He treated it as a vocation, even if a short-term one, and for the sake of doing it, rather like a temporarily holy man going into a monastery and renouncing the temptations of the flesh, he gave up the practice at which he was best and therefore enjoyed the most, which was the flailing of the opposition parties. In view of his office and his policy within it, which was to hasten the drive to independence and give paramountcy to the interests of the black majorities, he had no choice. There were no battles to fight with Labour or the

Liberals. They were on his side. His potential opponents were the African whites (or at least most of them) and their sympathizers in the Conservative Party at home. He was successful, particularly in his first year, in disarming a lot of the latter. In doing so he could not resist a few party flicks (the dismissive phrases came to him so easily), but he could not get much leverage out of them. The peroration of his 1960 Conservative Party Conference speech, which secured a thunderous ovation from an audience much of which had little enthusiasm for his policy, illustrates the skill with which he could put together familiar, even hackneyed, phrases in an order that was resonant, persuasive and applause-provoking:

> I cannot promise you a popular colonial policy. There will be toil and sweat and tears; but I hope not blood and I hope not bitterness – although in the turmoil that is Africa today, of even that one cannot be certain. But this is the road we must walk, and we can walk no other. The Socialists can scheme their schemes and the Liberals can dream their dreams, but we, at least, have work to do. I make you one pledge only; nothing more than this and nothing less – that we will at all times, and to all peoples, in all these territories, carry out our duties faithfully, steadfastly and without fear.

By the end of 1960 he had achieved a lot. Nigeria had reached independence. Tanganyika (Tanzania) and Sierra Leone were well on the way to it. There had been a successful conference on the future of Nyasaland (Malawi) and considerable progress had been made towards a reconciliation in Kenya, the most difficult nut to crack because of the combination of the Mau Mau revolt and a higher proportion of white settlers. Outside Africa a settlement and independence, although hardly stability for the future, had also been achieved in Cyprus.

Nineteen sixty-one was a more difficult year for Macleod. He got himself impaled on three nasty bits of barbed wire: Sir Roy Welensky, the fifth Marquess of Salisbury, and Duncan Sandys, who as Commonwealth Secretary was the Cabinet colleague with whom his responsibilities marched most closely. Welensky was a formidable although ultimately unsuccessful leader of the white settlers and wrote disparagingly of Macleod's 'mixture of cold calculation, sudden gushes of undisciplined emotion and ignorance of Africa'. Salisbury had become sour and malevolent. The implication of his notorious House of Lords attack was that Macleod was an upstart card-sharper. It caused a lot of resentment and damaged Salisbury. But it also damaged Macleod who was much interested in his own future, which Salisbury no longer was. Sandys was a minister of monumental stubbornness. Macleod and he got their horns completely locked, which was a natural posture for Sandys but an unnatural one for Macleod, who had a darting not a stolid personality. Furthermore, their constant conflict bored Macmillan, who blamed the one who seemed to be acting out of character. Macleod began to lose the Prime Minister's confidence and his days at the Colonial Office became numbered.

He was again reshuffled in October 1961. In form certainly, and to some extent in substance, he was promoted not demoted. He replaced Rab Butler as Leader of the House of Commons and Chairman of the Conservative Party. The press hailed his promotion as the creation of a new crown prince, and the days after his appointment to these posts were the apparent peak of his position in the Prime Ministerial stakes. Yet there were a number of maggots in the cheese, and the reality was that he was then like one of those countries – Britain in 1890, the United States in 1960, maybe Germany in 1990 – whose competitive position was already weakening when their power and affluence looked greatest.

The first of the maggots was that he had made a lot of Conservative enemies as Colonial Secretary and that he had been moved for negative reasons as well as promoted for positive ones. The second was that the leadership of the House and the chairmanship of the Party are two wildly incompatible horses to ride. The first requires its incumbent to be the least partisan of ministers and the second requires him to be the most. Even Butler with his built-in ambiguity had found the dual role diffi- cult and unsatisfactory. Macleod, who was more brittle and had less depth than Rab, found it bifurcating. Third, and least impor- tant, the sinecure office which he was given in order that he might have a salary, that of Chancellor of the Duchy of Lancaster, was well below the prestige of the Lord Presidency of the Council or the Lord Privy Sealship which normally goes with leading the House of Commons. In any event, while he was by no means an abject failure at either of his incompatible posts, they did not give him the pivotal position in the government and Party that the two in combination might have been expected to do. The leadership (not just of the House but of the Conservative Party) was twice to fall vacant in the next four years. On neither occa- sion was Macleod a possible runner or even a seriously consulted kingmaker.

The first occasion was when Macmillan precipitately resigned in October 1963. This was announced on Thursday 10 October. By Saturday 19 October Alec Home had emerged as Prime Minister and had got all the members of the outgoing Cabinet, save only Macleod and Enoch Powell, to serve under him. It was a disastrous ten days, not only for Butler, the obvious although passed-over candidate, but also for Macleod. Macleod was more anti-Home than he was pro-Butler, who was in some sense his mentor but for whom his support in the last leadership contest in 1957 had been to say the least equivocal, and who he regarded, with some justification, as behaving with hopeless softness at the 1963 crunch. But Macleod also seems to have been activated by some inner sourness. His friendly 1973 biographer, Nigel Fisher, then an MP and a supporter as well as a friend, hints strongly at this. He partly attributes Macleod's temporary lack, not merely of higher judgement, but of basic political common sense to the severe illness of his daughter at the time, but he did not feel that this was the whole explanation.

Hailsham began as the front runner, or at least the most noisy one. When he began to fade Macleod believed that he himself might emerge between the *fainéant* Butler and the too rumbustious Hailsham. His only excuse was that his Blackpool conference speech (on n October) had been as great a success as usual, in contrast with the dank efforts of Butler and Maudling. But he ought to have noticed that Home got as good a reception as he did for a much less powerful speech. A politician who is applauded without deploying rhetoric is like a comedian who provokes laughter without saying anything funny. Neither can fail to succeed. But Macleod refused to take Home's candidature seriously for nearly another week. As a result he was late and ineffective (despite inherent strength) in organizing his junta against him, and was left gesticulating rather than conducting. Macmillan, who over-reacted to his prostate condition but did not allow it to detract from his anti-Butler dedication, took not the slightest notice of Macleod throughout.

Fisher does not doubt that these days finished off Macleod's chances of becoming leader of the Conservative Party, which had already been gravely weakened by his liberal courage as Colonial Secretary. If, however, the coffin required the knocking in of any nails Macleod abundantly provided the hammer during the next few months. Out of office, he became editor of the *Spectator* and a director of Lombard Banking, not one of the great names in the City but a finance house which at least had enough resources, even in those relatively austere days, to provide him with an enormous motor car and a chauffeur. I remember his assuring me that the most important thing for an office-less politician was to secure this facility (he may well have been right). I also remember seeing him frequently step out of it in New Palace Yard looking like a discontented gnome in spite of his golden coach.

His *Spectator* editorship, at which he was rather a success, led him much more astray than did the motor car. In January 1964, at the beginning of what was certain to be an election year, he wrote and published a long denunciation of 'the magic circle' of privilege, prejudice and complacency which had put Home in and kept Butler out. Macleod wanted to provoke a row, but he got more than he bargained for. Even the Enfield Conservative executive censured him for the article, although only by fifteen votes to fourteen, and with seven abstentions. A rare foray of his into the House of Commons smoking room met with a proportionately still less friendly Tory response.

He contemplated withdrawal from politics, but instead set about the slow process of working his passage back. That did not start well. His old luck seemed: to have deserted him. Home welcomed his return to the Shadow Cabinet after the 1964 election, but probably unintentionally gave him a dud portfolio. It was thought that the new Wilson Government was about to

57

nationalize steel and that if Macleod were made steel spokesman he could redeem his reputation in the most bloody part of the battlefield without at first being given too senior a command. But the government wisely procrastinated and Macleod languished. There was even a debate in which he allowed himself to be badly worsted by as normally grey a ministerial spokesman as Fred Lee. The humiliation was made greater by the fact that the newspapers had been briefed for several days previously to trumpet Macleod's coming triumph. Fisher, always loyal but never blind, says it was the one really bad speech that Macleod made in the House of Commons.

In the summer of 1965 Home resigned the leadership, and Macleod had to stand on the sidelines and watch a battle between Maudling and Heath (with Enoch Powell as a semi-irrelevant third candidate), both of whom were his juniors in age and had been substantially so in rank as recently as 1961. He broke an old compact with Maudling (that they would both support whichever of themselves looked stronger at the time of any future leadership contest) and voted for Heath. If he carried even two handfuls of votes with him this would have been decisive, for the margin was narrow. He was rewarded with the shadow Chancellorship, although I do not think this consideration had affected his vote. The promotion did, however, mark the completion of his penance and his return to the central councils, but only when his last likely chance of leadership had gone by. He was no more than fifty-one but he was in poor health and Heath was four years younger.

Macleod was shadow Chancellor for almost five years, the longest time for which he ever did any job. For the last half of this period I was too close to his performance to be able to judge it objectively. Looking back, and leafing through his speeches, I am struck by the contrast between the splendour of his phrases and the vacuity of his economic prescriptions. In so far as he endeavoured to be constructive (which was not much, for he was a great believer in the Churchillian doctrine that the business of an Opposition is to oppose), it was about taxation rather than the management of the economy. On the latter he claimed no expertise and preferred scepticism to precision. Even on taxation, however, he operated with a broad-brush blandness which is today treated as the hallmark of a would-be profligate Chancellor. His speech at the 1967 Party Conference was thus summarized by Nigel Fisher: 'He promised that a Conservative Government would abolish the Selective Employment Tax and reduce the burden of direct personal taxation. He did not think it necessary to increase indirect taxes by an equivalent amount because he relied on larger savings and a higher growth rate to fill the revenue gap under a Conservative Administration.'

He was much happier at general raillery. In the same speech he said: 'Secretaries of State come and go. We started with George Brown. Happy days. Three per cent mortgages. The National Plan. Where have all the flowers gone? Gone to the graveyard, every one. Then you will remember Michael – [pause]. No, of course you do not remember Michael Stewart ... In nominal charge we have the Prime Minister himself, a man whose vision is limited to tomorrow's headline.' He always liked getting Harold Wilson in his sights. In that same year in the House of Commons, having described Wilson as persuading himself and trying to persuade the country that he was in turn Napoleon, Churchill, Abraham Lincoln and the Duke of Wellington, Macleod moved to his cheer line: 'J. F. Kennedy described himself in a brilliant phrase as an idealist without illusions. I could describe the Prime Minister as an illusionist without ideals.'

When it came to my period as Chancellor I thought Macleod was much better at Party Conferences than in the House of Commons. I sat before a TV set lost in reluctant and apprehensive admiration as he riveted the faithful at Blackpool or Brighton, but I never found him especially formidable across the despatch boxes. I think he was bored and frustrated as his sixth year out of office turned into the seventh and also the last year of his life. I cannot say that I believe he would have been a great Chancellor. He was too concentrated on taxation, perhaps too much of a politician, and above all too ill for that. He was also curiously and obsessively unrealistic about unemployment. His mind was struck in the early post-war years on the issue and he genuinely believed that any level much over 300,000 was a certain sign of socialist incompetence and bureaucratic indifference. How he would have accommodated himself to the Conservative performance in the 1980s I cannot imagine. But he would certainly have been a very much better Chancellor than Anthony Barber.

He was also a considerable general loss to the Heath Government. 'We have lost our trumpeter,' someone said when he went. But he was more than that. He had an empathy which eluded Heath and a sense of direction which eluded every other member of that administration. He would not have succeeded Heath had he survived to 1975, when he would have been sixty-one and old for his years. Also he had some quality of self-destructiveness which made him not nearly as *papabile* as he sometimes looked. But he might have prevented a Thatcher succession. As it is, he remains an ambiguous figure, romantic and perverse, with a capacity for leadership which frustrated itself by his incapacity to conciliate those who were not under his spell.

Dean Acheson

Dean Acheson is best remembered in this country for his 1962 speech at the West Point Military Academy in which he said: 'Great Britain has lost an empire and not yet found a role.' It touched a sore spot only six years after Suez and on the threshold of General de Gaulle's veto on our first but belated application to join the Common Market (as it was then called). But he should be still more remembered for his part in the Marshall Plan, in the putting together of NATO, and in the rallying of the Western world from a post-1945 slough of despond which led on, after forty years of long and often tense waiting, to the great bloodless victory of 1989. Acheson was not an unduly modest man, but when he called the second (1969) volume of his memoirs *Present at the Creation* it was an under- rather than an overstatement.

The late 1940s and very early 1950s were as dangerous as they were creative, and Acheson's nerve was as good as his vision. With Truman and Bevin, Robert Schuman and Jean Monnet, he was an architect who built a Western world which was first a secure bastion and then a lighthouse that sent out a beam of attraction which destroyed the Soviet empire. Yet, to illustrate the paradoxes of life, he ended his four years as US Secretary of State (1949–53) under heavy attack from Senator McCarthy and his allies as a quasi-Communist, and ended his life, twenty years later, by embracing some views of which the deplorable Senator, had he still been alive and with the intelligence to understand Acheson's typically taut and sophisticated expression of them, might have been proud.

Acheson, born in 1893, was the son of a British-born clergyman who had emigrated to Canada at the age of sixteen, trained at Toronto and then crossed the US border to settle in the quiet university surroundings of Middletown, Connecticut. Edward Acheson and his wife none the less remained British subjects until quite late in life. In 1905 he became Episcopal Bishop of Connecticut (a tautological designation, it might be thought, but one habitually used). Dean Acheson (Dean was also an odd name for such a high-ranking clerical gentleman to give his son) was thought in middle life to look like the epitome of an Englishman. At first sight, with his black Homburg hats, his bristling moustache, his waistcoats, his dark town suits and occasional severe tweeds, this was so. Item by item he looked like Anthony Eden. But not in the ensemble, and indeed his 'Englishness' was only superficial. This was not because he was trying to look English and failing. On the contrary, what he really looked like was an East Coast American gentleman showing the English how they ought to look if they pulled themselves together and exhibited more leadership and moral fibre. Of his English opposite numbers as Foreign Minister he made Bevin look lumbering, Morrison slovenly, and Eden too consciously negligent. Acheson looked crisp, self-confident and a little bossy. As befitted the grand vizier of American foreign policy at the height of United States power, his clothes owed more to Brooks Brothers than to Savile Row.

Although his mother was the daughter of an Ontario whiskey distiller and bank president, Acheson did not belong to the plutocracy or even strictly to fashionable society, much admired and sought-after by the cognoscenti though he mostly was. He was never a New Yorker. From his upbringing in Connecticut to his school in Massachusetts, his university back in Connecticut, his law school once more in Massachusetts, his law firm and his high government posts and elegant pre-Civil War house in Washington, DC, his farm in Maryland, and his many trips to Europe and the Far East, he managed to skip over the city of wealth and fashion on the Hudson. Of course he visited it, but he never lived there. His wife, Alice Stanley, whom he married in 1917 when he was twenty-four and who is still alive, came from Michigan via the good New England women's college of Wellesley.

Yet, although he eschewed the Manhattan glitter of the super rich, everything was always of very high quality, including Alice Acheson. The school was Groton, which the Reverend Endicott Peabody, a product of Trinity College, Cambridge, had founded in 1884 with the object of creating a less easy-going and more high-minded Eton in the green and pleasant land of northern Massachusetts. Franklin Roosevelt went there in 1896 and thirty-six years later Peabody, still headmaster, was able to appear in night-shirt and night-cap in the dormitory of FDR's youngest son and say: 'Boy, your father has just been elected President of the United States. Whether this is a good thing I do not know. But I thought you ought to know. Goodnight, boy.'

The hesitancy of the second sentence came from the fact that although after a hundred years its three best-known alumni were probably Roosevelt, Harriman and Acheson, Democrats to a man, the spirit of the school, certainly of the majority of the parents, was strongly Republican. This thought was, however, tempered in Peabody's mind by his liking for worldly success. He allowed the official school history to perform the statistical feat of pointing out that, if all American schools had produced high public servants on the scale of Groton's first thousand graduates, the country would have had 37,000 Presidents, 350,000 ambassadors and 110,000 Senators, which might be regarded as a remarkable tribute to the classlessness of American society.

The university was Yale, which in 1911, when Acheson went there, and for two or three decades afterwards, probably had a stronger corporate loyalty and a more close-knit élitist identity than Harvard. It was chosen by Scott Fitzgerald, who had himself been at Princeton, the third of America's 'gold coast' universities, as the epitome of privileged education for fictional representation in both *Tender is the Night* and *The Great Gatsby*. And at Yale, as opposed to Groton, Acheson was a success and enjoyed himself. However, in his first volume of memoirs he ignored both Groton and Yale and wrote about the two-month period which he spent between them, in very rough conditions in northern Ontario, working as a tree-feller for the building of the second transcontinental Canadian railway. This tempted me to contrast Acheson's slightly self-conscious American toughness with Eden's old world effeteness, until I remembered that Eden spent the equivalent nineteenth summer of his life in incomparably worse conditions on the Somme.

The law school was Harvard, where Acheson shared an apartment with Cole Porter, also a 'Yalie', who defected to the music school. Acheson there fell under the intellectual influence of Felix Frankfurter, who enjoyed a dazzling academic reputation before becoming a Supreme Court Justice in 1939. It was, however, an older Jewish Justice (and as a Supreme Court judge, although not as an academic, still more distinguished figure), Louis Dembitz Brandeis, who first took Acheson to Washington as his law clerk. He stayed two years (from 1920 to 1922) with Brandeis, and then joined a Washington law firm with the splendidly wasp (white, Anglo-Saxon, Protestant) name of Covington and Burling, with which through various mutations he remained intermittently associated to the end of his life.

He was professionally sought after, both as an advocate and as an adviser. While still in his early thirties he argued many cases before the Supreme Court, and apparently lost every one of the first fifteen. But if his clients went down his reputation went up. He became prosperous enough to buy during the 1920s both his Georgetown house which dated from the time of James Polk's presidency (1845–9) and his horse-country farmhouse at Sandy Spring, Maryland, which dated from that of George Washington.

Yet through all this privileged education, highly successful use of it, and rise to repute and limited affluence, he was essentially a product of the upper professional classes and not a magnate. This did not mean that he was modest. He was about as modest as Quintin Hailsham or Richard Crossman, who were almost exactly his social equivalents. But it did mean that he saw life differently from his fellow Grotonians Franklin Roosevelt and Averell Harriman. They were the American equivalents of Cecils or Rothschilds. He was the equivalent of a 'poor Etonian', more alike in social outlook although not in personality to a Robert Armstrong or a Douglas Hurd. This made him in a sense a servant rather than a ruler of the state. But it did not deprive him of a splendid and careless independence. Psychologically he needed office less than did Harriman, who desperately felt that it was both his duty and his pleasure to be 'in'.

This difference was vividly illustrated by Acheson's behaviour in his first government office. When Roosevelt was constructing his administration in early 1933 Acheson hoped to be Solicitor-General. However, the Attorney-General (Homer Cummings) vetoed him. Some said it was because Bishop Acheson had refused to bless the divorced Cummings's second marriage. Others said that it required no assistance from the father to make the son's grand manner unacceptable to the Attorney in a subordinate. Acheson was lucky in the circumstances to be offered the under-secretaryship of the Treasury, which office he accepted with enthusiasm but not with happy results. Woodin, the Secretary of the Treasury, soon became ill, so that Acheson was effectively head of the second major department in the US Government by the time he was forty. Roosevelt wanted to devalue the dollar by gradually raising the price of gold from $20.67 an ounce to $35.00, where it remained until 1968. Acheson got locked in with the conservative financiers in the government, of whom Lewis Douglas, later Truman's ambassador to London, was the most prominent, and said this was illegal.

Roosevelt did not want Under-Secretaries who said what was right and what was wrong. He wanted those who could remove road-blocks. He became irritated with Acheson. Acheson in turn quickly ceased to be a Roosevelt fan, foolishly resenting being treated with a familiar condescension. 'It is not gratifying to receive the easy greeting which milord might give a promising stable boy and pull one's forelock in return,' he wrote. What he particularly disliked was Roosevelt's habit of calling everyone 'from his valet to his Secretary of State' by his first name or even a nickname, and responded by never in my experience referring to FDR (fifteen years dead when I first knew Acheson) as anything other than a cool 'Mr Roosevelt'. He allowed him neither a

'President' nor a place in history without a prefix. It was reminiscent of the old lady in Henry James's *Aspen Papers* who always spoke of the poet as 'Mr Shelley'. Elsewhere Acheson wrote of his attitude towards Roosevelt as being 'one of admiration without affection'. That quality, extending even to devotion, he said, and accompanied by a still larger dose of admiration, he reserved for Roosevelt's successor, Harry S. Truman, superficially an improbable hero for the patrician Acheson.

Following the dollar devaluation dispute Acheson was dropped from the Roosevelt administration in the autumn of 1933 and did not re-enter the government until February 1941, when he became an Assistant Secretary of State (for economic affairs) under Cordell Hull in the State Department. Relations with Roosevelt had recovered their equilibrium in the mean time and Acheson had even written one of the President's more important speeches of the 1940 election campaign. In the later stages of his period out of office Acheson had been a resolute campaigner for American assistance to Britain and France.

He served four and a half years as one of four Assistant Secretaries, nearly all the time under Cordell Hull, the longest-serving but not the most influential Secretary of State (for Roosevelt encouraged him to concentrate on trade policy not high politics), and then under Edward Stettinius whose distinction of appearance many people, including Acheson, regarded as about ten times that of his mind. The shunting of Hull away from the political mainline suited his Assistant Secretary for Economic Affairs quite well, and Acheson was able to play an effective role in negotiating Lend-Lease and the Bretton Woods currency agreement. In both cases he enjoyed having Keynes, ten years his senior, as an interlocutor. Keynes sometimes offended Americans by his impatient intellectual speed, and

67

Acheson sometimes offended his own countrymen and others by his inability to suffer fools gladly. But in this relationship neither wanted to or could patronize the other, and they got along well, with the distinct but not excessive superiority of Keynes's mind balanced by the superiority of the national power which was behind Acheson.

In the summer of 1945 Acheson thought the time had come to resume his lucrative private practice of the 1920s and 1930s. The war against Germany was won, and that against Japan was unexpectedly on the brink of following. Roosevelt was dead and Truman was President. First Hull and then Stettinius had resigned. James F. Byrnes, who had the fatal flaw for a Secretary of State of thinking that he and not the incumbent ought to be President, had taken over the State Department. Acheson achieved a week of freedom from office in early August and was then summoned back to become Under-Secretary, that is, number two man as opposed to one of four number three men in the Department. He held this office for twenty-two months until January 1947, and achieved almost as much in it as he was subsequently to do in his four years in full charge of the State Department. Byrnes spent a great deal of time abroad. This was partly because of the leisurely rhythm of mid-century diplomacy. Bevin did the same, sometimes being away from London for six weeks at a time, as was Byrnes from Washington. But it was also because Byrnes did not respect Truman and Truman did not trust Byrnes. They were like a husband and wife who could keep going only if they did not often coincide in the same house. As a result Acheson came increasingly to be both the co-ordinator of US foreign policy in Washington and the man who kept the White House and the State Department, then only a couple of hundred yards from each other, within hailing distance.

The Truman-Acheson relationship was at once bizarre and crucially beneficial for the Western world. They were utterly unlike each other, yet became locked in an alliance of mutual respect and affection. The key date was 6 November 1946. Nineteen forty-six was the nadir of Truman's presidency, although the first half of 1948 and even 1952 with its end-of-regime wave of petty scandals were both pretty bad. Although Truman's reputation has stood so high for the past twenty-five years, he enjoyed no similar esteem when he was actually doing the job. At all three periods his poll ratings were abysmal. But by early 1948 he had gained confidence and a sense of direction, and in 1952 he knew that he had steered the country through seven testing years. In 1946 he was unproven and floundering. There were quite serious suggestions that he ought to resign the Presidency. He took no notice of them but he did accept the humiliating advice that he should play no part in the mid-term congressional elections. The only hope for the Democratic candidates, it was suggested, was that the Democratic President should neither open his mouth nor show his face.

He insisted on going home to vote in Missouri, but his journey across half the continent in the presidential train was conducted in silence and almost in solitude. There were no whistle-stop speeches. On the way back he was informed of the results, the disastrous nature of which had not been avoided by his abstinence. The Democrats had lost control of both houses for the first time since 1928. At Union Station, Washington, there was no one to meet the President except for the unmistakable figure of Dean Acheson, solitary and distinguished, who had gone there of his own volition, way beyond the duties of his office, partly because the disdain which made him suffer fools so badly also made him perversely loyal to those who were down. When the Alger Hiss security scandal broke three years later Acheson pretended that he had known Hiss much better than was the case. (It was Hiss's brother with whom he had worked closely.)

Acheson's 1946 presence on that railroad platform also became symbolic of the transition from the first to the middle phase of the Truman presidency. At first Truman felt at home only with Missouri cronies and with very political politicians. At the time of the Chicago convention which had nominated him as Vice-President he would have been amazed to be told that he would rather have been greeted by the acerbic Acheson than by the manipulating Byrnes, still Acheson's nominal superior, although soon to be eased out. Yet such was the case. Truman took Acheson back for an assuaging gossip at the White House and thereafter a special bond existed between them. Two months later General George Marshall returned to Washington from his long mission to China and immediately replaced Byrnes as Secretary of State. Acheson and Marshall were as different from each other as they both were from Truman, but they together constituted the twin and essential props for the creative international success of Truman's presidency. Yet they did not do it like crutches supporting a lame man. Their regard for Truman was just as high as was Truman's for them. They constructed a tripod of American leadership which shaped the Western world of the next forty years and, despite the hazards of the cold war, gave it unprecedented prosperity and unusually long-lasting peace.

It was as well that the tripod was in place and Truman's confidence underpinned by January 1947, for that month was the beginning of a peculiarly testing year for Europe and hence for American leadership. France and Italy looked on the brink of revolution. Russia, moved by a mixture of truculence and

70

fear, had become wholly unco-operative, iron-handed in Eastern Europe and menacing beyond. Of the victorious countries, Britain, snowbound and fuelless in a cruel winter, was forced to begin the long process of withdrawing from its world power illusions and responsibilities. On two successive days in February a date was fixed for withdrawal from India and the almost immediate cessation of aid to Greece and Turkey was announced.

The only country with any surplus energy and resources was the United States. Would they deploy them? Acheson was central to the positive answer. First he argued with almost excessive vigour the case for the proclamation of the 'Truman Doctrine'. This replaced British with American aid to Greece and Turkey on the grounds 'that it must be the policy of the United States to support free peoples who are resisting attempts at subjugation by armed minorities or by outside pressure'. Viewed favourably, the doctrine proclaimed several decades of the *Pax Americana*. Viewed unfavourably, it set the country on course to the débâcle of Vietnam. Viewed from any point of view, it was a momentous decision.

No sooner had it been taken than Acheson set about preparing the ground for Marshall's speech at Harvard four months later, which launched the European Recovery Programme or, as by Truman's shrewd and generous decision it came universally to be known, the Marshall Plan. The President knew that a Republican Congress would not vote a vast programme of civil aid to Europe (the Truman Doctrine was military and therefore less vulnerable) under a name as controversial as his own. Marshall, at least until Senator McCarthy got going, was a name almost beyond criticism. But although Marshall provided the eponym, as well as one or two insights of simple but crucial

71

importance, it was Acheson who organized the work, provided the most persuasive arguments, and even tried out the substance of the speech before the less august audience of a Teachers' College in Mississippi a good month before the Harvard Commencement Day. None of this would have worked without the dependable commitment of Truman, but it is none the less the case that Acheson's State Department work in January–June 1947, carried out from only the number two position, had more constructive impact than that of Cordell Hull, Stettinius and Byrnes put together. This was made stranger by the fact that he did it all under a self-imposed sentence of retirement. He had told Marshall in January that, after six years of (poorly paid) public service, he proposed to return to private legal practice on 30 June. It was odd to sound such a tocsin to America and the world in the spring and then to find compelling a return to Covington and Burling at midsummer. But it all worked out for the best as it enabled Acheson to replenish his energy and finances during Marshall's period of maximum effectiveness and then to come back as his successor at the head of the State Department when the General's health failed after the 1948 election.

Acheson was Secretary of State for four years from January 1949 to January 1953. He brought the North Atlantic Treaty into the (relatively) safe harbour of completion and signature, he saw the end of the Berlin blockade, he was the Secretary who stood at Truman's side and organized crucial UN majorities during the hazardous first year of the Korean War, and he was the one who took the brunt of the first wave of McCarthyite attack. Of course he despised McCarthy and, unlike many people from Eisenhower downwards, he had the courage not to conceal his contempt. There is a famous story of a chance encounter in a Senate elevator. McCarthy, away from the television cameras or reporters' pencils, liked to assume towards those whom he was tormenting the false bonhomie of a travelling salesman in one line of spurious goods to another. They both had their rackets to pursue and there was no need for cut-throat competition to affect their off-duty relations. This often produced an ingratiating response from weak opponents whom he had just been excoriating. He tried the technique on Acheson. 'Hiya, Dean,' he optimistically began. The murderously cold silence and apoplectic forehead of the Secretary of State penetrated even to McCarthy.

Yet, although Acheson could squash McCarthy, he could not immunize himself against him. McCarthy did not care about his own reputation. He hardly understood what the word meant. This gave him the deadliness of a terrorist who is indifferent to losing his own life. He made a misery of Acheson's last two years at the State Department. He threw Acheson on to the defensive, as he was also to do to General Marshall, who was then back in the administration as Secretary of Defense. He forced Acheson to retire several foreign service officers whose loyalty was impeccable except in the distorting eyes of the destructive Senator from Wisconsin, and as a result gave him a morale-shattered Department over which to preside. It considerably weakened his usefulness to the US Government, although probably more at home than abroad.

Acheson was sustained by a fierce loyalty from his President which was important for the buoyancy of his spirits, although Truman in those days did not carry a very thick mantle of prestige or authority that he could throw over the Secretary of State. Ernest Bevin was also a pillar of earthy support. Acheson recorded Bevin as saying on a 1950 occasion when there were

Republican congressional demands for his resignation: 'Don't give it a thought, me lad. If those blokes don't want yer, there's plenty as does.'

In the tangled skein of Anglo-American personal relations in the critical post-war years Bevin and Acheson got on crucially well. There is a general easy belief that after the years of wartime partnership there was a natural camaraderie between American and British leaders and public servants, which by comparison left the French, the Germans and others out in the cold. The position was more complicated than this. Bevin rather admired Marshall, but he did not have easy relations with him, and Marshall in turn, who was in some ways priggish, believed that Bevin was, of all things, unreliable, and in any event rather a crude fellow. With Truman, Bevin's relations were vitiated by Israel, and by his belief that the President played politics with the issue. Nor were Attlee-Truman relations particularly close, although they once had a convivial evening together, under the surprising aegis of Ambassador Oliver Franks, singing World War I songs. Acheson both failed to understand and discounted Attlee. Furthermore, to underline that this was no special feature of Democrats or Labour ministers, Dulles's relations with Eden were abysmal, and very little better with Churchill and Macmillan. So the Acheson-Bevin bond of affectionate respect, the more impressive for being across a chasm of dissimilarity, stood out as both valuable and unusual.

Acheson, however, was not Anglo-Saxon-centric. He got on almost as well with Robert Schuman, the ascetic-looking Lorraine lawyer who had been brought up in Metz under the German occupation of 1870–1918 and was the key early architect of Franco-German rapprochement, as he did with Bevin. He was also good with the pointed gothic arches of Konrad

Adenauer's appearance and personality. The Federal Republic of Germany with which he had to deal was immensely weak compared with what subsequently emerged, but he none the less had the foresight to treat its first Chancellor with a respect that laid secure foundations to a Bonn-Washington axis which persisted for thirty years as a salient world feature until Helmut Schmidt became disenchanted with the leadership of Jimmy Carter. Acheson was also crucial to bringing Italy into NATO. Truman was at first against. But the French, influenced by Mediterranean solidarity, persuaded Acheson, who persuaded Truman. There was thus avoided a major misfortune for the Alliance and a disaster for Italy, which with its big Communist Party and ambiguous location needed both Europe and NATO and would have been desperately adrift without either one of them.

Acheson was also at his best at the outbreak of the Korean War. In June 1950 the sudden eruption of a strongly Soviet-backed (so it was thought; Stalin, it subsequently emerged, had given only reluctant acquiescence) North Korean invasion of the South carried with it the clear threat of World War III. Equally clearly the brunt of resistance was certain to fall upon the United States. This combination of circumstances exactly suited Acheson's capacity for quick decision, his national self-confidence, and his lack of fear at peering into the abyss. By the time that Truman got back to Washington from a brief weekend in Missouri, Acheson had already procured a UN Security Council vote of nine to nil with one abstention (the Soviet Union was luckily and foolishly boycotting the Council) in favour of action. 'You are a great Secretary of State,' Truman wrote to him at the end of the week. 'Your handling of the situation has been superb.'

75

The Korean War proved a major but necessary defensive undertaking in which the United States suffered 157,000 casualties, including 34,000 dead. Truman and Acheson survived it together, unsubdued but not, at the time, honoured either, with the bond of mutual respect between them growing closer. When the Truman presidency came to an end in January 1953 the brunt in Korea was well over, although the armistice had not been negotiated. The final act of the presidency was a Cabinet luncheon for the Truman family at the Achesons' Georgetown house. At it Truman thawed from his icy excursion with Eisenhower to the Capitol, and the party was described by his daughter as 'an absolutely wonderful affair, full of jokes and laughter and a few tears.' Truman went back to Missouri, and Acheson, once more, to Covington and Burling. Subsequently, such is the role of circumstances in personal relations and in spite of their mutual respect and survival of shared vicissitudes, they did not see much of each other for their remaining two decades, although they exchanged some good letters. Acheson died on 1 October 1971, at the age of seventy-eight, and Truman followed two months later and nearly ten years older.

In these later years Acheson wrote a moderate amount (two slim volumes of reminiscence and a serious, sharply amusing but none the less too long tome of memoirs). He earned substantial fees for Covington and Burling but was never ensnared in the obsessive pursuit of mammon. He remained a firm although increasingly right-wing and hardline Democrat. I remember staying a weekend in 1959 at John Kenneth Galbraith's house to which the host returned from a meeting of the Democratic Advisory Committee in a state of half-controlled exasperation at the cold war intransigence of the former Secretary of State.

Acheson never had much view of Adlai Stevenson, who was

too hesitating and ambiguous for his taste. Nor was he an early Kennedy supporter, but he responded to the success and verve of the young President. At the time of the Cuban missile crisis he was temporarily recruited back into active service, and became a rash and leading 'hawk' in Excom, as the directing body was called. Although discontented with the President's desire to get a negotiated solution, Acheson undertook crucial missions to Britain, France and Germany with the photographic evidence of the Soviet build-up. In the first and the third countries the evidence was studied with sympathetic interest. In France it was swept aside as police court stuff. General de Gaulle asked one central question. Was he being consulted or informed of a decision already taken by the President? Acheson had the firmness to say clearly that it was the latter. De Gaulle expressed himself satisfied by the directness. He was in favour of independent decisions, he said. 'You may tell your President that on this occasion he will have the support of France,' he grandly concluded.

The last time I saw Acheson was at the end of 1970. He expressed some fairly outrageous opinions, partly as a tease. Unfortunately Senator Muskie, who was present and who was desperately trying to get Acheson's support for his then strong bid for the Democratic presidential nomination, purported to take them seriously, but adding the gloss that policy had to be democratically decided. Acheson turned on him like a matador on an old bull. 'Are you trying to say, Senator, that United States foreign policy should be determined in a series of little town meetings in the State of Maine? Don't ask them, Senator, tell them. When I believe you will do that, I will support you. Until then, not.'

It was one of the last cries of the thirty-year history of

Democratic Party world leadership. Acheson was a splendid exponent of it, arrogant, élitist, courageous, and very clear-sighted to the middle distance. He was in many ways too unsqueamish for British taste in the third quarter of the twentieth century, but Britain was none the less fortunate to have him 'present at the creation' of so many of the institutions of the post-war Western world.

Konrad Adenauer

K onrad Adenauer was the oldest statesman ever to function in elected office, beating Gladstone by a good two years. He became the first Chancellor of the Federal Republic of Germany in 1949 at the age of seventy-three, and very reluctantly gave way to a successor in 1963 at the age of eighty-seven.

If explanations are sought for the remarkable success of West Germany during its forty-one years of separate existence, the simple answer of the quality of its Chancellors should not be ignored. There were few of them – only six as opposed to ten British Prime Ministers and nine American Presidents during the same period – and they have all, with the sole exception of KurtGeorg Kiesinger, the handsome and somewhat vacuous Würtem-berger who survived in office only from 1967 to 1969, been men who in their different ways were dominant world statesmen: Erhard, the animator of the German economic miracle, who, however, shared with Anthony Eden the characteristic of being better in a second position than at the top; Brandt, who had vision and courage and the capacity to inspire even if not always to administer; Schmidt, who was much the better manager and saw to at least the middle distance with greater clarity; and Kohl, who may look lumbering, but has with exceptional decisiveness both reunited a nation and fostered a dynamic half-decade of European integration.

Yet the achievements of Adenauer, the first, the oldest, the least flexible and by no means the most amiable, must be set above those of all the others. He began with a Germany that was shattered, impoverished and reviled, and he ended with one which, while likely to remain indefinitely divided, was rich, respected and even admired. Its real national income had grown threefold under his Chancellorship, its exports by fifty times or more, it had regained such sovereignty as was possible in an interdependent world (although Adenauer always had the sense not to set too much store by sovereignty), had become America's most dependable and valued ally as well as the economic power-house of the Common Market, had buried a hundred years of Franco-German enmity and begun a partnership which was to run the European Community for at least a quarter of a century.

These achievements removed much of the jaggedness of the post-war German mood in which guilt jostled with resentment and poverty with pride. Objectively Adenauer's role was a calming one, but he was a divisive not a healing figure in West German politics. I doubt if he ever had a friendly relationship with a 'Sozi', the not very respectful term by which SPD members were known in CDU circles, although he was on good terms with Hans Bockler, the first post–1945 leader of the German trades unions, and he was always a Christian Democrat and not a Conservative in industrial and social policy. Nor was he very well disposed towards members of his own party who showed an independence of view like Gustav Heinemann, whom he got rid of as Minister of the Interior in 1950 and who subsequently became an SPD-supported President of the Federal Republic, or who achieved too much independent success like Ludwig Erhard. He reserved his affection not for his ministers but for his blood relations or for those who by working for him in the Chancellery constituted an official family, although in the latter case at least a half of them eventually fell out with him.

He was not very forgiving or tolerant of his fellow men, so little so that his successor (Erhard) said that his salient characteristic was 'contempt for humanity'. But this was after Adenauer was reported as having said of Erhard (then his Vice-Chancellor): 'I'm told that I ought to nail him down. But how can you nail down a pudding?' Adenauer's dislikes extended from political parties and individuals to nations, and it was said that the three principal ones amongst them were 'the Russians, the Prussians and the British'. Of the three it was certainly the second group, the Prussians, who aroused his most consistent dislike, and quite possibly the strongest as well. The Russians did not much obtrude upon him until they overran and lopped off half (but mainly the Prussian half) of his country in 1945, nor the British until they sacked him as Mayor of Cologne in the autumn of that same year. But for the Prussians his dislike was much more immanent and life-long. He disliked them not just for what they did, which is a curable dislike, but for what they were, which is not.

He was born a Prussian subject, but as an ardent Catholic in an area of the Rhineland that had merely been thrown to Prussia at the 1815 Congress of Vienna his loyalty to Berlin was negligible. As a child he lived through the anti-Catholicism of Bismarck's *Kulturkampf*. As a young man he found Bach 'too Protestant' for his taste. As a middle-aged Weimar Republic politician he claimed that his nights in the *Schlafwagen* between Cologne and Berlin always became disturbed when the train had crossed the Elbe, and, more seriously, he objected to working with such a respectable figure as Stresemann because of his bullet-headed 'Prussianism'. As an old man he was content to subordinate his commitment to German unity to the prior need for the integration of the Federal Republic in the West. He had no burning desire to upset the religious and political balance in West Germany by the infusion of too many Prussians, particularly as they might have been subject to Communist indoctrination.

Romantically Adenauer was a Carolingian, whose *annus mirabilis* was 800, when Charlemagne was crowned at Aachen as Frankish Emperor. But he was not remotely a cosmopolitan. In reality as opposed to romance he was a provincial citizen of Cologne, the centre of whose world was the small area of that Rhineland city which contained the Cathedral, the palace of the Cardinal-Archbishop and the *Rathaus,* from which, however, he much preferred the westward to the eastward prospect. He had no real command over any foreign language, except perhaps for Latin, and although he had made a student visit to Florence and Venice his travels in the next fifty years were confined to a couple of holidays in (German-speaking) Switzerland and a two-day visit to a Paris conference.

Yet his European vision was extraordinarily clear-sighted. He was determined to transcend the problem of Germany's past by tying the country into a European future; he saw that the key to that was the partnership with France, and he pursued this goal relentlessly, undeterred by setbacks like the collapse of the European Defence Community and undeflected by side issues like several years of fairly intolerable French behaviour over the Saarland. He also took in his stride the change from the weak Prime Ministers of the Fourth Republic, compared with whom he was manifestly more famous and more permanent, to General de Gaulle, compared with whom he was not.

The strain between these two old eagles was that Adenauer, Carolingian though he was, knew how necessary America was to Europe, and in particular to Germany, at a time when Khrushchev was about to build the Berlin wall, whereas de Gaulle was eager to cock snooks at Washington. Had this been compounded by an equal difference about Britain's relationship with Europe the gap might have become uncontainable. But in fact, although not in theory, there was no such difference on this issue. The official position of the German Government was in favour of British entry, and Atlanticists like Erhard and Foreign Minister Schröder genuinely cared about it. But Britain in Europe was no part of Adenauer's Rhenish vision. He was a clandestine Gaullist on the issue, privately believed that the General was quite right to veto the negotiations for British entry, and had no intention of applying the only effective German sanction, which was to hold up the signing of the Franco-German Treaty of friendship. So, within six days of the veto, he went to Paris and signed the Treaty. Britain's hope of relying on 'the five' (which meant Germany plus four) to counteract Paris was in ruins.

Was the unhelpfulness based on a desire by Adenauer to avenge past British insults? Not directly, I think, for it was deeper rooted than that. Adenauer was a 'little European' and he could not see Britain fitting into his idea of a tightly integrated group-ing. And, in view of Britain's behaviour over the twenty years of her delayed membership, who is to say that he was wrong? The danger he saw was compounded in early 1963, when de Gaulle's veto was applied, by the looming threat of a British Labour Government. Adenauer not only disliked socialists in general; he

83

had a particularly strong view against British ones. Almost para-noically, he regarded the generals, brigadiers and colonels who had been the agents in Germany of the Attlee/Bevin Government after 1945 as having grossly favoured the SPD and increased his own difficulties in coming to power. He saw the radio stations and Hamburg-based newspapers, such as *Die Welt*, which the British occupation had fostered, as being centres of left-wing propaganda, and continued to bear a grudge for this.

It was not, however, purely political, for I do not think that Adenauer ever got on to the friendly terms with any British politician that he achieved with Eisenhower, with Dulles (perhaps above all), with Acheson, with Schuman and with de Gaulle: not with Churchill, not with Eden, not with Macmillan, although it was with the last that he may have come closest to so doing. When Macmillan had him to Chequers in November 1959 and showed him the somewhat doubtful glories of the 'Tudor' hall, including the 'Rembrandt', in the corner of which Churchill had painted a small mouse, Adenauer's reported comment was '*das ist kein Rembrandt*'. While recent research strongly suggests that this comment was more than justified it was not perhaps the most welcome or warming to be expected from a friendly guest.

A great deal of Anglo-German reconciliation went on during the Adenauer years. The *Deutsch-Englische Geselschaft* began in 1950 the continuing series of Koenigswinter Conferences between politicians, journalists and academics of the two countries, which became amongst the most influential because the most spontaneous international colloquia ever held. But these and other fructuous activities were at a level a few steps below that of Adenauer.

Franco-German reconciliation leading into close partnership

came essentially from the top downwards, alike in the Adenauer–Schuman, the Adenauer-de Gaulle and the Schmidt-Giscard days. It was not for this reason artificial or fragile, for it could be observed seeping downwards like water to the roots of a plant, and it produced very effective political co-operation. Anglo-German reconciliation was more of an unofficial and spontaneous affair and arguably produced more cultural cross-fertilization. Certainly it was more linguistically fecund on the German side. But it did not produce comparable political results. This was substantially due to British detachment from Europe, although there were also strong personal factors at work. Adenauer set the pattern for these, although it must be said that they also made Schmidt less than enchanted with Harold Wilson, and Kohl still less enthusiastic about Margaret Thatcher. Adenauer, moreover, had a belief in grace through the calm and patient endurance of vicissitudes, accompanied by a concentric view of Europe, which made him more at home with the Catholic statesman from the border regions of the defeated continent than with those who had led more oceanic and victorious lives.

The other salient truth about Adenauer was that he was immensely old for those with whom he was mostly dealing. He was Churchill's contemporary within fourteen months but then Churchill was himself immensely old in his second period of office, and was eight and a half years gone when Adenauer at last ceased to be Chancellor. But Adenauer was fifteen years older than both Eisenhower and de Gaulle, nineteen years older than Macmillan, and forty years older than Kennedy. He was born in the heyday of the Second Reich of Wilhelm I and Bismarck. He liked its apparent stability and burgeoning success as Germany (and America) bounded ahead of Britain to become the leading heavy industrial powers in the world. But he was always somewhat detached from both the militarism and the Protestantism of the Berlin-centred Empire.

His father was a minor law-court official, who had surprisingly fought with sufficient enthusiasm for the Prussians against the Austrians at Koeniggrätz (or Sadowa) in 1866 that he had been commissioned in the field. But he had no money with which to support a wife in a style adequate for an officer in the caste-ridden Prussian army, and when he wanted to marry he had to resign. He then became a petty bureaucrat, short of money but of some force of character. He was hesitant as to whether he could afford to send his third son to university but eventually Konrad Adenauer got to both Freiburg and Munich and then came back to become a successful Cologne advocate.

In 1904 he married several ranks up into the *haute bourgeoisie* of the city. His bride's father was dead but her paternal grandfather had been a small-scale Frick, building up a gallery of six hundred or so significant paintings, and her mother was a Wallraf, which family was soon to provide an Oberbürgermeister (or Lord Mayor) of Cologne, which was important to Adenauer, for in 1906 he entered the city administration, rose rapidly through it, and in 1917, when Wallraf was enticed to Berlin as Under-Secretary at the Ministry of the Interior, succeeded him as Lord Mayor. By then his wife, who had long been sickly, had died at the age of thirty-six, leaving him with three young children. She had also provided him with the route to becoming a prosperous notable, although this was not the motive for the marriage, for he was a devoted husband and a desolated widower. He was married again after three years to the daughter (eighteen years his junior) of a medical professor who was his next-door neighbour. They were Protestants, but Gussi Adenauer was converted to Catholicism before the marriage. They had a further three children. She died in 1948, leaving him to live the last twenty years of his life and the whole of his Chancellorship as a second-time widower. He was close to his children, but the reconciliation to and endurance of loneliness was an important strand in his make-up.

In early 1917 he was seriously injured in a motor crash. His municipal limousine ran into a tramcar in the centre of Cologne. It was a very civic accident. The confusion and agitation must have been worthy of a street scene in an early German film. Adenauer walked the short distance to hospital, but his head injuries were severe. He was in hospital for four months. The shape of his face was permanently changed, and when a deputation from the City Council came to visit him in convalescence in the Black Forest they took a long time in conversational gambits somewhat ponderously designed to explore whether his brain was functioning normally. Then they offered him the Lord Mayoralty, which he accepted.

His brain was certainly not impaired, but nor was it ever very nimble or original or fluent. He always employed a small vocabulary and expressed simple ideas, but with force and persistence. His wit, which was considerable, was dry and deflating. His oratory was far from charismatic, and its force came not from his words or gestures but from his inner certainty. He had a capacity for hard work and for the complete preparation of a case, whether legal or political.

The Lord Mayor of Cologne, whether under the Empire or the Weimar Republic, had almost *ex officio* an influence in German national politics. Cologne was the fourth-largest city in the Reich, and its history, its Cardinal, and its Rheinbrücke, which made it the great gateway to the west, then gave it a traditional preeminence over Düsseldorf which it has not fully maintained in the last fifty years. In 1918, with the armistice and the fall of the Hohenzollerns, it was the focal point for the disorderly demobilization of the defeated Imperial army making its way back from the Western front. First in the confusion of the disintegration and then with the mutual prickliness involved in dealing with the British occupation force, Adenauer had a more testing time than most major mayors.

Later, under the Weimar Republic, his life as Lord Mayor involved more of Berlin than he would have wished. From May 1921 onwards he was President of the State Council, the second house of the Prussian Parliament, which retained a separate although not perhaps very pointful existence under the Republic as it had done under the Empire. In the endless round of shifting governments that undermined Weimar, he was three times suggested for the post of Reichskanzler. The first two suggestions in May 1921 and November 1922 were only glancing propositions. The third, substantially later in May 1926, was more serious. He was summoned to Berlin by two leading members of his own party, the Centre Party, which in spite of its name was more confessional than middle of the road, being rather right-wing and almost exclusively Catholic, and told that he would be acceptable to the other parties as head of a broad-based coalition.

After two days of talks he decided that he would rather stick to Cologne. The People's Party were not reconciled to joining with the Social Democrats, and the Social Democrats feared that Adenauer was too far to the right for them. In addition, Adenauer and Stresemann (People's Party, who had been Chancellor, was Foreign Minister and would insist on remaining so) were each frightened that the other would be too strong-willed for them to work together in partnership. Adenauer went home, Wilhelm

Marx became head of a more limited government, and the Republic staggered on through six more governments and nearly seven more years to Hitler's coming to power. Throughout these years of Weimar failure Adenauer was more than a provincial mayor, but none the less just short of achieving the international fame which gave the names of Ebert or Rathenau or Stresemann or Brüning a resonance outside Germany. I doubt if Brigadier Barra-clough, the intrepid British officer who in October 1945 sacked Adenauer from the Cologne mayoralty (to which he had been reappointed by the Americans in March of that year), knew what Adenauer had been before the war, let alone what he was about to become.

One of Adenauer's sensitivities was whether he had or had not been a Rhineland separatist in the inter-war years. Both in 1919 and in 1923 he had been involved in movements for the setting up of a Rhenish Republic. The key questions were whether he intended this to be little more than the equivalent of a modern *Land* within the Reich, and how far he was working with people who were in effect French agents intent upon the disruption of Germany. On the answer to these questions there depended the issue of whether he could reasonably be accused of having tried to turn his back on the 'Vaterland'. What he undoubtedly wanted to do was to get the Rhineland out of Prussia, in which it had been incongruously placed after 1815. But not out of Germany, he rather obsessively subsequently insisted, even causing his authorized 1957 biographer to blow up an account of Berlin meetings in November 1923 at which, he claimed, Stresemann and others, panicked by currency collapse and the French occupation of the Ruhr, tried to force him against his will to follow the autonomous course. All accounts leave an impression of his protesting too much on the issue.

There is also some ambiguity about Adenauer's life during the twelve Nazi years. What is certain is that he declined to join the bandwagon of the incoming Führer in 1933 and consequently found himself quickly dismissed from his mayoralty. Hitler was appointed a minority Chancellor by President Hindenburg on 30 January and immediately announced Reichstag elections. On 17 February he came to Cologne. Adenauer declined to meet him at the airport (admittedly at 11 p.m.) and then ordered swastika flags to be taken down from the pillars of the municipally owned Rhine bridge, although saying that they could be flown in front of the Trade Fair Hall (where Hitler's meeting was to take place). On 5 March Hitler won a landslide victory, with a strong vote in Cologne. A week later, warned of impending danger, Adenauer fled and/or was dismissed from his office and his city.

It was never wholly clear which came first, the dismissal or the flight. And his destination was also surprising. He went to Berlin and made a personal petition of complaint to Goering, of all people, against the local conditions that had made him flee from Cologne. And he took up residence as president of the second chamber in the state apartments of the Prussian Government, situated in the Wilhelmstrasse, of all places. He had gilded furniture but no money and no security. The former deficiency was repaired by a sudden cash gift of 10,000 marks (the equivalent today of about £20,000) by a Jewish American admirer, a businessman resident in Belgium. (There is some evidence that this vital subvention had a permanent effect on Adenauer's attitude to Jews and Israel; no doubt as a post-war German Chancellor he would in any event have felt it necessary to show evidence of guilt, but he did so with more spontaneous conviction than might have been expected from a central

European Catholic of his generation.)

The security deficiency was less easily repaired. After a few weeks he clandestinely left Berlin and took refuge, without his family, in a remote Benedictine monastery in the Eifel mountains, of which the abbot was a former school-fellow. He stayed there until the beginning of 1934. Then he was offered and accepted the tenancy of a lavish house whose owner was leaving Germany, which probably drew attention to it and which was most inappropriately situated for Adenauer, very near to Berlin and in flat, sandy, Prussian pine forests. There most things went wrong. He was accused of massive municipal peculation in Cologne, succeeded in destroying his accuser and in establishing his innocence of dishonesty (although it was clear that he had been most handsomely remunerated), but was none the less arrested and harshly interrogated in Potsdam at the time of the Röhm 'blood-bath' in June 1934.

Then he was released, as suddenly and irrationally as he had been arrested. He spent a few months – or was it a few weeks, or a few quarters, details are curiously imprecise – more or less on the run, and settled in Rhöndorf, a village across the Rhine and a little above Godesberg, at first in a rather mean house. Rhöndorf was to remain his base for the rest of his life. Then he was expelled from the Cologne rural district, in which Rhöndorf was just situated, and moved about four miles. Then he was allowed back, then mysteriously his Cologne city pension was half restored at a rate sufficient to give him about £40,000 (at present-day values) a year. Out of this, and some compensation for his sequestered Cologne property, he built a substantial house, with mounting terraces, a lovingly tended rose garden, and a striking westward view across the river to the Eifel mountains.

91

There he lived unmolested for seven or eight years. He was detached from the regime, but not its active enemy. His three sons served in the German army. He declined to have anything to do with the 'July plot' against Hitler, but was none the less arrested in August 1944. He then hovered on the brink of Buchenwald and extermination for a few months, but survived through a mixture of luck and the respect in which he continued to be held by most Rhinelanders, even if they were serving as policemen or guards or doctors in Nazi camps. He was back in Rhöndorf well before the Americans arrived in March 1945 and drafted him to his old post in the Cologne *Rathaus*.

Adenauer's experiences under Nazism remind me of Sakharov's extraordinary life in the last years of Soviet oppression. As Sakharov travelled to protest at the trial of a fellow dissident he was in constant danger of arrest. But until it actually happened he was allowed to flash his pass as a member of the Soviet Academy of Science and get priority travel to his point of protest. Both Nazi Germany and Soviet Russia were oppressive societies, but they were also onions of civilization (Germany more than Russia) with a lot of leaves to be peeled off before pluralism could be destroyed.

On this record Adenauer could never be accused of having given a flicker of support to Nazism. But he treated it more as an aberration which had to be endured than as an evil that had to be opposed at all costs. His attitude to it was rather like that of the Catholic Church to unwelcome and potentially hostile regimes. They would sooner or later perish. The Church would endure. As a result, while he had the utmost distaste for a system that had predictably brought Germany so low, a sense of anti-Hitler solidarity, as opposed to a determination to correct the mistakes of the past, never seemed part of his motivation.

He was content to have some former Nazis in his governments. And he was able within days of the erection of the Berlin Wall in 1961 to pronounce the most self-damaging sentence of his political life against the Governing Mayor of that city, who was also his principal opponent in the Federal elections then taking place. When the monstrous barrier sprang up in the middle of an August night Willy Brandt immediately interrupted his campaign for the Chancellorship and flew to what was then the most exposed sector of the Western world. Adenauer, after the briefest pause, went on electioneering, and in Bavaria a few evenings later said with almost incredible insensitivity: 'If ever anyone has been treated with the greatest consideration by his opponents, it is Herr Brandt, alias Frahm.' Brandt had been born illegitimate in Lübeck and was brought up in Germany as Herbert Frahm. After Hitler came to power he emigrated to Norway and in 1940, joining the resistance movement there, he assumed the name by which he was known to the world. He resumed German citizenship after the war and became Mayor of West Berlin in 1957. But for Adenauer, at least during the election, he was more an émigré 'Sozi' than a noble fellow-resister. Hence the clanging remark.

In spite of or perhaps because of this partisanship Adenauer was a great election winner. When he was dismissed (for the second time) from the Cologne mayoralty in 1945 he was also banned from taking part in politics in the British zone. Noël Annan, as a colonel in the Control Commission, was instrumental in getting this ban lifted. For the next three years Adenauer devoted himself to building up the CDU and to securing as absolute a personal control of it as is possible in a democratic party. He eliminated his old Centre Party rivals from Berlin, Jakob Kaiser and Andreas Hermes, as effectively as, seven years later,

93

he was within a few weeks to make Heinrich Brüning, who reappeared in Germany trailing the clouds of glory of being Weimar's last hope before Hitler, feel that he would do better to return to the New England groves of academe from whence he had come. (Brüning, at once amazingly for a pre-Hitler Chancellor but also typically for a possible Adenauer rival, had the dangerous attribute for being ten years his junior.)

By September 1948, when the Parliamentary Council began its nine months of work on the Basic Law (or constitution) for the Federal Republic, Adenauer had the CDU under full control and was able (for once with SPD support) to become the President of the Council. He then got his way on most constitutional issues. Bonn (almost in the shadows of the spires of Cologne Cathedral) became the capital. Frankfurt, with its past in the lay revolution of 1848, its present in the SPD *Land* of Hesse, and its future as the city of mammon and the D-Mark, was the rejected rival. Moreover, the main weaknesses of Weimar were corrected. The electoral system, while roughly and adequately proportional, kept out splinter parties by its 5 per cent threshold for representation in the Bundestag; and that Bundestag, once it had elected a Chancellor, was prevented from undermining him by a vote of no confidence unless and until it was able to provide a majority for an alternative candidate.

The first elections in the late summer of 1949 produced a near equality of members for the CDU and the SPD, but with a slight edge for the former, and with an almost equal third being divided amongst a variety of other parties of which the FDP was the biggest. From this somewhat motley assembly Adenauer succeeded in getting an absolute majority of one – 202 out of 402 – for his election as the first Chancellor of the new Germany. One hundred and forty-two voted against, and fifty-eight, in one way or another, failed to cast a valid vote. He was nearly seventy-four years old, but he did not hesitate to vote for himself.

That narrow victory gave him four years of coalition power, not a big coalition with the SPD, which much of the CDU favoured but which Adenauer firmly rejected, but a more limited one with the FDP and the German (or refugee) Party. During these four years he negotiated the effective return of German sovereignty with the three occupying western High Commissioners, turned Germany from a pariah amongst nations to a member of the Council of Europe and of the Coal and Steel Community, with membership of the European Defence Community and, through it, of NATO on the near horizon. In addition, the German economic miracle was already burgeoning although not yet in full bloom. On the other hand, German politics became rent with bitter division. The SPD, under the incorruptible intransigence of the war-crippled Kurt Schumacher, opposed all these developments and dug themselves into a bunker of resentment. 'Federal Chancellor of the Allies' was Schumacher's Bundestag epithet for Adenauer. But this nationally divisive factor joined with the favourable ones to strengthen Adenauer's political position. Schumacher was not only incorruptible but also unelectable. The result was that on a very high poll the CDU plurality of votes over the SPD moved up from 400,000 to 4½ million, and its strength in the Bundestag less dramatically went to a bare but absolute majority. Adenauer none the less continued the centre-right coalition.

The first of the next four years was bad. The rejection of the European Defence Community by the French National Assembly in August 1954 was one of the two worst setbacks of Adenauer's Chancellorship. It not only upset his central policy of rapprochement with France, but also temporarily blocked Germany's route to full rehabilitation in the Western community. However, an alternative route for Germany's entry into NATO was quickly found through the Western European Union treaty. The French Government made some amends by relaxing its grip on the Saarland and allowing that coal- and steel-rich territory to begin its return to Germany in late 1955. The European unity train was triumphantly put back on the rails at the Messina Conference in the summer of that same year, which led on to the signature of the Treaty of Rome and the inauguration of the EEC in 1957. The *Wirtshaftswunder*, which was a little too imbued with the Protestant ethic and the personality of Ludwig Erhard for Adenauer's ideal taste, but which none the less greatly redounded to the credit of his Chancellorship, got fully into its stride. And Adenauer basked in the glow of easy transatlantic relations with Eisenhower, and shared with Dulles, then at the peak of his moralizing powers, a suspicion of all attempts to soften the asperities of the cold war. In 1955 Adenauer surrendered the foreign affairs portfolio, which he had carried jointly with the Chancellorship since 1949, but to a wholly pliant acolyte, Heinrich von Brentano. His government did not lack strong figures, however. Both Erhard and Gerhard Schröder, Interior Minister until he succeeded Brentano as Foreign Minister in 1961, were their own men.

The 1957 elections were an even greater triumph for Adenauer than the 1953 ones had been. Schumacher had died and his angularities were replaced by the pedestrian fuzziness of Erich Ollenhauer, who made the SPD election slogan 'Instead of Adenauer, Ollenhauer' into a sad boomerang. The CDU vote rose by another 2½ million to over 50 per cent of the poll and their Bundestag representation to an absolute majority of forty-three. This time Adenauer dropped the FDP and continued only in alliance with the German Party which had become his creature. He was eighty-one.

In the next four years he had three major international developments to which to accommodate, one bed of nails which he made entirely for himself, but which, when he got up from it, left some nasty scars, and one hidden climacteric in his career to pass. To the first of the international developments he adjusted brilliantly, the second threw him considerably, and to the third he was curiously indifferent. The first was the replacement as his French opposite number of the transients of the Fourth Republic by the General de Gaulle of Verdun, of the Cross of Lorraine and of the Liberation. In six bilateral meetings the two old men (or so they seemed, although de Gaulle was a boy compared with Adenauer), beginning at Colombey-les-Deux-Eglises within a few months of de Gaulle coming to power and including a triumphant tour of Germany by the General in 1962, surmounted strains to keep their two countries in a Carolingian direction. It showed a great sense of purpose and proportion on both their parts.

The change that threw Adenauer was that from Eisenhower to Kennedy as the captain of the West. Neither the old Chancellor nor the young President appreciated the other. Perhaps the age gap was simply too large, particularly as the power discrepancy ran in the opposite direction. Even their common religious affiliation, because it sprang from such different traditions and left such different personal imprints, was more a barrier than a bond. Adenauer referred to Kennedy as 'a mixture of a junior naval officer and a Roman Catholic boy-scout'. Kennedy thought Adenauer's outlook on world affairs was sclerotic. Dulles's death in May 1959 made the Atlantic prospect less bright for Adenauer. Kennedy's inauguration in January 1961 made it positively uncomfortable.

The third event was the return of Berlin to the centre of the cold war battlefront for the first time since the end of the blockade in 1949. This came with the erection of the Wall in August 1961. The reactions in Washington, London and Paris were greater than in the Bundeskanzlerei. Berlin was well beyond the Elbe, and Adenauer never took too much notice of what the Russians were up to. He was implacably opposed to them, he expected no good of dealings with them, he left it to the Allies to look after the security aspects, and he got on with his own job of making a success of the Federal Republic and tying it ever more firmly into the West. This bore several resemblances to his attitude to Nazism.

The bed of nails was constructed out of his ambiguity as to whether to exchange the Chancellorship for the Federal Presidency in the spring of 1959. The term of President Heuss, a Free Democrat, was coming to an end. The SPD had a strong candidate in Professor Carlo Schmid, whom Adenauer was determined to stop. At first he tried to persuade Ludwig Erhard to provide the road block. But Erhard did not want to become President. He wanted to become Chancellor, and was supported in this desire by most CDU members of the Bundestag. Adenauer was then tempted himself, and was encouraged in this direction by most of his blood and official families. But they wanted him to make the move as a form of honourable semi-retirement. He wanted to make it in order to give himself at least half of de Gaulle's powers, and in particular the right to nominate a Chancellor other than Erhard. Erhard and most of the CDU made it clear they would not have this. Adenauer then decided that he would rather remain as Chancellor, which meant that he made an ass of himself before the public, to whom he had announced his presidential intentions eighteen days earlier, and an affronted enemy of Erhard. His power and his prestige were never quite the same again.

This was partly because he was approaching the most dangerous milestone in a democratic leader's career. Three months after the presidential débâcle he began his second decade as Chancellor. There is now overwhelming evidence (more than there was at the time) that it is a mistake for any elected head of government (maybe any unelected one as well) to stay more than ten years in office. It has been so with Roosevelt, with de Gaulle, with Margaret Thatcher, with François Mitterrand. It was equally so with Adenauer. He did survive the 1961 election – up to a point – but the further two years of provisional power, like a prisoner on licence, which it gave to the Adenauer tenure were a sad travesty of his former glories.

The 1961 election cost the CDU its absolute majority. Its vote fell by nearly a million and its number of seats declined from 277 to 241. The SPD under Brandt by contrast polled an additional 1 ½ million and went up from 181 to 198 seats. The FDP did proportionally even better, increased their vote by over 50 per cent and their number of seats from forty-three to sixty-six. Some form of coalition was essential. Erich Mende, the FDP leader, was perfectly prepared for one with the CDU, but he wanted it under Erhard not Adenauer. Erhard of course wanted the same, had nominally an impregnable position from which to get it and plenty of grievances against Adenauer. But, like R. A. Butler in Britain two years later, he did not have the cold steel to hold out for his own ends. Adenauer went through the motions of negotiating with SPD for a 'grand coalition' (which in fact came about under Kiesinger five years later), but in 1961 this was not a serious Adenauer intention but merely a ploy to frighten Mende

99

and Erhard. At the price of some indignity and even dishonour he succeeded. Eventually he was elected Chancellor for the fourth time, but by a margin almost as small as in 1949. He was eighty-five, but age was still setting no limit to his appetite for office. What did set a term was a secret letter that he had been forced to write to Mende. In it he promised to resign after about two years, in any event in good time before the 1965 elections.

In this twilight period he brought his great purpose of Franco-German reconciliation to a ceremonial conclusion with the signing of his treaty of friendship with de Gaulle, silently sustained the General in his rupture of negotiations for Britain's entry into the European Community, and got badly stained by the fall-out of the *Spiegel* affair in 1962. (Franz-Josef Strauss, then Minister of Defence, was allowed to behave towards that not always admirable journal with a brutal intolerance which was alien to the whole spirit of the Federal Republic.) After this Adenauer made a last and fairly ludicrous attempt to block Erhard as his successor, wildly nominating almost any alternative whose name he could think of, until eventually even one of the most loyal and anonymous members of his government was reported to have cruelly said 'don't make me laugh' to the hitherto intimidating face of the old statesman.

He was at last forced to accept a date in October 1963 when he was removed from the Chancellery like a crustacean from a rock. He lived another three and a half years, discontented despite his vast achievements, and ungenerous towards his successor to whom he owed the solid economic base that was the foundation of his rehabilitation of Germany. This last phase brought him the irritation of seeing Erhard do much better in the 1965 elections than he himself had done in 1961, accompanied by the satisfaction of seeing Erhard's Chancellorship collapse only a year after this.

Adenauer's gothic arches had proved themselves to have much more staying power than the baroque rotundity of his successor and junior by thirty-one years. But even Adenauer was not ultimately indestructible. He died in April 1967, aged ninety-one, a little younger than Macmillan, a little older than Churchill. He had accomplished much more than the former, almost as much as the latter, compared with whom, however, he had enjoyed his life much less. Triumph over despair, achieved by endurance and guile, was his motto for himself and his country. It was a recipe for quiet strength rather than for rumbustious joy.

Charles de Gaulle

Compared with his companions on the world stage, Charles de Gaulle had mostly to play a poor hand from a weak seat. He believed from an early age that he was a great man, and he always acted like one, often to the fury of those who thought he should have been a supplicant. He behaved in a way which, seeking grandeur, invited ridicule, yet always escaped it. He was the frog that puffed itself up but instead of bursting became almost as big as it wanted to be.

Although indisputably a man of action, he was also a notable man of words, the story of whose life could be measured out in his own transfixing phrases. And the governing phrase, the one that most informed his whole career and best expressed his guiding purpose was *'une certaine idée de la France'*. He wrote it in the first volume of his memoirs (published in 1954) about his boyhood attitude, and defined it in terms at once romantic and impersonal. France to him was like 'a princess in a fairy tale or a madonna in a fresco'. If France performed mediocrely then the fault must lie with the mistakes of the French people rather than with the genius of the land. But France could only fulfil itself through grandeur: 'only great enterprises can neutralize the poisons of disunity which her people carry in their veins'. France must 'hold itself erect and look to the heights if it is not to fall into mortal peril'.

His eighty years of life in the Third, Fourth and Fifth Republics gave him a full experience of the poisons of disunity, of mediocre performances and of mortal perils. He was born in 1890, when France was at once a defeated and defensive power and the centre of world civilization. He spent most of his childhood in the Paris of *la belle époque, la ville lumière* and the mixture of cultural flowering and uninspiring politics that marked the midstream years between the two wars against Wilhelmine Germany. Yet he never seemed very Parisian. Proust's world of Swann searching frantically for Odette in the cafés of the *grands boulevards,* or of Gilberte and Marcel playing in the gardens of the Champs Elysées, or of the Guermantes or Verdurin *salons,* or even of Saint-Loup's smart cavalry barracks at Doncières all seem very remote from him. He described himself as *un petit Lillois de Paris,* for although his father taught at the Jesuit school of the Immaculate Conception near the Luxembourg Gardens he had been born at his maternal grandparents' house in the dour northern industrial city of Lille, and always carried a whiff of the more austere and enclosed parts of France about him. His father's family *were petite noblesse de province* before the Revolution. They lost their property then but kept themselves on the edge of gentility for the next hundred years. His mother's (and indeed his maternal grandmother's) family were of bourgeois substance in Dunkirk.

When the Jesuits were expelled from France at the height of Third Republican anti-clericalism in 1905, Henri de Gaulle established his own Paris school, but Charles de Gaulle went with the Society to Antoing, just over the Belgian frontier and in the purlieus of the forbidding round towers of Tournai Cathedral. When he joined the army in 1909 it was at Arras for a year of non-commissioned service in that hard landscape of the Pas-de-Calais. St Cyr provided two years in the softer surroundings of the Ile-de-France, but then it was back to Arras. His World War I service (three wounds, two in the first six months, the third at Verdun in March 1916, which led him to his spending the rest of the war as a prisoner) was all in the north-eastern approaches. When he married Yvonne Vendroux in 1921 it was in NotreDame de Calais. His wife's family were biscuit makers in the port which faced but did not emulate England. When he acquired a modest country property in 1934 it was in the Haute Marne on the western edge of Lorraine at Colombey-les-Deux-Eglises (of which one was missing) a thousand feet up and 140 miles from Paris in a lonely forest landscape uniquely far from even a one-starred Michelin restaurant. There were very few beakerfuls of the warm south, or even of the cosseting countryside of the core of France in this experience.

Between the wars Captain de Gaulle, as he was in 1919, or Colonel de Gaulle, as he became in 1937, had an interesting career for a professional soldier grinding through the slow process of promotion in a peacetime army. He was a dedicated officer but an awkward one. He was an intellectual who devoted much of his interest to the four books, admittedly on military topics, that he produced during these years, and he positively enjoyed standing alone against the conventional wisdom. They were neither of them qualities that naturally eased his progress up the military ladder. The fact that they did not do his career more harm was largely because he had a most powerful patron in the surprising shape of Marshal Philippe Pétain.

Pétain had been his battalion commander at Arras. When de

Gaulle was wounded and captured at Verdun Pétain was his commanding general and signed the citation that led to his decoration. Then in 1925 Pétain had de Gaulle recalled to work under him at the Supreme War Council from a dreary quartermaster staff job with the occupying forces in Germany to which he had been assigned after two not very successful years at the École Supérieure de Guerre. By then de Gaulle had already published his first book, *La Discorde Chez l'Ennemi,* a study of German military errors in 1914–18, and it was this that commended him to Pétain. In a very French way Pétain wished to sustain his then superb military reputation with an equivalent intellectual distinction, and in particular to surpass the literary output of Marshal Foch. De Gaulle he believed was the best writer in the army. He wanted him on his staff for this reason, and set him to work on a series of studies of the history of the French army with which the Marshal had been toying since 1921.

At first Pétain's appreciation of de Gaulle's literary talents brought mutual satisfaction. He even avenged de Gaulle's semi-humiliation at the École Supérieure by arranging for him, still only a captain, to give three compulsorily attended lectures to the whole École with himself presiding over the first. These were to form the core of de Gaulle's second book, *Le Fil de l'Epée* (The Sword's Edge), which was published in 1932, and set out the qualities, many of which bore a flattering resemblance to those of Marshal Pétain, that would be required in a great captain general who could save France in a war of the future. The lectures were a plea, presented with much historical allusion and some shafts of iconoclastic wit, for the training of élite commanders disposed to improvisation as opposed to the doctrine of defence by the book which was then favoured by the French

High Command. They caused considerable offence amongst the many officers far senior to himself who were forced to listen.

Even with Pétain relations began to fray, but more for reasons of literary jealousy than of strategic disagreement. Pétain wanted a ghost-writer but de Gaulle wanted a literary reputation of his own. When Pétain became War Minister in 1934 he recoiled from his original thought of making de Gaulle his *directeur de cabinet* because of warnings that de Gaulle had become too much his own man. De Gaulle was relieved because the post might have prevented him publishing his third and best-known pre-war book, *Vers l'Armée de Métier* (Towards a Professional Army). This was a plea for a small, highly trained, highly mobile corps of 100,000 men. Although it did not decry the supplementary use of fortifications, it was essentially hostile to the Maginot Line mentality.

It was, however, his fourth book, *La France et son Armée*, that provided the final irritable chapter in de Gaulle's literary relations with Pétain. The basis of the book was the historical material that de Gaulle had prepared when working under Pétain in 1925–7, which Pétain had wanted to publish under his own name in 1928 but which de Gaulle had successfully resisted. Ten years later Pétain less successfully resisted de Gaulle's claim to copyright and eventually agreed, subject to a negotiated dedication, the form of which de Gaulle slightly changed. Pétain was furious, and de Gaulle tried to appease him by promising that any second edition would carry the proper version. It was a supreme example of a storm in a teacup, particularly as publication took place at the height of the Munich crisis and was little noticed. Even without that diversion, however, the work would have been unlikely to sell much. All of de Gaulle's books of that epoch had rippling repercussions but small sales – *Vers l'Armée de*

Métier sold only 700. It was reminiscent of the joke that 'the reason academic disputes are so bitter is that the stakes are so small'. In France at least the habits of the Champ de Mars could rival those of the groves of academe in this respect. But few professors achieve the positions that Pétain and de Gaulle were to do within two years of the fracas.

De Gaulle, apart from producing his books, spent the twelve pre-war years first as a light infantry battalion commander in Trier, the Moselle city in which Karl Marx was born, then as a staff officer in Beirut, then for nearly six years in Paris with the French equivalent of the Imperial General Staff, until in the summer of 1937 he was promoted to full colonel and given command at Metz of one of the very few fully armoured regiments. It was the first time he had been in charge of troops for eight years. It was a crucial test of his soldiering qualities, for he had written so much about the deployment of tanks that if he could not make a success of handling them himself he was going to look fairly foolish.

There is considerable dispute about how good he was at this practical task. In any event he was promoted in May 1940 and given command of a newly formed armoured division. He engaged it with the enemy in the last weeks of May and is claimed by his biographers to have inflicted one or two dents on the advancing Germans. There is also a view, however, that he was essentially a theoretical and political rather than a tactically competent fighting general, and it is adduced in support of this view that not a single one of his officers of that armoured division subsequently joined the Free French. What is certain is that he did not have to exercise his command for long. On 5 June he was recalled to Paris and made under-secretary for National Defence in the Reynaud Government. It sounded a junior political assignment, but as Reynaud combined the National Defence portfolio with the premiership de Gaulle was in effect in charge of the department and was close to the centre of the crushing chain of events that unfolded between then and the surrender on 18 June.

He was next to Churchill at the dinner on the evening of the conference at the French High Command on 11 June, and fortified the favourable impression that he had made on the British Prime Minister when they had first met in Downing Street two days before (de Gaulle was on a six-hour mission to London to persuade Churchill to commit more resources to France, but was already being converted to the contrary doctrine that it was crucial for Britain to retain the capacity to fight on alone). He appeared to Churchill like a lofty island of calm resolution sticking up out of a sea of defeatist confusion. This was of determining importance for the reception that de Gaulle received in London when he left France on 17 June. Without this strongly positive personal impression he would have been an unknown two-star general. As it was, he was received by Churchill within hours of landing, allowed to broadcast in the name of France on both the second and third evenings of his exile, officially recognized by the British Government as the leader of the Free French on 28 June, given a subsidy of £8 million a year, and showered with Churchill invitations to Downing Street luncheons and Chequers weekends during the next desperate two months (de Gaulle left for eleven weeks in Africa on 28 August) when Britain's fate hung in the balance.

De Gaulle as an allied leader was thus very much Churchill's creation, and at a certain level of consciousness he knew this perfectly well, and even felt persistent stirrings of subterranean gratitude. But he believed that gratitude had no place in the relations of statesmen. And although his early resources of 7000 scattered men entitled him to be no more than the commander of a motley brigade, it was a statesman that he was determined to be – on his own behalf and on that of France.

The display of nerve by which he achieved this remains awe-inspiring. His position was far more difficult and dangerous than that of the groups of Homburg-hatted gentlemen who constituted the half dozen or more other allied governments in London. They clustered together for comfort, mostly had the legitimacy of their sovereign's support and had left nothing with any claim to be an indigenous government behind them. De Gaulle was alone. He was also a soldier subject to the harsh discipline of the still extant even if defeated French army, in which he had spent his whole life. His old commanding officer and patron-general had become head of state, was cosseted by Roosevelt, who alone could lead the free world to full victory, and was recognized by the Vatican, the Soviet Union and even Britain. De Gaulle was recalled to duty by Weygand on behalf of Pétain in July, and was condemned to death for desertion by a Vichy military court in August. It required great self-certainty to stand against the military hierarchy and the French state, which even in degradation had a continuing centralized tradition. But what rendered the performance breathtaking was that at the same time he bit the British hand which fed him and defied the latent power of American leadership before which even Churchill almost prostrated himself.

When Anthony Eden, who was de Gaulle's most effective friend in Britain, exasperatedly asked him why the Free French were twice as much trouble as the rest of the allies put together, he replied with the grand simplicity of an illogicality erected on a false premise: 'Because France is a great power.' France was nothing of the sort at the time, but it had been, and thanks largely to de Gaulle it came as near to being so again, particularly in the 1960s and 1970s, as any fifty-million nation could hope to be in the age of Washington/Moscow bipolarity.

De Gaulle, whose attitudes were to an unusual extent historically governed, no doubt had a full sense of traditional Gallic rivalry and even antipathy towards the British. '[He] did not like England,' his principal French biographer (Jean Lacouture) wrote. 'He admired her.' He once expostulated to General Spears that he did not particularly want England (which was the term he always used) to win the war. He only wanted France to be victorious, to which end he accepted that an English victory was also necessary. He knew that his own objectives would be compromised if he appeared as an auxiliary fighting under the Union Jack. There had to be a great deal of the Cross of Lorraine. And the weaker he was the more intransigently he had to uphold its dignity. He also had to keep his distance. He saw this need in almost astronomical terms. Many years later he wrote in relation to America that 'a small or medium-sized [country] cannot stand too close to a very great power without risk of being drawn into its orbit'. Throughout his life his reaction to setback was always to try both to distance and heighten himself. And he had the nerve to take frightening risks in the pursuit of this tactic. His definition of a great statesman was 'a man capable of taking risks', and the fact that the definition so manifestly did not exclude himself no doubt increased its attraction.

His behaviour in the early autumn of 1940 encapsulated these various attributes. On 23–25 September he suffered the humiliating failure of an Anglo-Free French naval assault on Vichy-controlled Dakar. The failure was joint but the humiliation was his. He was blamed by Roosevelt for the foolhardiness

110

of the concept and by his British collaborators for the deficiencies of Free French security which was thought to have made a substantial contribution to the defeat. And many (although conspicuously not Churchill) noted without too much dismay that his name and his appeal had carried little resonance with the garrison. Immediately afterwards he was almost suicidal. He retired to Lagos, not one of the most recuperative cities in the world. A natural human reaction would have been to hope for and half to invite messages of reassurance and support. Instead de Gaulle plunged off on a tour of various French equatorial outposts where he received some of the first of the *bains de foule* (immersion in an enthusiastic crowd) which subsequently became one of his few necessary forms of psychological massage. Then, at Brazzaville in the French Congo, barely five weeks after the débâcle of Dakar, having indisputably distanced himself from the British, he proceeded to heighten himself by proclaiming 'We, General de Gaulle' as the true and legitimate heir to all the sovereignty of the French Republic. He compounded his insolence by summoning the American Consul from Léopoldville (now Kinshasa) across the river and offering to negotiate with the United States over the occupation of western hemisphere islands currently under the control of the Vichy Government which Washington was anxious to propitiate. It was dangerously on the edge of bathos, but de Gaulle just got away with it. The State Department never replied. The Foreign Office was appalled but de Gaulle was too far off and too necessary for them to do much about it. Churchill got de Gaulle to come back to London in mid-November, but more by cajolery than by discipline.

Thus was the pattern set for the next few years. De Gaulle continued to push his luck almost unbelievably far. In Syria in the summer of 1941 he practically provoked a war within a war. After he got back to London at the end of August Churchill suspended all communication with him for nearly two weeks. When the Prime Minister eventually saw him he was determined to give him a tremendous dressing down. It did not work. De Gaulle was impervious and Churchill's wrath was not cold enough. There is a hilarious description of the occasion in Colville's diaries. It was partly Churchill's belief that he could speak French that undermined him. First he thought that he would make his disapproval clear by declining to do so and conducting the interview through an interpreter. Colville was deputed to act in an amateur capacity but was quickly discarded because Churchill claimed that he was rendering his phrases in a way too polite to the General. A bilingual Foreign Office official was then sent for, but Churchill found him equally unsatisfactory. So he plunged on alone with de Gaulle. This meant in his own inimitable French, in which he had little command over the nuances of what he was saying and was also anxious that de Gaulle should pay him the compliment of comprehension. This self-imposed weakness destroyed his chance of being successfully magisterial. After an hour and a half they had moved to sit side by side, the Prime Minister was declaiming in French and de Gaulle was smoking the peace-offering of a large Churchillian cigar.

A year later, when Madagascar was added to a repeat of Syria as a scene of de Gaulle-induced trouble, they had a more serious quarrel. The atmosphere was vitiated by the presence on that occasion of four other people, so there could be no smoke-wreathed tête-à-tête on a sofa. And by then – 30 September 1942 – the tension for Churchill was increased by the looming proximity of the Anglo-American landings in North Africa and by de Gaulle's complete inability or unwillingness to make himself acceptable to Roosevelt. Just over three months later there occurred the farce of the shot-gun 'embrace' (actually it was only a hand-shake in spite of their being French generals) between Giraud and de Gaulle in Casablanca, with Roosevelt and Churchill seated behind them and looking like duennas who had each produced an offspring for the nuptial. De Gaulle was summoned from London in a British aeroplane to be received as a client in an American security enclave on sovereign French territory. He arrived truculently but he none the less achieved as great a star role in Casablanca in 1943 as Bogart and Bergman together had done in 1942. In 1942–5 American power was nearly always decisive. It defeated Keynes at Bretton Woods in 1944. But in 1943 it did no good for Giraud against de Gaulle. By November the four-star general had been eliminated by the two-star one (it was part of de Gaulle's strength that, although he referred to himself as General de Gaulle as automatically as the US Chief of Staff and future Secretary of State called himself General Marshall, he never advanced his military rank and eschewed both the polished field boots and 'scrambled egg' *képis* to which most French generals were then attracted; he dressed as a junior general, but modestly so, almost as a desk-bound one).

Churchill frequently contemplated withdrawing support from de Gaulle and trying to eliminate him as leader of the Fighting French (as they had become in 1942) and on one occasion delivered himself of the immortal phrase: '*Si vous m'obstaclerez, je vous liquiderai.*' But he knew that he could not do so for three reasons of mounting order of importance. First, he had Eden as a sometimes exasperated but courageous and persistent ally of de Gaulle sitting on his doorstep. He set higher store by Roosevelt, but Eden was more present. Second, he did not in the last resort wish to ditch de Gaulle. He was sentimental and the General was for him part of the magic myth of 1940. Third, de Gaulle's strength in France (and his popularity in Britain) grew almost inexorably with every wartime year that went by. The unknown and presumptuous brigadier of 1940 became the national leader of 1942, 1943 and 1944. In the second half of the war he could not have been jettisoned without the most appalling consequences on the French internal resistance movement.

De Gaulle was not allowed much of a role in the Normandy invasion. On 4 June, two days before D-day, he was summoned to Britain after an absence of a full year in North Africa and given a briefing by Churchill. The military part of the discussion went well, the political part much less so. De Gaulle wrote in his memoirs that Churchill had said: 'How can you expect us to differ from the United States? We are able to liberate Europe only because the Americans are with us. Any time we have to choose between Europe and the open seas *(le grand large)*, we shall always be for the open seas. Every time I have to choose between you and Roosevelt, I shall choose Roosevelt.' These do not strike me as *ipsissima verba*, but no doubt they approximate to the reality, and in any event were what de Gaulle believed Churchill had said, which was what counted for the future.

After some hesitation de Gaulle was allowed to pay a forty-eight-hour visit to the bridgehead starting on the eighth day of the invasion. His visit was regarded as an irritating distraction by both the Americans and the British, but not by the French population. In Bayeux he was received with an emotion and an automatic acceptance of his authority that was wholly spontaneous because he was not expected and people at first had difficulty realizing that it was he. This first *bain de Joule* on metropolitan French soil was a major fortification of his self-confidence. It did not make him more amenable but it made him calmer. He accepted a further two months away from France, mostly with his provisional government in North Africa, but interspersed with visits first to the Pope in Rome and then to Roosevelt in Washington. The latter did not go as badly as it might have done.

He returned to France (from North Africa) only after the allied troops had broken out of the Normandy peninsula and the liberation of Paris seemed imminent. He came in an American plane which broke down on the way, and he was full of suspicion. But he reached Eisenhower's headquarters on 20 August and mostly got his way with him. Leclerc's French division was allowed to lead a direct assault on Paris and de Gaulle himself entered the city on 25 August. His objectives then were a mixture of the warm and the cold. He wanted to savour, in joyous unity with some of those who had helped him achieve it, one of the most remarkable turns of fortune in a span of fifty months ever brought about by any individual. He also wanted to make clear to the leaders of the Resistance, many of whom were Communists, who was boss.

In the glow of the first he never lost sight of the second objective. Thus, after a rendezvous with Leclerc and a Resistance representative at the Gare Montparnasse, he went first, not to the Hôtel de Ville where the other Resistance leaders were awaiting him, but to the Ministry of War in the rue St Dominique where he installed himself in the office (curiously quite unchanged) out of which he had been prised by the government's evacuation of Paris on 10 June 1940. Then, having established both continuity and a grip on the levers of authority, he did go to the Hôtel de Ville, but via police headquarters (thus putting his hand on another lever), and when he got there announced his triumphant parade down the Champs Elysées for the following afternoon. He thought that 'perhaps two million people' attended. *'Ah! C'est la mer,'* he recorded himself as saying, 'And I, in the midst of it all, feel not a person but an instrument of destiny.' From the Concorde he went to Notre Dame for a *Te Deum*. Thus did he seek a reunion of state and Church which had been rare since 1870, and only intermittent since 1789.

Three days later he organized a more surprising parade over the same mile and a half of grand avenue. He and General Omar Bradley reviewed an American march past. Eisenhower said it was at de Gaulle's request. He wanted to show the Resistance that if there was any trouble he had the big battalions on his side. If the explanation was correct it was a striking illustration of his ability not only to use pride when he wished but also to subordinate it when that too served his purpose.

Ten weeks later on 11 November there was a third Champs Elysées parade. At a time of severe adversity Churchill had said to de Gaulle: 'One day we'll go down the Champs Elysées together.' He was determined to do so, and de Gaulle recognized that he had to discharge the obligation. But in the pictures they do not match. Churchill looked determinedly happy. De Gaulle looked sour. He did not like sharing occasions. It was the less attractive side of his character. By then, however, he was engaged not in looking forward to governing a liberated although impoverished and divided France but in the more intractable task of actually doing it, and, this first time round, was proving by no means adept.

The last months of 1944 were not, however, too bad. He was mostly as well received in the provinces as in Paris. He made his writ run throughout the country, and successfully surmounted the biggest obstacle to the authority of the state by insisting on the incorporation of the Resistance militias into the regular army. He established a coalition government, including two Communists, but presided over it with an icy discipline rather than a democratic camaraderie. In 1945 he was excluded from the Yalta and Potsdam conferences but given, thanks to Churchill's pressure on Roosevelt, an occupation zone in Germany and a permanent seat on the UN Security Council. In spite of these concessions he continued to provoke his more powerful allies. He refused an invitation to meet Roosevelt in Algiers on the President's last journey back to the United States. And two months after Roosevelt's death Churchill was telling Truman that de Gaulle was 'the worst enemy of France in her troubles' and 'one of the greatest dangers to European peace'.

Nineteen forty-five also brought victory, but that for de Gaulle was no more than a postscript to the Liberation. In addition it brought the re-emergence of party politics in France. De Gaulle wished to be above them and in July took the decision not to field candidates for the October elections to a new Assembly that was not only to control the government but to frame a new constitution for a new Republic. This Constituent Assembly, in which the Communists were the largest party but were closely followed by the new MRP (which was loosely but not loyally Gaullist) and they by the Socialists, proceeded in November unanimously to elect de Gaulle President of the Government, but then to spend the remaining six weeks of the year in ensuring that he had as little power as possible. The Fourth Republic, just as much as the Third, was to be dominated by the shifting alliances of a legislative chamber which neither the head of state nor the head of government had power to dissolve. This was wholly contrary to de Gaulle's ideas, and his mind began to move towards resignation, a destination at which it arrived on 20 January 1946.

His resignation statement was brief, in a way brutal for it set out the alternative with an almost unnecessary starkness, yet it was essentially unchallenging, for it deliberately turned away from 'a general on a white horse' scenario. 'The exclusive regime of the political parties has returned. I condemn it. But, unless I use force to set up a dictatorship, which I do not desire, and which would doubtless come to a bad end, I have no means of preventing this experiment. So I must retire.'

He did not want a coup. But he certainly expected more dismay at his departure than was manifested. The politicians, even the MRP, did not mind. Nor, it appeared, did the public. And France's allies were rather relieved. Colombey-les-Deux-Eglises was not rehabilitated until five months later, and de Gaulle at first merely went to Marly in the royal forests of the Ile-de-France. His proximity to Paris led to no press of crowds to draw him back. In June he began his nearly twelve years of retreat in the Haute Marne. They were, however, divided sharply into two parts. Until 1953 he endeavoured to come back to power through the RPF (Rally of the French People), the programme for which he had outlined at Bayeux nine months earlier and the launch of which he proclaimed at Strasbourg in April 1947. His choice of locations was fully exploitative of his reputation: the Norman town where he had first re-mingled with the French people at the beginning of the Liberation and the Alsatian city that he had saved from reoccupation by the Germans in rough encounters with Eisenhower and Churchill as a consequence of the last Ardennes flourish of the Third Reich at the end of 1944.

He became neither the first nor the last man to use the back-cloth of national glories for partisan political purposes. What was

118

more surprising was that he did so with only modified success. His rallies were commanding, perhaps a little too much so for democratic taste, but his supporters were not entirely satisfactory, too few of his left-of-centre adherents of London days and too many of those who had been content to go along with Vichy, and a feeling that more than at any other stage of his career he was being driven towards the shores of reaction. The electoral performance followed a pattern sometimes experienced by new political movements. Seven months after its launch the RPF polled 40 per cent in municipal elections. But municipal elections do not determine political destiny. When the next national elections came the RPF was down to 21.5 per cent of the vote. This gave them 120 seats in the Assembly. But what were they to do with them? Eventually half their deputies decided they wanted to play the game of parliamentary power broking and drifted out of the General's control and into successive Fourth Republican governments.

That was effectively the end of the RPF, which had throughout been one of the less glorious chapters of de Gaulle's career. For the remaining five years before his return to power he was in almost full retreat at Colombey. He worked at his memoirs, and the first two volumes appeared to great acclaim in October 1956 and June 1958. He tried one more political manifestation. In May 1954 on the feast of Joan of Arc he announced that he would appear at the Étoile and lay a wreath on the tomb of the Unknown Soldier, and implicitly invited a mass silent demonstration. It was not a success. As he got into his car after the ceremony he murmured 'Le *peuple n'est pas tellement là.*' He gave only one press conference in four years, his very occasional speeches were commemorative rather than political, and his solitude was broken only by occasional visits from faithful adherents, Courcel, Guichard, Debré, Malraux, or, still less frequently, from one of two more independent politicians – Mendés-France, for example, for whom he had a certain regard.

The flame of his hope of a return must have flickered very low as the years advanced – he was sixty-seven in the autumn of 1957 – and his body was manifestly ageing. This sense of time running out may have pushed him to sail as close as he did to the shores of illegality, and even of disrepute, on the route by which he came back to power. He did not mount a military coup and therefore did not directly contradict his abnegatory dictum of January 1946. But he allowed the explicit threat of a military rebellion in Algiers, and the implicit threat that it would spread to Paris, to destroy the Pflimlin Government, the last of the Fourth Republic, and to cause both Pflimlin and President Coty to seek a legal transfer of power to de Gaulle. Until this was secure de Gaulle declined to curb the rebellious generals. On the contrary he heightened the tension by referring to 'the collapse of the state' and announcing his own readiness to assume once more, as in June 1940, 'the powers of the Republic'. If this did not happen, he would leave the regime to die in the ditch of its own weakness.

Coty was convinced that de Gaulle was the only alternative to civil war and determined to commission him as Prime Minister. There were still difficulties with the political groups. The Socialists were the key. De Gaulle received the two most prominent, Mollet, the Premier of the Suez adventure, and Vincent Auriol, President of the Republic from 1947 to 1954, at Colombey and persuaded them of his attachment to Republican democracy. Nevertheless, they were able to carry the Socialist parliamentary group by only seventy-seven votes to seventy-four. The majority of the minority then accepted group discipline and with it de Gaulle was endorsed in an Assembly vote by 329 to 224 with thirty-two abstentions. The margin was not vast, particularly in view of the Socialist 'block vote'. The meat the Assembly had been required to swallow was, however, very strong. The next day it had to vote special powers for the new head of government to restore order in Algeria and in France and to draw up a new constitution, and then put itself into recess, at one of the most critical moments in the history of post-war France, for four and a half months. Once elected, de Gaulle's democratic behaviour was almost as impeccable as he had managed to convince Mollet and Auriol that it would be, but the methods by which he came to power remain less admirable. It is rare for so much that is respectable and desirable to come out of such an ambiguous beginning.

De Gaulle was Prime Minister for seven months, and then, with a new constitution approved in a referendum by a 79 per cent positive vote, President for ten years and four months. During this too-long reign his popular support varied enough for him to contemplate resignation on at least two occasions, but until 1969 it was never insufficient for survival. Although the Fifth Republic was based on a great tilt of power from the legislature to the executive there was not at first a directly elected presidency. De Gaulle was elected in December 1958 by 78 per cent of the votes in college of a few thousand notables. A month before that the new Gaullist organization had won two-fifths of the seats in the Assembly and had no difficulty in finding enough parliamentary allies to provide a majority. Then in 1962 de Gaulle decided to strengthen the presidency by moving to direct election. This was opposed by a majority of the Assembly which carried a vote of censure. De Gaulle ordered both a referendum and a dissolution of the Assembly. The former produced a 'yes' vote of 62 per cent, which, however, he regarded as disappointing, being not quite a half of the total electorate. The parliamentary elections none the less gave for the first time a small absolute Gaullist majority of seats.

The first presidential elections under the new system did not take place for another three years and then, ironically, gave a much less satisfactory result for its instigator than had the old system in 1959. He started in an apparently commanding position, but was placed *en ballotage* by the combined votes of his two opponents, Mitterrand and Lecanuet. On the first round de Gaulle got 44 per cent against 32 per cent for Mitterrand and 16 per cent for Lecanuet. On the second he got 54.5 per cent against Mitterrand's 45.5 per cent. It was decisive but not glorious. Then in the spring of 1967 the Gaullists lost their independent majority in the Assembly.

The next significant elections were the legislative ones of June 1968. They followed the disastrous month of May, when student riots eliding into industrial unrest led to the collapse of de Gaulle's nerve and to his putting on a very passable imitation of Louis XVI's flight to Varennes. Louis XVI got only to the edge of Champagne by coach but de Gaulle got to Baden-Baden by helicopter, where, according to General Massu and to some extent to Lacouture following Massu, it required a bracing lecture from Massu, one of the old Algiers junta of 1958, promoted to commander of the French occupation forces in Germany, to turn him round. It was amazing in view of the far more awesome dangers de Gaulle had faced in 1940 and afterwards that he should have cracked so badly. Maybe it was a classic example of the rule that nobody is much good in his second decade of continuous office (it was actually his 120th month). Maybe Massu exaggerated his own role and de Gaulle

122

always intended the retreat to Baden-Baden as a tactic that would give him the advantage of surprise on the rebound. Whatever the reason, he returned fortified, and with his return there was a dramatic and favourable reversal of the situation. One result of this reaction was the electoral triumph of a month later. The Gaullists moved to a substantial absolute majority, but de Gaulle himself remained wounded and vulnerable. Ten months afterwards, when he forced an unnecessary referendum on a couple of minor ill-matched and unpersuasive constitutional questions, he lost by a margin of 5 per cent and resigned within six hours.

There is no close link between the fluctuating combination of daring, vision and irresponsibility that marked de Gaulle's performance as President and these ups and downs of electoral fortune. He was consistent in working always for the greater glory of France, but by no means predictable in the means he employed to this end. He loved *coups de théâtre* and the surprise of paradox. Perhaps he remained a natural tank commander who believed that the unexpected approach was half the battle. Out of government he had opposed European integration and the Treaty of Rome. In office he found that Pflimlin, the man of Strasbourg who was later to be President of the European Parliament, had sent Maurice Faure, a great orator of the European cause, round the capitals of the other five original members to warn them that France could not meet the 1 January 1959 deadline for the dismantling of customs barriers. By December 1958 he was able to reverse that policy of hesitant weakness and say that France, after all, would be ready. His devaluation and subsequent stabilization of the franc made France fit to participate in and to benefit from the Common Market.

123

Then he achieved an almost mystical rapprochement with Adenauer and laid the foundations of the Franco-German partnership which was to lead Europe for the next thirty years. In early 1963 he scuppered Macmillan and displeased Italy, Benelux and half the German Government, but not Adenauer, by consigning Britain to *le grand large*. And in 1965, with Adenauer gone, he brought the first phase of the Common Market to a juddering halt with his quarrel with Hallstein, the presumptuous (as he thought) German President of the Commission.

His Algerian policy was both a greater reversal of alliances and his most signal presidential service to France. The conditions for his coming to power had been created by a cabal of generals who thought that the politicians of the Fourth Republic were hopelessly wet in their weak underpinning of the permanence of *Algérie Française*, and over the next four years he proceeded to show that they were indeed hopelessly wet because they would never have had the courage to sever the link and get the poison of *la sale guerre* out of the veins of France. De Gaulle did precisely this, and in the course of doing so employed one of the most memorable ambiguities in the history of politics. When he looked at the hysterical crowd of *pieds noirs* outside the Governement- Général in Algiers on the evening of 4 June 1958 and said '*Je vous ai compris,*' it was interpreted as a commitment of support, may well have been delivered with mixed emotions at the time, but turned out to be a disdainful dismissal.

Freed of the incubus of Algeria and responding unexpectedly well to the stimulus of the Common Market, France enjoyed a period of rapid growth, currency stability and mounting prosperity in which much of the work done by Monnet's *Commissariat du Plan* under the Fourth Republic redounded to the credit of the Fifth. But it was due to de Gaulle that its benefits did not drain away into the sands of Algeria and that the new France had the political panache to turn the economic success into international influence. At first de Gaulle, while preaching against too much subservience to an American-dominated NATO, played a hard cold war hand at moments of crisis. When the Berlin Wall was built in 1961 he was the only Western leader in favour of reacting with force. In 1962 when Kennedy confronted Khrushchev in the Cuban missile crisis he was more forthright in his support than either Macmillan or Adenauer. From 1963 onwards, however, with the Algerian war behind him and with the Khrushchev threat greatly reduced after Cuba, he began to take an increasingly anti-American line: on Vietnam; on the growing weakness of the dollar, which made the United States' assumption of currency hegemony increasingly intolerable; on the nuclear test ban treaty; on the independent cultivation of relations with both China and the Soviet satellites; and on the attempt to build up a special French position in South America.

On some of these points de Gaulle was more sensible than Washington. But in his last years of power he began to go over several tops. Nineteen sixty-seven was a vintage year. In June, at the time of the Six-Day War, he switched from the traditional French pro-Israeli line and half-denounced the Jews as 'an élite people, self-confident and dominating'. In July he went to Canada and proclaimed *le Québec libre* from the balcony of the Montreal City Hall. His visit had to be cut short before he got to Ottawa. In September he went to Poland and there made remarks almost as offensive to the Soviet Union as his Quebec ones had been both to Ottawa and to Washington. In October he was actively supporting the Biafran revolt against the Nigerian Government, a policy that was regarded as hostile in both London and Washington. In November he dismissed Britain's second application to join the European Community before the negotiations had even opened. Later that same month he encouraged his Chief of Defence Staff to announce that the French nuclear deterrent would be *à tous azimuts,* in other words targeted in all directions, including America. (No French missile could have begun to reach there, but that introduced bathos rather than moderation into the proposition; *tous azimuts* did, however, help to give the French deterrent support *from* all directions, including the Communist Party, within France.)

Inside as well as outside France 'the shipwreck of old age' was felt to be beginning. He was seventy-seven, much younger than Adenauer had been at the end of his Chancellorship but wearing less well. And so it proved to be. The year of 1968 was downhill nearly all the way; 1969 was a year of defeat and resignation, followed by six weeks of retreat in Ireland and a coldly unhelpful attitude towards the presidency of Georges Pompidou, who had been his Prime Minister throughout six years of great Fifth Republican success. Nineteen seventy brought almost complete solitude (except for the company of his wife) at Colombey, rather hasty work on his second and post-1958 series of memoirs, and sudden death, at an age two weeks short of eighty, on 9 November. 'France is a widow,' said Pompidou in what was probably the best phrase of his life. He could not compete with de Gaulle in that or many other respects, but nor could any other figure of the mid-twentieth century, except for his two old enemies/allies, Churchill and Roosevelt.

John Henry Newman and
the Idea of a University

*This is a lightly edited version of a lecture given in the
Examination Schools at Oxford in February 1990. It was part
of a series organized for the centenary of Newman's death. All
the other participants were considerable Newman and/or
theological scholars. I was asked as Chancellor of the
University: hence the occasionally defensive tone.*

I have found the preparation of this lecture one of the most formidable tasks I have ever undertaken, and am inclined to the view that my sense of cancellarian duty to the University – which I interpret as meaning that I should not refuse a serious engagement which it is physically possible for me to fulfil – has led me to take leave of my senses. A few months ago I knew little about Newman, beyond the facts he was a Trinity undergraduate, an Oriel fellow in the years when that college led the awakening from the Oxford slumber of the eighteenth century, and Vicar of St Mary's. I had some vague knowledge of his part in the launching of the Oxford Movement and of his retreat to Littlemore.

Forty years ago, which is nearly a third of the time back to his sojourn there, I addressed an election meeting in the Anglican schoolroom at Littlemore, but got little response from the small and stolid audience for what I hoped was my felicitous reference to their former parish priest. I think I would have got the correct year for his conversion to Rome, but I was hazy about the exact date of his move to Birmingham, although during my long years as an MP for the other end of that city I was aware of the presence of Oratory and the Church of St Philip Neri and of their Newman connection. I knew that Pope Leo XIII had shown that he was not Pope Pius IX by making Newman a cardinal, and I thought that was a good thing, rather like Cinderella being taken to the ball, and one in the eye for Cardinal Manning, although whatever else may be said about Manning he was neither ugly nor a sister. I had read *Apologia Pro Vita Sua* as a very young man and had found it surprisingly easy going. But that was about it.

I therefore found myself committed to spend quite a lot of time immersed in Newman, in the Discourses that make up *The Idea of a University* in particular, and in the circumstances in which they were delivered and/or composed. This concentration left a number of impressions, some of them contradictory, upon my mind. First (a blinding truism) that Newman was a man of exceptional interest. There seems to me to be more room for argument about his piety, although I would hesitate to pronounce on that, his charity, his simple niceness, or even his modesty, than about his fascination. This stems partly from his brilliance as a stylist, even though his imagery could be lush and his use of words was rarely economical, as an ironist, and as a polemicist. But it was more than that. He could write dull passages, sometimes it seems almost intentionally so, because he was getting round a corner in his argument with which he did not feel wholly at ease. But whether or not it was intentional he was always conscious that he had written a relatively dull passage. You can almost feel him waiting in slack water, hardly moving his paddle, yet preparing to swoop into the next stage of the argument as soon as a favourable current developed.

He had star quality, as surely as did, amongst his contemporaries, Gladstone or Tennyson or Carlyle. It is possible to confuse Keble with Pusey, or Pusey with Keble and to wonder which was doing what at a particular time. It is never possible to confuse Newman with anyone. It is possible to be irritated or to be muddled by Newman, but very difficult to be bored by him. This is the more striking because I felt throughout that Newman's *mentalité* (my excuse for using the French rather than the English word is that I fondly imagine it to embrace not only the working of his own mind but also the intellectual climate in which he operated) is an ocean away not only from my own but from that of almost anyone, inside or outside the University, with whom I have frequent contact.

Next week these centenary celebrations culminate with a Newman sermon (from the Archbishop of Canterbury) and service in St Mary's. It will be a notable occasion, but I doubt if any service can recapture the atmosphere in which Newman, having slipped across the cobbled and trafficless High from Oriel, or in later days walked in from Littlemore, and then, in Matthew Arnold's words, 'after gliding in the dim afternoon light through the aisles [of St Mary's] [and] rising into the pulpit, in the most entrancing of voices breaking the silence with words and thoughts which were a religious music – subtle, sweet, mournful'. Yet we are told from another source that Newman's 'sermons were read, with hardly any change in the inflexion of the voice and without any gesture on the part of the preacher,

129

whose eyes remained fixed on the text in front of him'. The two descriptions are only superficially incompatible, and whatever was or was not the histrionic quality of Newman's sermons there was a still more remarkable quality about the later ones, and that was their capacity to excite and divide the University. What would the Vice-Chancellor think? Would the Regius Professor of Divinity retaliate? What would the Heads of Houses do? How might the Provost of Oriel navigate between his peers and his turbulent fellow? Would Convocation censure Tract Ninety, which was a Newman sermon in print, or would dedicated Tractarian Proctors, as happened in February 1845, veto the censure being put to the vote? What would be done by poor Bishop Bagot of Oxford, a High Church sympathizer, who liked a quiet life and found himself presiding over the cockpit of whether or not Anglicanism could be Catholicism.

Even the Duke of Wellington, as Chancellor of the University, and the last who was not himself an Oxonian, could not remain entirely remote from these quivering controversies. In the mid-thirties he had inclined to the High Church side, at least to the extent of being hostile to R. D. Hampden, another member of the Oriel constellation of *circa* 1820 and Melbourne's nominee as Regius Professor of Divinity. But he soon thought the Tractarians went too far in trying to torment Hampden. Schism was the great evil, he admonished the Vice-Chancellor, worse even than heresy or impiety. And by 1844 Wellington was determined, to the brink of threatening to resign, that his nomination of the Evangelical Warden Symons of Wadham as the new Vice-Chancellor should be accepted. The Tractarians forced a vote but were overwhelmingly defeated in the Sheldonian, and Wellington responded to this victory with suitable lack of magnanimity by announcing that he would never allow such a vote again. The power of the Chancellor to nominate the Vice-Chancellor is now temporarily in abeyance, but I have found looking into these matters very instructive.

All this was well past and it was nearly nine years since Newman had last entered St Mary's and six years since he had seen Oxford, except from the railway, when he went to Dublin in May 1852 and delivered on five successive Monday afternoons the lectures that became the first half of *The Idea of a University*. He records at the end – a sympathetic thought to me today – that they 'have oppressed me more than anything else of the kind in my life'. However, he did not allow this to put him in a compromising mood towards his audience. Ladies, to his surprise it appears, were present. But he did not pay too much attention to them and wrote: 'I *fancied* a slight sensation in the room when I said, not Ladies and Gentlemen, but Gentlemen.' This may have owed less to a sense of affront at female presence, although Newman was certainly capable of feeling that, as to the fact that he constantly employed the word 'gentlemen' as a sort of alpenstock to lever him up the hill of an important stage in his argument. Perhaps it was to remind himself of the difference between delivering a lecture and preaching a sermon. Indeed he carried it to the almost ludicrous extent of spattering the texts of the last few Discourses, which were never publicly delivered but form to my mind the more interesting half of the whole, with this form of address.

The five delivered lectures themselves were a considerable on-the-spot success. They were listened to by high-quality attendances of about four hundred, and Newman was delighted with the quick perception of the Irish audience, just as they were with the distinction of the lecturer and the elevation of his thought. This was as well for the book for which they were written, which

Newman called 'one of my two most perfect works, artistically' (a strong statement for any author), attracted much less critical notice and much smaller sales than his previous recent works. By contrast, its long-term resonance has been enormous, so much so that it has become impossible to dissociate from Newman the evocative phrase of *The Idea of a University.* John Sparrow made some attempt in his 1965 Cambridge Clark lectures to divert it on to Mark Pattison, who had a more solid influence in nine-teenth-century university life than did Newman, but who lacked his capacity to arouse excitement. But Warden Sparrow, who allowed Newman, together with Matthew Arnold, a status equal to Pattison in the relevance to contemporary problems of his mid-Victorian pronouncements on universities, did not succeed in his diversionary attempt. Pattison stands with Jowett as one of the two dominating Heads of Houses of the second half of the nineteenth century, but 'the idea of a university' belongs to Newman, even though he never set foot in the only university that he understood between 1846 and 1877, between the ages of forty-five and seventy-six, which was by any standards a substan-tial and significant segment of his life. And when Professor Jaroslav Pelikan of Yale published *The Idea of* the *University* in 1992 the choice and slight variance of title was a deliberate obei-sance to the persistent centrality of Newman's thoughts on the subject.

The circumstances of Newman's Dublin sojourn were unfa-vourable from a number of points of view. Just over a year earlier the Roman Catholic hierarchy in Britain, with its panoply of territorial bishops, had been established. Newman was unenthu-siastic. He thought seminaries and education were more important than sees. But he was far too new a convert to be able to protest, even though he bore some of the brunt of the reaction against what was widely regarded as aggressive Catholic presumption. The Achilli case in which he was prosecuted for criminal libel against an unfrocked Dominican, who had subsequently been taken up by the Evangelical Alliance and had toured the country denouncing the corruption of Rome, is one of the most curious and ill-fitting episodes in Newman's life. In a Birmingham lecture in the summer of 1850 Newman had drawn, without checking, on an anonymous pamphlet (in fact written by Bishop Wiseman, later Cardinal Archbishop of Westminster) which denounced the personal immorality of which Achilli had been convicted by a papal court in Rome. Achilli, with his Low Church sponsors, got Newman indicted. The evidence that was essential for his defence was constantly on the point of arrival from Rome, but in spite of a special mission by two Birmingham Oratorians, it was never there when it was needed.

There were a series of portentous court hearings before the very anti-Catholic Chief Justice, Lord Campbell. It must have been a great *cause célèbre*. Newman's counsel, as was permissible in those days of private fees for Government Law Officers, was the Attorney-General, Cockburn, who was later to be Chief Justice himself and to achieve fame by inventing the definition of obscenity as 'a tendency to deprave or corrupt those into whose hands [the complained of publication] may fall', which subsequently stood for ninety years. Cockburn was almost as full of anti-Catholic prejudices as was Campbell, and only attempted to defend Newman by holding the complained-of passage like a piece of soiled linen in his fingertips. In Dublin in 1852 Newman thought that the main hearing would come on at any moment, and faced the real prospect of imprisonment for a year or so. On 24 June the verdict was given against him, but the sentence, for which he had to wait another seven months, was only a fine of

£100 (the equivalent of about £4000 today), which led Newman's supporters to proclaim, almost as though he were a modern Sunday newspaper editor, that the result was a moral victory. But all this lay heavy on his mind in Dublin. In addition, he was barely settled into the new Oratory in Edgbaston. To deal with these concerns he made the inconvenient journey across St George's Channel and by the new railway between Birmingham and Holyhead several times during the series.

More important, however, was the fact that Newman had embarked on a largely impossible task in Ireland. In 1851 he had accepted an invitation from Archbishop (later Cardinal) Cullen of Armagh to become founding Rector of a Catholic university in Ireland. Cullen, after many years in Rome, where he had developed an authoritarian cast of mind, had returned to Ireland only in 1849, had been appointed apostolic delegate for the foundation of the university, and was to be translated to the see of Dublin in 1852, which meant that he had still more opportunity to interfere with Newman's plans, although not apparently to reply to his letters. And he was interested only in the new university providing a strictly religious education. He attended at least some of Newman's lectures, but he must have regarded them as containing a good deal of froth, some of it dangerous.

The position was even more complicated than that. There were also two powerful factions in the Irish hierarchy (and Newman was in some sense responsible to the bishops as a whole) which diverged from Cullen in contrary directions. Archbishop Murray of Dublin (until 1852) was attracted by the London government's scheme for Queen's Colleges (one of which in Belfast has survived both in fact and in name, while two others, in Cork and Galway, have survived under different names), which would be open equally to Catholics and Protestants. And

Archbishop MacHale of Tuam wanted an Irish Nationalist university, a Fenian college as those of a different view, including Cullen and Murray, might have described it.

What did Newman want? Essentially, he wanted a Catholic Oxford on the banks of the Liffey. And the Catholicism, while it was to infuse its heart, was not to be restrictive of the movement of the limbs, as Dr Cullen might have wished. Nor really was the Dublin location important to Newman. Outside the city might have been better, outside Ireland would have done had the Papal authority not been given for a *Catholic university in Ireland*. Newman was free of much nineteenth- (and twentieth) century educated English Catholic impatience with the Irish, but he was not much interested in Irish nationalism, and certainly not in a nationalist university. He wanted his university to be for Anglophone Catholics, for England as much as for Ireland. (I am not sure if he embraced the thought of America.) And he wanted it to be a university for gentlemen. In Discourse VIII he came as near as could be to saying that gentlemanliness was next to godliness. Admittedly, he defines (or rather describes) gentlemanliness in a peculiarly self-effacing way. After stating 'that it is almost a definition of a gentleman to say he is one who never inflicts pain', he goes into a famous description of high but gentle good manners:

> The true gentleman … carefully avoids whatsoever may cause a jar or a jolt in the minds of those with whom he is cast – all clashing of opinion, or collision of feeling; all restraint, or suspicion, or gloom, or resentment; his great concern being to make every one at their ease and at home. He has eyes on all his company; he is tender towards the bashful, gentle towards the distant, and merciful towards the absurd; he can recollect to whom he is speaking; he

guards against unseasonable allusions, or topics which may irritate; he is seldom prominent in conversation, and never wearisome. He makes light of favours when he does them, and seems to be receiving when he is conferring. He never speaks of himself except when compelled, never defends himself by a mere retort, he has no ears for slander or gossip ... He is never mean or little in his disputes, never takes unfair advantage, never mistakes personalities or sharp sayings for arguments, or insinuates evil which he dare not say out. From a long-sighted prudence, he observes the maxim of the ancient sage, that we should ever conduct ourselves towards our enemy as if he were one day to be our friend. He has too much sense to be affronted at insults, he is too well employed to remember injuries, and too indolent to bear malice. He is patient, forbearing, and resigned, on philosophical principles; he submits to pain, because it is inevitable, to bereavement, because it is irreparable, and to death, because it is his destiny.

The tests sound as though they would leave most of us to fall by the wayside. In Discourse V, however, he gives a more succinct account of the relation of gentlemanliness both to a liberal education and to religion:

> Liberal Education makes not the Christian, not the Catholic, but the gentleman. It is well to be a gentleman, it is well to have a cultivated intellect, a delicate taste, a candid, equitable, dispassionate mind, a noble and courteous bearing in the conduct of life; – these are the connatural qualities of a large knowledge; they are the objects of a University; I am advocating, I shall illustrate and insist

upon them; but still they are no guarantee for sanctity or even for conscientiousness, they may attach to the man of the world, to the profligate, to the heartless …

Yet for all Newman's stress on self-effacement and his insistence that refinement is not saintliness (although it 'may set off and recommend an interior holiness just as the gift of eloquence sets off logical argument'), he leaves us in no doubt that it is not rough diamonds with hearts of gold or 'nature's gentlemen' that he is talking about. It is those who have acquired their urbanity through the traditional processes of a privileged liberal education. In 1856 he put it even more sharply when he wrote that he had gone to Dublin because 'the Holy See had decided that Dublin was to be the place for Catholic education of the upper classes in these Islands …'

So the conflicts between the desires of the different sponsors, and between aspiration and what was realistically possible, pile up. Newman wanted an idealized version of collegiate life under the dreaming spires, undefiled by the Reformation, trans-shipped to Leinster. And he wanted it to be filled with devoutly Catholic young men who combined the Whig virtues of an easy-going and cultured tolerance with the Tory virtues of a natural acceptance of authority and revealed truth. But neither economically nor sociologically was there room for a Christ Church on St Stephen's Green, within a quarter of a mile of Trinity moreover, and Archbishop Cullen would not have dreamt of letting him have it even had it been practicable. And to compound the contradictions much of Newman's thought was conditioned by the pluralism of Oxford, while the minds of others and the constitution with which he had to work were much more influenced by the model of the centralized and professorially controlled Catholic University of Louvain in Belgium.

In the circumstances, what seems to me remarkable are not the considerable disappointments but that the scheme was not a more dramatic failure than it was. Newman survived in Dublin for six and a half years from the date of his 1852 lectures. For only four of them was he formally Rector, and there were frequent absences in Birmingham because he gave at least an equal priority to the affairs of the Oratory, which was another cause of dissension with Cullen. He established a house with about ninety students in the heart of Dublin, and indeed a University Church, with the somewhat disproportionate capacity of 1200. And the Catholic University as such survived until 1882, and then left substantial educational legacies, of which perhaps the most considerable has been the medical school, which could be regarded as ironical in view of the secondary role to which Newman relegated vocational education.

To what extent was Newman irrevocably Oxford-conditioned, even when he had spread a trail of intellectual and liturgical upheaval in that university and spent long years as exiled from the city as was the Scholar Gipsy? It was my predecessor in this series, A. N. Wilson, who, without himself uttering so obvious a thought, aroused in my mind the Scholar Gipsy comparison with his evocative television portrait last autumn, which left me with the loose impression of Newman haunting the Cumnor Hills and looking down with ineffable sadness at a Turneresque view of the Oxford skyline.

On the other hand, I. T. Ker, Newman's 1988 biographer, wrote that it was 'leaving Littlemore, unlike leaving Oxford or St Mary's, [that was] very painful for Newman'. It was part of Newman's fascination that he was frequently capable of unexpected judgements about places, as about people. He would be as good an example as one could possibly imagine of a figure who was quintessentially Oxonian rather than Cantabrigian. Yet, when he first saw Cambridge, at the surprisingly late age of thirty-one, he wrote, 'I do really think the place finer than Oxford'. And when in 1846 he was on the most symbolically important journey to the Eternal City of any nineteenth-century person from England he perversely decided that Milan was 'a most wonderful place – to me more striking than Rome'. He appears to have rated Milan Cathedral together with the chapel of Trinity College, Oxford – an unusual pair – as almost his favourite ecclesiastical buildings.

Yet, despite some unwillingness to worship at predictable shrines, I think Newman did carry a half-visible Oxford canopy around with him for the forty-five years of his Roman Catholic life. In the seventh Dublin Discourse, for example, there is the panegyric of Oriel. It is worth citing at length for it is a typical, although by no means the most brilliant, example of Newman's cumulative style, by which he uses cascades of words to build up an idea like a range of hills with each summit rising a little higher than the previous one, but also steers through this mountain chain in order to get into position for the next axis of aggressive advance. I say 'aggressive' for I find it beyond dispute that John Henry Newman, for all his portrait of that 'parfit gentil knight' which was his ideal of a gentleman, was a polemicist of an elegant deadliness that is met only once in a generation. The only comparable figure in this respect that I have encountered in our recent University is Professor Hugh Trevor-Roper, who deserves his nobility as Lord Dacre even more for his sword than for his robe.

Newman's quarry in this early part of Discourse VII was no less a figure than John Locke. Newman had perhaps a keener sense of intellectual than of ecclesiastical hierarchy, and he knew that Locke was too strong a fortress to be attacked without a considerable preliminary investment. Lesser (although by no means negligible) figures like former Lord Chancellor Brougham or Bishop Mattly of Durham he would engage more directly. Even in these lesser cases, however, there is an aesthetic pleasure in watching Newman get into position for the attack. His old adversary Dr Arnold of Rugby could hardly have prepared for a flogging with more loving care than Newman does for an intellectual joust. Just as Arnold, while rolling up his sleeves, might have referred to the eminence of the boy's parents and the promise with which he came to the school, so Newman pays preliminary tribute to the general respect in which the right reverend prelate or the most learned lord is held and the lucidity with which he expresses his ideas; perhaps even (although not I think in the case of Brougham) to the probity of his personal life. Then comes the thrust, delivered like a matador's deadly lunge.

But Locke, who although not well-treated by Christ Church at the time, had become almost as great a talisman for seventeenth-century Oxford as Newton had for the same period in Cambridge, could only be assaulted after a more elaborate approach march. So we have a eulogy of the recently dead Dr Copleston, Provost of Oriel in Newman's early days and later Bishop of Llandaff, and with him of John Davison, another member of the Oriel galaxy whose devastating attack on R. L. Edgeworth's fallacies on *Professional Education* was really, Newman says, an attack on the luminaries of the *Edinburgh Review* and behind them 'an a far greater author … who in a past age had argued on the same side'. So the siege gun was at last in position for the engagement with Locke.

But in introducing his Irish and Catholic audience to 'the Protestant Bishop of Llandaff' Newman felt that he had a peg on which he could hang some of his feelings about Oriel, which had nurtured him for a quarter of a century but which in 1852 he had not seen for nearly a decade. As a further convolution he does so sufficiently archly that the name of Oriel, as though it were that of a modest mistress, is never mentioned, and I was indeed far into the passage before I was certain which college he was talking about:

In the heart of Oxford there is a small plot of ground, hemmed in by public thoroughfares, which has been in the possession of and the house of one Society for about 500 years. In the old time of Boniface VIII and John XXII, in the age of Scotus and Occam and Dante, before Wyclif or Huss had kindled those miserable fires which are still raging to the ruin of the highest interests of man, an unfortunate King of England, Edward II, flying from the field of Bannockburn, is said to have made a vow to the Blessed Virgin to found a religious house in her honour ...

The visitor, whose curiosity has been excited by its present fame, gazes perhaps with something of disappointment on a collection of buildings which have with them so few of the circumstances of dignity or wealth. Broad quadrangles, high halls and chambers, ornamental cloisters, stately walls, or umbrageous gardens, a throng of students, ample reserves or a glorious history, none of these things were the portion of that old Catholic foundation; nothing in short which to the common eye sixty years ago would have given tokens of what it was to be. But it had at that time a spirit working within it, which enabled its inmates to do, amid its seeming insignificance, what no other body in the place could equal …

One of the things it did was to elect fellows solely on the basis of what Newman rather oddly described as 'public and patriotic grounds', and without regard not only to connection but also to university class lists. The result was that Newman's disastrous schools results of 1820 were compensated for by his being elected a fellow of Oriel sixteen months later. For this he remained grateful, but his feelings towards that college, in spite of some fluctuations in his years of crisis, were I think based on a more lively emotion than that of gratitude. Oriel's diversity of intellects and religious positions, as well as his memory of other colleges with broader quadrangles and more umbrageous gardens, infused much of his unrealistic hopes for what he might create in Dublin.

The Oriel passage I have dealt with at length not only to illustrate Newman's attitude to Oxford but also to exemplify both the circumlocutory and the rhetorical nature of his style. He was a great rhetorician. He was so in both the favourable and the less favourable sense of the word. He was certainly a persuasive and impressive speaker. But he was also given to the use of words more for ornamentation than for meaning. Disraeli's jibe about Gladstone, 'a sophistical rhetorician, inebriated with the exuberance of his own verbosity', could, with the word sophistical, which is not appropriate, left out, be applied just as well to Newman. His style is less portentous than Gladstone's. It reminds me more of Chrisopher Fry out of whose plays in the 1940s and 1950s felicitous words tumbled like stars from a magnificent firework. Newman was moderately austere in the physical surroundings of life, but not in his use of words or imagery, where he was luxuriantly self-indulgent. He was as addicted to never using one word where ten words would do as Mr Kinnock is accused of being, although his phrases were substantially better chosen.

An outstanding example is provided in Discourse I of *The Idea,* where Newman has to deal with the awkward fact that the Pope had laid it down that there must be a purely Catholic university. Newman makes no attempt to pretend that it is not awkward: 'It is the decision of the Holy See. St Peter has spoken, it is he who has enjoined that which seems to us so unpromising.' He does not attempt to argue for this decision on its merits. Instead he asks for it to be accepted on the basis of the proven record of the Papacy over 1800 years: 'He has spoken, and has a claim on us to trust him.' Newman then a little implausibly says, 'These are not the words of rhetoric, Gentlemen, but of history'; and then proceeds to sweep into a prose-poem of quasi-historical rhetoric that uses every possible evocative name and image not only to extol the early Christian cause but to bind England and Ireland together in a tradition of civilizing holiness.

> ... the two islands, in a dark and dreary age, were the two lights of Christendom. O memorable time, when St Aidan and the Irish monks went up to Lindisfarne and Melrose, and taught the Saxon youth, and when a St Cuthbert and a St Eata repaid their charitable toil!

And so he continues for several hundreds of words, through the Christian exploits of Mailduf and St Aldheim and St Egbert and St Willibrod and 'the two noble Ewalds' to Alcuin, 'the pupil of both the English and the Irish schools' who was sent for by Charlemagne to 'revive science and letters in France'. 'Such was the foundation of the school of Paris, from which, over the course of centuries, sprang the famous University [which was] the glory of the middle ages.'

So the awkward decision was dissolved in this paean to Anglo-Irish partnership which elided encouragingly into the suggestion that it had led to the foundation of the great University of the Sorbonne. And the lecture concluded by saying that England and Ireland had changed but 'Rome is where it was, and St Peter is the same ... And now surely he is giving us a like mission, and we shall become one again, while we zealously and lovingly fulfil it.' If that is not rhetoric, I do not know what is.

Equally, at the end of Discourse IX, entitled the *Duties of the Church Towards Knowledge,* he ends with the most tremendous *tour de force* that owes more to oratory than to relevance. He is attempting first to sum up what he has previously said, which he is rarely good at, for his thoughts live in his phrases and fade when they are reduced to summary form. Second, he is attempting to reconcile his strong shafts of instinctive tolerance with his respect for the authority of the Church, and gets himself, perhaps only to my inadequately spiritual mind, into a very great muddle. He has just proclaimed a firm libertarian doctrine on literature: 'I say, from the nature of the case, if Literature is to be made a study of human nature, you cannot have a Christian Literature. It is a contradiction in terms to attempt a sinless Literature of sinful man.' And he adds, 'we would be shrinking from our plain duty, Gentlemen, did we leave out Literature from Education.' The university, he adds, is not to be a convent or even a seminary. 'It is a place to fit men of the world for the world.'

But how is this to be reconciled with the authority of the Church over every aspect of this university? Is he advocating and defending such pervasive authority? In Discourse II he

144

seems to be taking up a much more modest position in regard to Catholic authority: 'As to the range of University teaching certainly the very name of University is inconsistent with restrictions of any kind.' In this Discourse he proceeds from this only to the limited claim that as theology is part of knowledge it cannot be excluded from the subjects taught at a true university. It is at least entitled to a chair (or chairs) amongst many. From there he advances to an intermediate position of refuting that which he calls the Lutheran advocacy of the complete separation of science and religion. He postulates a modern philosopher of science, asking him, 'Why cannot you go your way and let us go ours?' and says, 'I answer, in the name of the Science of Religion, when Newton can dispense with the metaphysicians, then may you dispense with us.' But he is still confining himself to an argument for the wholeness of knowledge and to religion's claim to a place in it.

Then in Discourse IX, quite close to the liberal passage on literature, he suddenly goes much further: 'If the Catholic faith is true, a University cannot exist externally to the Catholic pale, for it cannot teach Universal Knowledge if it does not teach Catholic theology. That is certain, but still, though it had ever so many theological Chairs, that would not suffice to make it a Catholic University; for theology would be included in its teaching only as a branch of knowledge, only as one of many constituent portions, however important a one, of what I have called Philosophy. Hence a direct and active jurisdiction of the Church over it and in it is necessary, lest it should become the rival of the Church with the community at large in those theological matters which to the Church are exclusively committed ...'

Much of the rest of this final Discourse, with the exception of the passage on literature, is Newman at his uneasiest. His words

145

do not flow with their usual spontaneity. There are a great number of 'Gentlemens' and 'that is certains', the latter in fact a certain sign of Newman's uncertainty. And then suddenly he escapes from this viscosity by hitting on the idea of bringing the whole thing to an end by throwing everything into a panegyric of St Philip Neri – 'my own special Father and Patron' as he refers to him. It is like the finale of an open-air concert I once attended, which brought the 1812 Overture to a conclusion with cymbals banging, cannons pounding, fireworks exploding and the conductor exhausting himself with enthusiasm:

Nay, people came to him, not only from all parts of Italy, but from France, Spain, Germany and all Christendom, and even the infidels and Jews, who had ever any communication with him, revered him as a holy man. The first families of Rome, the Massimi, the Aldobrandini, the Colonnas, the Altieri, the Vitelleschi, were his friends and his penitents. Nobles of Poland, Grandees of Spain, Knights of Malta could not leave Rome without coming to him. Cardinals, Archbishops and Bishops were his intimates, Frederigo Borromeo haunted his room and got the name of Father Philip's soul. The Cardinal-Archbishops of Verona and Bologna wrote books in his honour. Pope Pius IV died in his arms. Lawyers, painters, musicians, physicians, it was the same with them. Baronius, Zazzara, Ricci, left the law at his bidding, and joined his congregation to do its work, to write the annals of the Church, and to die in the odour of sanctity. Palestrina had Father Philip's ministrations in his last moments. Anninuccia hung about him during life, sent him a message after death, and was conducted by him through Purgatory to Heaven. And who was he, I say all

146

the while, but a humble priest, a stranger in Rome, with no distinction of family or letters, no claim of station or of office, great simply in the attraction with which a Divine Power had gifted him? And yet thus humble, thus unennobled, thus empty-handed, he has achieved the glorious title of Apostle of Rome.

It was a magnificent extravaganza, even if veering at times towards being a Jennifer's Diary of life in sixteenth-century Rome, but it was hardly a satisfactory synthesis of the competing roles of liberal culture and religious authority in the scheme of an ideal university between which he had veered throughout the nine Discourses. The dust was stardust, but he was frankly throwing it into the eyes of his audience while he escaped under its cover from the dilemma into which he had put himself. When, therefore, the whole series came to an end, and the work to which it led was complete, only one paragraph after the end of this pyrotechnical exhibition, I was left dazzled but intellectually unsatisfied. Newman had mostly held me spellbound in the grip of his prose, but he had convinced me neither that he had a practical plan for an Irish university in the 1850s or that he had left guidelines of great relevance for a university of any nationality or any or no faith today.

This does not mean that he did not shine splendid shafts of light on to particular issues. I greatly enjoyed his attack on Victorian materialist values, where Nassau Senior, the first Professor of Political Economy in this University, is set up with many compliments, both to his own eminence and to the 'unsordidness' of Oxford, to be the bull which is felled. '… the pursuit of wealth …' he exposes Nassau as saying, 'is, to the mass of mankind, the great source of *moral* improvement.' Then he says:

'I really should on every account be sorry, Gentlemen, to exaggerate, but indeed one is taken by surprise, one is startled, on meeting with so very categorical a contradiction of our Lord, St Paul, St Chrystostom, St Leo, and all Saints.'

Equally firm was his rejection in Discourse VII, many years ahead of its time, of the principle of contract funding for universities: 'Now this is what some great men are very slow to allow; they insist that Education should be confined to some particular and narrow end, and should issue in some definite work, which can be weighed and measured. They argue as if everything, as well as every person, had its price; and that where there has been a great outlay, they have a right to expect a return in kind'.

Then, again, there is his exhortation, in Discourse VI, against losing one's way in detail and specialization. He starts with a little text: 'A great memory does not make a philosopher, any more than a dictionary can be called a grammar.' Soon afterwards he goes into a fine passage which expands the need to command facts from a hillock, a sort of 'Wellington at Waterloo' theory of knowledge.

I say then, if we would improve the intellect, we must ascend … It matters not whether our field of operation be wide or limited; in every case, to command it, is to mount above it. Who has not felt the irritation of mind and impatience created by a deep rich country, visited for the first time, with winding lanes and high hedges, and green steeps, and tangled woods, and every thing smiling indeed, but in a maze? The same feeling comes upon us in a strange city, when we have no map of its streets. Have you not heard of practised travellers, when they come first into a place, mounting some high hill or church tower, by way of reconnoitring its neighbourhood. In like manner you must be above your knowledge, not under it, or it will oppress you; and the more you have of it, the greater will be the load.

So Newman could have been expected to be pretty strong on all the main issues that beset universities today. He would have been against contract funding, he would have supported tenure and academic freedom, certainly against any depredations from the state and probably instinctively against any from Archbishop Cullen, although he would have found it more difficult to speak unequivocally about this. Student loans, I think, he would have found difficult to engage with, although he would not have been in favour of encouraging the pursuit of careers of mammon in order to repay. I am not sure that he told us much about how to strike the balance between research and the teaching of the young, although his emphasis was all on the latter. He respected science, but I do not think that he regarded the advancement of the frontiers of knowledge as the most important form of human activity, any more than he did the pursuit of wealth. And there can be no doubt that he would have been on the restrictive side in recent controversies about experiments on the embryo.

I agree with the view of Professor Owen Chadwick (in his little book in the *Past Masters* series) that although Newman professed himself to have spent his life fighting liberalism, this was only true on his own very special and religious definition of liberalism, which almost equated it with intellectual brashness, and that some of his work had a considerable liberalizing influence. Yet, from the High Toryism of his outraged opposition to Catholic emancipation when he was a young Fellow of Oriel to his view when he was a very old man that issues should not be pursued

149

when the results of the enquiry might unsettle 'simple people', his respect for ecclesiastical authority necessarily set limits to seeing him as the patron saint of universities as republics of ideas, as unfettered as they are broad-based.

I have talked more about Newman and less about universities than you might have expected me to do. That is partly because I have many more opportunities to talk about universities than I do to talk about Newman, and partly because I have found him a wholly absorbing even if sometimes provoking a subject.

Changing Patterns of Leadership: From Asquith via Baldwin and Attlee to Margaret Thatcher

This essay started life as a lecture given to the Institute of Contemporary British History at the London School of Economics in November 1987. It has been brought up to date mainly by the changing of tenses.

Asquith became Prime Minister eighty-five years ago and held office for eight years, two hundred and forty-one days, which was then the longest continuous period since Lord Liverpool, the only Prime Minister to have made a reputation out of longevity. Walpole and the younger Pitt were both longer in office but their fame had other less arithmetical components. Mrs Thatcher overtook Asquith's record on 3 January 1988. I am convinced that it is essential to have a cumulative period in office of at least five years in order to rank as a Prime Minister of major impact. No one of the last one hundred years who does not fulfil this criterion has achieved the front rank. Not Rosebery, not Balfour (although, despite the electoral ignominy of his fall, he comes nearest to being the exception), not Campbell-Bannerman, not Neville Chamberlain, not Eden, not Home, not Heath, not Callaghan. That leaves three Prime Ministers who served over five years in peacetime within my eighty-five-year span and are not mentioned in my title: MacDonald, Macmillan, Wilson. I left them out partly because I have not written books about them. But nor have I about Mrs Thatcher. She however was there for so long and provided such an idiosyncratic style of government that she demands inclusion.

I begin my excursion with the currently ill-regarded and underestimated Asquith. A couple of years ago I came to re-read my life of him, first published in 1964, after an interval of nearly nine years. I was struck again by the quality of his mind and temperament and hence by his capacity to lead a government. It was not an adventurous mind which breached new frontiers, but he had knowledge, judgement, insight and tolerance. And for at least his first six years as Prime Minister he presided with an easy authority over the most talented government of this century. How would I illustrate his quality in government? I give two examples.

First, a memorandum on the constitutional position of the Sovereign, which he wrote on holiday in Scotland in September 1913 without any official advice, probably without any reference books to look at, and sent off direct to King George V. It was in reply to a rather pathetic *cri de coeur* from the King, complaining that he would be vilified by half his subjects whether or not he approved the Irish Home Rule Bill and almost suggesting that he had an equal constitutional choice between the two courses. Asquith's dismissal of this foolish idea was done with erudition and succinctness presented in a framework of muscular argument while treating the King with a firm courtesy untinged with any hint of obsequiousness. I can think of no other Prime Minister this century who could have written such a document out of the resources of his own mind with equal authority.

Second, as late as the eighth and penultimate year of his premiership he gave a brilliant and effective display of his talents as an effortless administrator. Kitchener (Margot Asquith's 'great poster' successfully masquerading as a great man) had by 1915 become a focus of indecision at the War Office. It could be held that Asquith ought to have sacked him, but given Kitchener's hold on public opinion that course was well beyond the limits of Asquith's courage. What he did was to encourage Kitchener to go on a month's visit to Gallipoli, temporarily himself to take over the War Office (as he had done four months after the Curragh mutiny in 1914) and quickly to lance several boils that Kitchener had allowed to fester for half a year or more. It was a last display of an exceptional administrative talent, and the fact that he enjoyed doing it contradicts the view that he was over the hill and had become indolently ineffective by 1914 at the latest.

Asquith was lazy only in the sense that because of his remarkable skill in the speedy (but perhaps too coolly detached) dispatch of public business he was able to keep a lot of time for pastimes outside politics. Nevertheless, I think he was in office too long and his style was unsuited to the demands of wartime leadership. It was not so much that Lloyd George, when he replaced him, was a better war leader. His errors of strategic judgement and his ineffectiveness in controlling a High Command backed by the King were just as great as were those of Asquith. But Lloyd George had the zest and the brio to behave as though he were a better war leader, and that was half the battle.

Asquith did not like the frenetic drama, the mock heroics, of politicians' war, although he certainly did not insulate his family

153

from the tribulations of soldiers' war, and he could not be bothered to pretend to an enthusiasm he did not feel. The lady who, as a conversational gambit in 1915, said, 'Mr Asquith, do you take an interest in the war?' was nearer to the bone than perhaps she imagined. His pattern of government should therefore be studied mainly in its peacetime manifestation, although part of the complaint against him was that this pattern was hardly changed when the war began.

Although in general his authority in the government was good, with no suggestion that he was frightened of strong ministers, of whom he had plenty, or that they were disrespectful of him, I do not think it could be said that he operated the Cabinet tautly. There was then no written record of its proceedings, apart from his own handwritten letters to the King after each meeting. That sounds unimaginable today, but it was a practice that he had inherited from all his predecessors, including one as efficient as Peel and another as energetic as Gladstone. I think the lack of tautness had other causes. He did not talk much in Cabinet himself. He had other Cabinet occupations. But he rather believed in letting discussion run on, almost exhausting itself before he could see developing what he liked to describe as a 'favourable curve' for bringing it to a satisfactory conclusion.

These methods made him good at holding rumbustious colleagues together and good too at avoiding foolish decisions. It made him less good at taking wise decisions ahead of time and at galvanizing the less energetic members of his government. This latter deficiency must be seen in the context of his indisputable achievement of presiding over one of the only two major reforming left-of-centre governments of the past hundred years. He did not greatly interfere in the work of departmental ministers and when he did it was to give them necessary but slightly reluctant

154

support where needed, rather than to correct them. Lloyd George, ironically in some ways, was the foremost beneficiary of this support, both in getting the Budget of 1909 through a reluctant Cabinet and at the time of his Marconi peccadilloes. Asquith allowed Edward Grey an almost complete independence at the Foreign Office, but as that somewhat insular and priggish bird-watcher was, in my view, one of the most overrated statesmen in the first half of this century the results were not altogether happy.

As a butcher of ministers, Asquith was in the middle grade, about half-way between Gladstone, who regarded his Cabinet colleagues, once appointed, as having the inviolate permanence of members of the College of Cardinals, and Macmillan, who in 1962 axed a third of them like junior managers in an ailing company. Asquith dropped Tweedmouth, his First Lord of the Admiralty, when he became seriously deranged, Herbert Gladstone, who was an incompetent Home Secretary but who was compensated with the Governor-Generalship of South Africa, Charles Masterman when he lost two by-elections running, and Haldane, Asquith's oldest political friend, because the Tories, foolishly from several points of view, demanded Haldane's head as the price for accepting a rotten lot of portfolios for themselves when they joined the 1915 Coalition. But he left the North Sea to engulf Kitchener and the Dublin Easter rebellion to destroy Birrell as Chief Secretary for Ireland. Birrell, in spite of splendid epigrams, ought to have gone much sooner before the rebellion also destroyed the prospect of Home Rule within a United Kingdom. He reshuffled some of his ministers a good deal, although not as much as Wilson, who had not a butcher's but a circus master's approach to reshuffling. Under Asquith, McKenna and Churchill in particular were subjected to a number of rather pointless changes.

155

Asquith's own attention was mostly concentrated on the high constitutional issues of which there were plenty in the peacetime life of his government: on relations with the Lords and with the Sovereign leading to the Parliament Act, on Irish Home Rule, on Welsh Church disestablishment, and on the failed suffrage reform. Although he had himself introduced the first old-age pension in his last Budget as Chancellor before becoming Prime Minister, he left the subsequent development of national insurance as much to Lloyd George as he did foreign affairs to Grey until late July 1914. Nevertheless, it would be quite wrong to think of him as other than the leading figure in his own government, the one whom his colleagues naturally accepted as the fount of praise or rebuke, with the greatest command over the House of Commons, and the best-known figure to the public. In this last respect, being well known to the public, and only in this last respect, Lloyd George was a near runner-up.

Stanley Baldwin came to the Prime Ministership in a totally different way. Asquith's was the calmest, the most certain, assured ascent this century, with the possible exception of Neville Chamberlain. But Chamberlain was twelve years older than Asquith at accession and for this, amongst other reasons, he will be seen in history as an appendage to the age of Baldwin, while Asquith, almost independently of merit, relegated his predecessor, Campbell-Bannerman, to being a prefix to the age of Asquith. Baldwin, in contrast to Asquith, came out of the woodwork a bare six months before he was in Number 10 Downing Street. Until then there were at least six Conservative politicians who were much better known than he was. Asquith had become the senior Secretary of State at the age of thirty-nine, Baldwin was fifty before he became even a junior minister. Baldwin was a

Conservative, Asquith was a Liberal. Baldwin was rich, Asquith was not. Asquith was fashionable, partly but not wholly through his wife. Baldwin was not. In spite of these differences, Baldwin wished to model himself more on Asquith than on any other of his twentieth-century predecessors.

Did he succeed? His main government, that of 1924–9, was less talented, although with Churchill, Balfour, Birkenhead and the two Chamberlains, Neville and Austen, it could not, by any stretch of the imagination, be regarded as negligible in this respect. He was as economical with the attention he was prepared to devote to politics as was Asquith. But his intellectual equipment was much less formidable. When asked what English thinker had most influenced him, he firmly replied, 'Sir Henry Maine'. When asked which particular aspect of Maine's thought had seized his mind, he said Maine's view that all human history should be seen in terms of the advance from status to contract. He then paused, looked apprehensively at his interlocutor, and said, 'Or was it the other way around?' This is totally un-Asquithian. Asquith might not have had many original thoughts but he could summarize the broad doctrines of any well-known philosopher or historian as well as giving you their dates at the drop of a hat.

Baldwin's authority within his main government in the 1920s was substantially less than Asquith's had been. Baldwin, by then, had escaped from the anonymity of 1923; he had won a great election victory and he had made his own Cabinet, unlike his first short spell in Downing Street in 1923 when he had merely inherited one from Bonar Law. But he had made it mostly of men who were used to being his political seniors. He inspired no awe. On the other hand, partly by the devotion of vast areas of time to sitting on the front bench in the House of Commons,

157

talking in its corridors, and hanging about its smoking room, desultorily reading the *Strand Magazine,* as was reported on one occasion, he acquired a considerable popularity in, and indeed mastery over, the House of Commons. His skill at the new medium of broadcasting was also a considerable and exceptional strength.

The *Strand Magazine* incident I use to epitomize certain differences between Baldwin and his predecessors and successors. Asquith would never have chosen the *Strand Magazine,* or the House of Commons as a place in which to read. He would have read more reconditely, but equally haphazardly, in some more private precinct. Churchill in office would never have wasted time in the smoking room without an audience. Lloyd George would never have wasted time there at all, but he might well have chosen the *Strand Magazine* had he been left waiting upon a railway platform. Neville Chamberlain would never have read haphazardly. Ramsay MacDonald would never have exposed himself so apparently free from the burdens of state. It could not exactly be said that Stanley Baldwin was wasting time. More likely he was not even reading the magazine, but sniffing it, and with it the atmosphere around him, ruminating, feeling his way, nudging towards a variety of decisions he had to make. He was not indecisive. Indeed, Birkenhead once unfavourably described his method of government as 'taking one leap in the dark, looking around, and taking another'. But he reached decisions much more by sniffing and then making a sudden plunge than by any orderly process of ratiocination.

Baldwin rarely applied himself to the methodical transaction of written business. Tom Jones, Deputy Secretary of the Cabinet who later became one of his closest confidants, at first thought him remarkably slow, with barely a fifth of the speed of his

158

predecessor, Bonar Law, in dealing with papers. It took Jones some time to realize that Baldwin did not work at all in Law's rather unimaginative accountant's sense. But his mind was none the less always playing around the political issues. In this way he was the opposite, not only of Law but of Asquith, who certainly did not have an accountant's mind. Churchill wrote of Asquith, 'He was like a great judge who gave his whole mind to a case as long as his court was open and then shut it absolutely and turned his mind to the diversions of the day.' With Baldwin the court was never either wholly open or wholly shut.

It followed from this method of work that Baldwin was even less inclined to interfere in the work of departmental ministers than was Asquith. He did not bombard his ministers with declaratory minutes like Churchill, or petulant ones like Eden, or nostalgic ones like Macmillan. Nor did he exercise much control over his ministers by headmasterly promotions, demotions or sackings. He made hardly any changes during his four-and-a-half-year period of office, except when Halifax (then Wood, about to become Irwin) went to India as Viceroy, when Curzon died, or when Birkenhead decided he could not live on his salary. He never seriously thought of getting rid of Steel-Maitland who was a useless Minister of Labour, stationed in the most crucial and exposed segment of the government's political front. This decision at least had the effect of involving and identifying the Prime Minister very closely with his government's handling of industrial relations. This was true both before and during the General Strike. His 'Give Peace in our Time, oh Lord' speech in February 1925 was then his most successful House of Commons foray, and the decision four months later to set up the Samuel Commission and to pay a temporary subsidy to the coal industry was very much his own work. During the eight days of the

General Strike itself he was also deeply involved, but once it (as opposed to the coal strike, which dragged on for another six months) was defeated, he rather lost interest.

There were five major developments in the life of his second and central government (1924–9), and this was the only one with which he was crucially concerned. The return to the gold standard in 1925 was very much Churchill's decision at the Treasury, even though he had at first been opposed to it. The Treaty of Locarno, and the European security system created by it, was overwhelmingly Austen Chamberlain's work at the Foreign Office. The housing and poor law reforms were even more decisively the work of his half-brother Neville at the Ministry of Health. Finally, the Statute of Westminster, which enabled the reality of Dominion independence to be combined with the dignity of the Crown, came from Balfour.

Baldwin was therefore more detached from the main policies of his government than was Asquith, and he was, in my view, a less considerable man, although not a negligible one either. He would not have had the intellectual grasp to write Asquith's constitutional memorandum. But he had the feel to deal successfully with the General Strike, although not the sustained energy to follow this up by dealing equally well with the miners' strike, which was both its cause and its aftermath. He dealt still more skilfully with the Abdication crisis ten years later. Like Asquith, he preferred to engage with constitutional issues more than with any other, though his lack of overseas interest (except for India and that he never visited) meant that that Statute of Westminster slipped by him almost unnoticed. He continued Asquith's practice, interrupted by Lloyd George, of performing as Prime Minister without a surrounding circus. He would walk about London or travel by mainline train on his own.

Attlee arrived in Number 10 Downing Street eight years after Baldwin had left for the last time. Unlike either Asquith or Baldwin, he inherited a vast government machine which the war had created, and which was used to dealing with a great part of the nation's affairs and spending a high proportion of its income. He was also the heir to a post-Baldwin Prime Ministerial habit of trying to run a large part of British foreign policy from 10 Downing Street, and believing that Britain counted for a great deal in the world. (The latter belief was pre- as well as post-Baldwin.) Attlee's first duty in his new office was to meet the Russians and the Americans at Potsdam. Neither Asquith nor Baldwin had ever attended an international conference as Prime Minister. Attlee, a very firmly established member of the English upper-middle-class, was not rich like Baldwin, or fashionable like Asquith, but he was similar to both of them in having a natural respect for conventional values and institutions. He liked almost all institutions with which he had been connected: cricket, Haileybury, where he had been at school, Oxford (and University College in particular), the Inner Temple, Toynbee Hall, and even the National Executive Committee of the Labour Party. It did not make him pompous, for his taciturnity gave him a natural talent for balloon-pricking, and it did not prevent his being the head of an effective radical government just as it had not prevented Asquith or, for that matter, Gladstone before him being in the same category.

Compared with Asquith and Baldwin, Attlee was the worst speaker, the least engaging personality, and by far the best Cabinet chairman. He developed this last quality even before he had the authority of Prime Ministership behind him. Many recorded tributes testify to the way in which he presided over the War Cabinet during Churchill's frequent absences: rhetoric disappeared, and decisions were taken with speed and precision. Yet Attlee was not the dominating figure of his government, either publicly or privately. Bevin, Cripps, Dalton, Morrison, Bevan, and latterly Gaitskell, constituted a formidable array of ministers. I do not think that they can quite be classed with Asquith's, partly because of the subsequent fame of Lloyd George and Churchill, but also because there was nobody in the Attlee Government to match the non-political distinction of Morley, Birrell and Haldane. That Liberal Government apart, however, they are unmatched this century and for most of the last, too. Attlee balanced them, steered them, kept them and himself afloat, but he did not exactly lead them. He was a cox and not a stroke. For his first three or four years he distributed their weight brilliantly, although latterly he failed to place Aneurin Bevan properly, which led to considerable trouble.

One of his strongest attributes was said to have been his capacity for laconic ministerial butchery. This may be slightly exaggerated. He despatched parliamentary under-secretaries with ease, but this was rather like shooting chickens. Of big game he was more cautious. He was probably relieved when an exhausted Dalton shot himself but he pulled no trigger on him. Arthur Greenwood he did dispose of but only when that figure had become unwilling to conduct even his morning's business from anywhere except the 'snuggery' (I think it was called) of the Charing Cross Hotel. Then towards the end he dismissed Ernest Bevin from the Foreign Office. That was an extraordinary feat. Bevin was the most important Foreign Secretary of this century, by which I mean that he was the one who left the biggest imprint on British foreign policy for a generation ahead. He was a massive but by no means a wholly amiable personality. He had been the sheet-anchor of Attlee's support throughout the life of

162

the government. He had given his support to 'little Clem' against Morrison, Cripps, and Dalton. Yet when his health made him no longer capable of doing the job, out he went, miserable and complaining, and died six weeks later. This was an act of cold courage more difficult even than President Truman's sacking of General MacArthur.

With what aspects of government policy did Attlee most concern himself? Like both Asquith and Baldwin, even though both of them had been Chancellors of the Exchequer, I do not think that he understood or was much interested in economics. But the 'dismal science' had become far more central to government by his day. He gave his Chancellors, and especially Cripps, a very dominant position. His Foreign Secretary had such a position by virtue of his own personality. Between Potsdam and Attlee's visit to Washington in December 1950, when Truman had falsely suggested that he might be about to drop an atomic bomb on the Chinese in North Korea and when Bevin was too fragile to cross the Atlantic in less than five days, Attlee intervened in foreign policy no more than Asquith had done.

However, the beginning of the end of the Empire meant that there was a great range of external affairs with which a Prime Minister could concern himself without impinging on the prerogatives of even the most truculent Foreign Secretary. On relations with America, Russia and the continent of Europe, Attlee supported Bevin. On India, with a rather weak Secretary of State, he made his own policy. And determining the future of 450 million people, now 800 million, was by any standards in the major league. Perhaps the two biggest impacts on history made by Britain during the past two hundred years have been first to govern and then to leave both America and India. So Attlee ranks as a major agent of Britain's world impact.

Internally, constitutional affairs engrossed Attlee less than they did either Asquith or Baldwin. On the other hand, he took more part in the social legislation of his government than did Asquith in the previous wave of advance in this field. The Attlee Government was also memorable for six or seven major measures of nationalization. Attlee did not much involve himself in the detail, but supported them all with commitment, even enthusiasm.

He presided over a highly interventionist government but he did not find it necessary to overwork. He once told me that being Prime Minister left him more spare time than any other job that he had done. It was partly, he said, because of living on the spot and avoiding the immensely long tube or Metropolitan Railway journeys, to which his modest suburban lifestyle condemned him, both before and after Downing Street. But his modesty should not be exaggerated. No other Prime Minister in British history was ever so richly honoured, as he noted in the little piece of doggerel which he wrote about himself:

> Few thought he was even a starter
> There were many who thought themselves smarter
> But he ended PM, CH and OM,
> An Earl and a Knight of the Garter

His reputation went steadily up and he and Macmillan were almost the only Prime Ministers who enjoyed themselves in retirement more than in active life. Not Lloyd George or Churchill, Rosebery, Asquith, Wilson, Eden or Heath. And I doubt whether Mrs Thatcher will be very content.

The government that Mrs Thatcher ran bore less relation to the three previous administrations I have considered than they each did to the other two. The comparison is by no means wholly to her credit. In terms of the quality of the other ministers, I think it must be regarded as the least illustrious government of the four. It is always necessary to be on one's guard against underestimating contemporaries compared to their predecessors. It is easier to admire those on whom the gates of history have slammed shut, and there is a fairly constant tendency to see things as always going downhill: to say that the younger Pitt was not as good as his father, that Canning was not as good as Pitt, that Peel was not as good as Canning, or Gladstone as Peel, or Asquith as Gladstone. Such constant regression is biologically improbable. But even with that warning I do not think that Messrs Howe, Lawson, Parkinson, Tebbit, Baker and Hurd can be put in the same league as the Asquith, Baldwin or Attlee lists as outstanding political personalities, nor can they match the Asquith list as men of distinction outside politics.

To some substantial extent this goes with the dominant position within the government of the recent Prime Minister. She certainly did not leave ministers as secure in their offices as did Gladstone or Baldwin. She was not as addicted to the annual gymkhana of a reshuffle, almost for its own sake, as was Wilson. But she none the less wrought great changes of personnel in her eleven and a half years. It is remarkable that there was no member of the Cabinet, other than herself, who survived throughout her term. In addition, her changes had far more of a general purpose than did those of Asquith or Attlee. They were not primarily made on grounds of competence. They were steadily directed to shifting the balance of ideology, or perhaps even more of amenability, within the Cabinet.

As a result of these various factors, she must be counted the most dominating Prime Minister within her government of any of the four. Her control over the House of Commons I would regard as much more dependent upon the serried majorities she had behind her than upon any special parliamentary skill. Her combative belief in her own rightness ensured that she was rarely discomfited and never overwhelmed. But she brought no special qualities of persuasiveness or debating skill that enabled her to move minds where others would have failed. Even an unsuccessful Prime Minister like Eden had, in my view, more capacity to do this than she had. And the serried majorities were a direct function of having a split opposition with a voting system designed for only two parties. She never exercised any special command over a medium of communication as Baldwin did in the early days of broadcasting, and for much of her fifteen and a half years as Conservative leader, before and after 1979, she was personally below rather than above her party's poll rating.

Her stamp upon every aspect of her government's policy, on the other hand, was incomparably greater than that of any of my other three Prime Ministers. There was no question of her reserving herself for major constitutional issues. Indeed, I doubt that she had much sense of what was a constitutional issue and what was not. There was no departmental minister who was able to sustain an area of prerogative. It was impossible to imagine her being asked for advice, and saying to Geoffrey Howe, as Baldwin said to Austen Chamberlain, 'but you are Foreign Secretary'. She was equally interfering in the military, economic, industrial, social security, Commonwealth and law and order aspects of the government's policy. She sought no respite from politics, in the sense that did Asquith, Baldwin and Attlee. Her impact was bound to be greater by virtue of her determination and longevity in office. She reduced the influence of the Cabinet:

if she had improved Britain's influence, that might have been taken as having been a fair exchange, but any improvement in this respect was distinctly temporary.

Over the nearly a century I have been considering, the scope of government obviously increased enormously. Public expenditure rose from approximately £170 million, perhaps £5 billion in present-day values, to about nine hundred times that in money terms and thirty times it in real terms. Great new departments, like Health, Social Security and the Environment, sprang up with an entirely different pattern of ministerial duties from anything remotely prevailing before 1914. The essential role of the Prime Minister did not change as much as this might lead one to believe. The function of a conductor is not greatly altered by introducing new instruments into the orchestra. The style is much more a product of a man or a woman than it is of the epoch. President Reagan at least showed that modern government need not be too strenuous. Mr Major would no doubt like to achieve a reversion to the calmer habits, if not of Asquith at least of Attlee, but that requires an authority which has so far eluded him.

What has changed permanently, however, is the necessary involvement of the head of the government of this or any other comparable country in external affairs. The interdependent world, not to mention the European Community, has changed that for ever. The calm insularity of Asquith and Baldwin, even to some extent that of Attlee, must equally have permanently disappeared.

An Oxford View of Cambridge

(With Some Reflections on Oxford and Other Universities)

This is a lightly edited version of the 1988 Rede Lecture delivered in the Senate House at Cambridge on 10 May of that year.

The last time a Chancellor of Oxford delivered a Rede Lecture was when Curzon gave it in 1913. In many ways he was a rasher man than I am, as he showed in India and then at Oxford, where in his first year as Chancellor he moved in, asserted his undoubted right to preside over the Hebdomadal Council, and generally set about ruling the university and not merely reigning over it. As in Calcutta and Delhi, his Oxford assertiveness ended in a mixture of achievement and chagrin.

In Cambridge, however, he behaved more circumspectly than I have boldly undertaken to do. His lecture was on *Modern Parliamentary Eloquence*. I would now find that a difficult subject. However, it would have been a much safer subject here to have lectured upon than my Oxonian view of Cambridge. When I

168

first suggested it to the Vice-Chancellor of Cambridge I think he was apprehensive. My understanding of his fears increased when, a little later, I told a distinguished Oxford historian of somewhat polemical temperament who recently retired from a seven-year spell as a Cambridge Head of House, that I was committed to this subject in this place. 'If by chance,' Lord Dacre said *con amore*, 'you feel at all unwell as the occasion approaches, do not hesitate to send for me as a substitute. There is no subject on which I would rather talk before an audience in the Cambridge Senate House, if necessary unprepared. I could do it spontaneously.' But I feel reasonably well, and intend to devote myself not to polemics or even to Oxford flippancy (of which more later) but to looking at the interaction of our two universities upon each other and to a glance at their relationship to others at home and abroad.

Exploring the history of Oxford and Cambridge for the purposes of this lecture I have been struck by the symbiotic nature of the relationship between the two universities. Over eight centuries they have greatly influenced and cross-fertilized each other. They have been more pacers than rivals. At times one has gone ahead (indeed it could, I suppose, be argued that in the Middle Ages Oxford was fairly consistently so) but the other has then caught up or overtaken, frequently building on a development initiated in the first one. The result has been an historical relationship a great deal more fluctuating and interesting than the average course of the sporting event for which we are best known in the world. During these fluctuations certain differences of style and even ethos have developed. About them one can generalize with mild amusement and a modicum of accuracy. But the similarities have remained much greater than the differences. Increased influence and prestige for one has usually meant the same, perhaps after a time-lag, for the other and neither has ever significantly gained from the other's misfortune.

We are clearly both federal universities, with great power and individuality residing in the colleges. I do not think such a degree of decentralization exists in any other geographically concentrated university in the world. California, yes, even London, but they are not concentrated geographically, and certainly not Harvard or Yale, which are. Harvard houses are merely dormitories with resonant names. Yale has colleges, but they are concerned only with living and not with teaching. Oxford and Cambridge are both highly collegiate universities, some would say Oxford marginally more so than Cambridge, in spite of the longer-term and more full-time nature of the Oxford Vice-Chancellorship (until 1991 when Cambridge accomplished a leap-frog in this respect), because the colleges in Oxford appoint many of those who are subsequently paid by the university. This being so, however, it is surprising that the history of both of them contradicts the normal pattern of federations, where, as in America, Switzerland, Australia, the component states came first and the federal authority was very much an afterthought. In Cambridge as in Oxford, on the other hand, the university was there nearly a century before the first colleges and it was not indeed until a good three hundred years after the beginning of the universities that the colleges came into their full insolent authority.

This was for the very good reason that the most lordly of them did not exist. Cambridge towards the end of the fifteenth century was a university almost as old as Harvard is today, was rapidly catching up on Oxford both in numbers and fame, but was still without Trinity (except in vestigial form) or St John's, as well of course as the late sixteenth-century trio of Caius,

Emmanuel and Sidney Sussex, and with King's looking no more than a muddy building site alongside a gaunt and roofless shell which was to become the chapel. Yet it was undoubtedly a much better period for Cambridge than for Oxford, where the mid-fifteenth-century foundation of Magdalen and All Souls did nothing to arrest a half-century of decline. Erasmus was at Queens' (Cambridge) for some time around 1510, and much though he complained about his living conditions and the climate, although I cannot think that he had been used to much better in his Low Countries, his presence was both an indication of Cambridge's rising prestige and a formative influence on teaching developments. Just as the college as a community for living was an Oxford idea, stemming essentially from Merton, which spread to Cambridge at the beginning of the fourteenth century, so the college as an institution for teaching was a Cambridge idea which spread to Oxford at the beginning of the sixteenth century.

Then in the second quarter of that century there came the outbreak of grandeur in both universities in the form of Trinity here and Christ Church at Oxford. Christ Church was born only after two false attempts, which made it first Cardinal College, then King Henry VIII College and only finally Christ Church, all within thirty years. It is to the best of my belief the only college in the world that has a cathedral tucked away in its purlieus. But however firmly it may have the diocesan church in its embrace it has not got the university in this position. The original intention was perhaps precisely this – 'a college which when finished will equal the rest of Oxford' was an early state-ment of aim. It has never quite achieved that, although it has achieved the worldly feat of producing more Prime Ministers than the rest of the university put together. So has Trinity.

171

Christ Church indeed in some ways resembles a bit of Cambridge in Oxford. It was wholly appropriate that its first dean – Cox – should have been imported from Cambridge. Perhaps for this reason it is more detached than is Trinity. Trinity may be uncomfortably large and rich for the rest of the university – like a province of an African state with an unbalancing amount of the minerals and therefore the wealth, a Katanga or a Biafra, although not I hope a candidate for secession, but it is also part of the core of the university and therefore its middle kingdom. Christ Church, both geographically and psychologically, is much more like a ship – some would say a luxury liner – moored off shore. However, they have both exhibited a worldly exuberance and physical splendour which make them suitable monuments to their royal founder as well as major moulders of the shapes of their universities.

In spite of these great developments the sixteenth century was a pretty rough time in Cambridge. Five of its nine Chancellors were executed, including the great Fisher in 1535. This was a degree of hazard to which my predecessors have never been exposed, which is surprising for, more recently, the Oxford tradition has favoured the choice, after contest, of more controversial Chancellors than has been the Cambridge habit.

The seventeenth century was one of almost equally great turbulence and fluctuating, almost contradictory, fortunes for both universities. Until the Civil War their numbers were rising strongly. Cambridge grew from a total of 1600 in 1550 to 3000 in the 1620s and 30s. Oxford moved more or less in step. Their influence rose proportionately. Oxford was particularly good at flattering the royal vanity of King James I. University MPs were introduced during his reign, but perhaps more significant was a very substantial increase to about a third in the proportion of the House of Commons that was Oxford or Cambridge educated.

The Civil War brought the increase in numbers to an end. Oxford became the Royalist capital, while Cambridge spawned the Earl of Manchester and Cromwell, although it was Oxford that had to accept the latter as its Chancellor in 1650. Cambridge saw ten of its sixteen colleges have their heads of houses removed from office – three colleges twice experienced the change – during the Civil War and Commonwealth period. Oxford took more enthusiastically to the Restoration and – a very Oxonian touch – led the way in establishing a one-day coach service to London and thus strengthening its links with court and government. In both universities, however, the long torpor of the eighteenth century was casting its shadow before it, numbers were falling heavily, and influence was declining. The intake of freshmen per year fell at Oxford from 460 in the 1660s to 300 in the 1690s. It became little more than a seminary for the Anglican church. Cambridge avoided such a complete retreat to a church bastion, but its total size was reduced by a third before the nadir of the 1770s.

Perversely, this period of academic and worldly decline was marked by the most glorious architectural flowering. Wren, Hawksmoor and Gibbs gave Oxford a large part of what one would most enthusiastically show to a first-time visitor. Between 1660 and 1730 there arose the Sheldonian Theatre, the Clarendon Building and the Radcliffe Camera in the university area, the Codrington Library and the North Quad of All Souls, Tom Tower and the completion of Tom Quad as well as Peckwater Quadrangle and the Library at Christ Church, Magdalen New Buildings and almost the whole of the Queen's College, including its baroque façade on to the High Street.

173

From the same architects Cambridge gained Trinity Library, the chapels of Pembroke and Emmanuel, the Senate-House and the Gibbs Building at King's. It is perhaps less dependent on the period than Oxford because it had more to show before. And for Cambridge the contrast between the splendour of buildings and the poverty of intellectual enquiry was less sharp, for it was the age of Newton as well as the age of Wren, although it could be argued that Newton found London and the Royal Society more stimulating than Trinity. After he had gone, however, and even though Bentley, the great classicist who was Master of Trinity for nearly fifty years, lingered on until 1742, the mid-eighteenth-century sleep into which Cambridge fell was even more profound than that of Oxford, which could at least claim to have sustained the century by educating Wesley, Johnson, Blackstone, Gibbon and Bentham, even though the last two did not think much of their *alma mater.*

What is the case is that the eighteenth century, the last century in which Oxford and Cambridge maintained their English university monopoly, and the century widely thought of above all others as that of the gentleman scholar, the easy-going squire/classicist who was as at home in his library as on his horse, at the production of which type they should have been so adept, was undoubtedly the first century amongst seven in which neither Oxford nor Cambridge was pre-eminent amongst the centres of learning of the territories within the realm of their sovereigns. Edinburgh was superior and so, after its foundation within his Electorate of Hanover by George II in 1737, was Göttingen.

The surprising thing is that Oxford and Cambridge, having been thus overtaken in the eighteenth century, regained their British intellectual pre-eminence in the nineteenth century

174

although some would say that they took longer and the assistance of several Royal Commissions to get back to the top European league. How did they do it? The short answer is that Cambridge did it through mathematics and Oxford through religion, and that mathematics being on the whole a more serious subject than religion (at least as pursued by the Oxford liturgical disputes of the second quarter of the nineteenth century), there stemmed from this a certain Cavalier/Roundhead bifurcation which had not really occurred in the seventeenth century but which in the nineteenth century sent Oxford in a more metaphysical, frivolous and worldly direction and Cambridge on a more enquiring, serious and austere course.

The remarkable achievement of eighteenth-century Cambridge was that within a clerical shell it shed theology as its central subject and hatched out mathematics as its replacement. The ladder of wranglers as well as the tripos was established, and already when George III came to the throne the Senior Wranglership was a coveted position strenuously striven for. Muscular intellectual competition began in Cambridge a good fifty years before cricket and rowing, the two first organized games to be brought into either university from the schools.

I last had occasion to write about the Cambridge mathematical tripos and its relationship to athleticism when, just over thirty years ago, I tried to describe the Leslie Stephen-inspired atmosphere of Trinity Hall for a life of Sir Charles Dilke, who went there in 1862, which I was then engaged in writing. 'Stephen', I wrote, 'believed in plain living and hard work. He had a high respect for the discipline of the mathematical tripos and the habit of cool, detached enquiry, founded upon intensive application, to which it led. He was as distrustful of enthusiasm in affairs of the intellect (or of the emotions) as he was respectful to its exhibition on the tow-path. He disliked obscurity and ambiguity of expression, and thought of them as inevitable results of speculative generalization. Let a man stick to his last, write or talk only about those subjects to which he had applied himself (without attempting to weave them all into a single metaphysic), and it could all be done in good, calm, clear Cambridge English.'

I added that Stephen, having been a poor oar, had made himself one of the great rowing coaches of the century, had written the college boating song, liked thirty-mile walks and had at least once walked from Cambridge to London to attend a dinner and back again during the night. He was also the son-in-law of Thackeray, the father of Virginia Woolf and Vanessa Bell, and the first editor of the *Dictionary of National Biography.* He was in addition, I suggested, 'almost perfectly suited to the Cambridge tripos system of the day, under which a man reading for honours was toned up like an athlete and won his awards by a combination of staying power during the long period of preliminary work and speed in the examination room.'

The key Oxford/Cambridge phrases in my attempted analysis of the intellectual style of Dilke's mentor, in which I suspect I was heavily influenced by Stephen's biography by Noël Annan, which had been the first book of the then recently elected 'boy Provost' of King's, were 'without attempting a single metaphysic' and 'calm, clear Cambridge English'.

This distinction after which I was groping was given somewhat farcical Cambridge expression thirty years after Stephen had left Trinity Hall, although I did not come across this until fifteen years after I wrote my Dilke book. H. S. Foxwell, notable St John's economist who lived in I Harvey Road for almost as

176

long as John *Neville* Keynes, Registrary of this University, lived in 6 Harvey Road, was disturbed by rumours in the early 1890s that his neighbour was about to be enticed away by the chair of political economy in the University of Oxford. 'Pray don't go,' he wrote in half-serious horror. 'Think of the effect your move may have on your son. He may grow up flippantly epigrammatical and end by becoming the proprietor of a Gutter Gazette, or the hero of a popular party; instead of emulating his father's noble example, becoming an accurate, clear-headed Cambridge man spending his life in the valuable and unpretentious service of his kind, dying beloved of his friends, venerated by the wise and unknown to the masses, as true merit and worth mostly are.'

Keynes *père* did not go, and Keynes *fils* was protected from the superficial worldliness of an Oxford education which Professor Foxwell rather oddly thought would necessarily follow from such a translation. John *Maynard* Keynes, it must be said, did not entirely eschew either epigram or fame, but he remained faithful, if not to the extent of emulating the 'warp and woof' Cambridge life of his parents, at least to that of becoming one of this University's greatest twentieth-century ornaments.

Was Foxwell expressing a truth in mocking language or was he merely being complacently denigrating of the university he did not know? I think he did have a fragment of reality concealed within his joke. It can be differently expressed by saying that although as a matter of simple geographical fact Cambridge is and always has been three miles nearer to London than Oxford, in most other senses Oxford has long been closer to the capital. And that is not only a function of the superiority of the Padding-ton over the Liverpool Street train service. It pre-dates the railway age. The operator of that fast coach from

Carfax to the court at Whitehall in the late seventeenth century had done his market research well. He knew that amidst the 'dreaming spires' below 'the soft-muffled Cumnor hills' and in 'the home of lost causes' there were plenty of moths who would respond to the prospect of a quick journey to the metropolitan candle.

Oxford gradually became more of a nursery of government. Of the fourteen eighteenth-century Prime Ministers, seven were at Oxford, five at Cambridge and two at neither. It should however be said that if stature is the test, both Walpole and the Younger Pitt were from Cambridge, with only the Elder Pitt of comparable quality from Oxford. Of the nineteenth century's nineteen (not counting the two who overlapped), nine were Oxonians, six Cantabrigians, three from neither. Oxford's stars were Peel and Gladstone, Cambridge's Palmerston. In this century Oxford has eight, Cambridge three and 'nowhere or elsewhere' seven. This time the greatest stars, Lloyd George and Churchill, were amongst the 'nowheres'. What is perhaps more significant is that because Cambridge had no nineteenth-century Prime Minister after 1868, the last 120 years give a score of Oxford eleven and Cambridge three.

Prime Ministers are the most obvious piece of litmus paper but also provide only a narrowly based test. However, if Lord Chancellors or Viceroys of India are put through the same sieve, roughly the same result is produced. In the past hundred years there have been thirteen Oxford Lord Chancellors to four Cambridge ones. In the ninety-year history of the viceroyalty there were fifteen Oxonians and five Cantabrigians.

Something the same has been true at the less elevated ranks both of politics and of administration, particularly overseas in the heyday of empire. Despite the tradition of the Butler family

178

amongst a number of other Cambridge examples, Oxford was always twice as strong in the Indian Civil Service and in the Sudan Political Service. In the words of Richard Symonds, historian of *Oxford and Empire:* 'No other university had a college such as [was] Balliol between 1870 and 1914, devoted to selecting and preparing young men for high office and then, through the network of old Balliol men, ensuring that they secured it. Nor elsewhere was there an institution comparable to All Souls … [which] appointed as its fellows the most brilliant graduates of each year who, as one commentator said in the 1930s, thus joined a committee which took upon itself no less a task than running the British Empire.' It is tempting to comment that the main direction in which they ran it was into the ground.

This Oxford approach was as much a matter of attitude of mind as of the statistics of jobs procured. Its late nineteenth- and early twentieth-century spirit and interest, as I have said, were more worldly, more metaphysical and less empirically enquiring than those of Cambridge. Nor, surprisingly, was the attachment to 'cool, clear Cambridge English' quite so strong. Oxford sometimes preferred obfuscating a question with an epigram to clarifying it with quiet diligence. The Franks Report – the 1966 result of a seven-strong internal enquiry into the affairs of the university – proclaimed its determination that 'reading and writing, rather than listening, should continue to be the salient characteristics of that Oxford system'. This was an illuminating comment and sensible declaration of intent, but it did not reveal the whole truth, which is that Oxford has now long been a university based hardly at all on listening, substantially on reading and writing, but above all on talking. The taciturnity of Whewell or the simple certainties of G. E. Moore would have sat ill with the unending and kaleidoscopic talk of Whateley or Bowra or Berlin.

Oxford at its worst has been glib and flippant: at its best it has constantly burnished with a new sparkle the store of humanistic learning of which it has been a crucial guardian; and in its median performance it has kept Britain well supplied with those good at the chattering occupations, such as defending the criminal classes, conducting television panels, and governing the country. But it cannot be denied that for nearly a hundred years after the important watershed of 1870 in the universities it unashamedly preferred the soft climate and lush meadows of a river valley leading smoothly to London, while being happy for Cambridge to live more robustly in the harsher East Anglian countryside and closer to the rugged frontiers of knowledge.

Cambridge had followed up the eighteenth-century birth of the mathematical tripos with the creation of the natural sciences tripos in 1849, but although this came after a period of very strong increase in numbers (substantially greater than any decline in the late seventeenth and early eighteenth centuries, and much concentrated in Trinity and St John's, which were between them responsible for half the admissions) it was not immediately followed by any significant provision of natural science facilities. In 1871, however, the lesser known of the two Dukes of Devonshire who between them occupied the Cambridge Chancellorship from 1861 to 1908 performed what turned out to be one of the rare significant acts of any Chancellor of either university for several centuries and made the gift that led to the creation of the Cavendish Laboratory. There was a good deal of scientific ferment in Cambridge before that. Darwin had come and gone at the end of the 1820s and the *Origin of Species* was published in 1859. Adam Sedgwick had completed his long but active period as professor of botany in 1861. F. D. Maurice and then Henry Sidgwick dominated successive generations of the Apostles, which society was already nearly fifty years old. And the great interlocking dynasties of Cambridge families were already setting up their encampments west of the Cam.

Nevertheless, it required the foundation of the Cavendish, as both a cause and a symbol of a line of Cambridge development, to set this university's first half of the twentieth-century style in a mould markedly different from Oxford. If in the 1920s or 1930s one had heard that a breakthrough in the natural or applied sciences, or in mathematics, or in economics, had occurred in a British university it would have been far more likely to have happened on the banks of the Cam than of the Isis. It would have been difficult for Oxford to have produced contemporary names that could stand in rivalry to Rutherford, Hardy, Russell, Keynes, Blackett, Dirac, Adrian, Chadwick or Aston. It could I think have been then fairly said that the baton not merely of British but of world pre-eminence on the frontiers of knowledge was in the hands of Cambridge.

Since then there have been two developments. First the war ran down Cambridge, England, in a way that was unreflected in Cambridge, Massachusetts. Harvard (and MIT) was fortified by the great bonus of its post-1940 ingestion of European refugee scholars and by the stimulating effects, both psychologically and materially, of the post-war economic and political pre-eminence of the United States. Just as an Oxonian should not deny that the flame of intellectual enquiry burned most brightly beside the Cam in the inter-war years, so I do not think that either of us, Oxonians or Cantabrigians, should deny that in the forties and fifties it had substantially migrated, for reasons outside our control, to the banks of the Charles River and the purlieus of Harvard Yard. Quite where it is today is more difficult to decide. Still in the United States, I think, but more disseminated in accordance with the westward tilt in the balance of the country, and with Berkeley and Stanford able to claim at least a piece of the true cross.

The second more domestic development has been Oxford's success from the late 1950s onwards in grafting on to its humanistic core a major new research capacity in the natural and applied sciences, including medicine. Its facilities in this respect now equal, possibly slightly exceed, those of Cambridge. And, having first been generous the other way I think it can now be said that a break-through would be at least as likely to occur in Oxford as in Cambridge.

Per contra Oxford has become somewhat less dominant politically. For the first time for many years there are more Cambridge alumni than Oxford ones in the present Cabinet, although there are not a great number of either. And it might I suppose be held that on power as opposed to numbers the edge was still with Oxford, even if dependent upon a not very enthusiastic member of that university.[1] Oxford's influence on the present-day Labour Party is hardly comparable with that in the first Wilson Government when it reached the extraordinary peak of fourteen Cabinet members out of twenty-one. And the new leader of the Liberal Democrats is not likely to be one of ours – or one of yours; this despite the fact that when we started out with the Gang of Four it was three-quarters Oxonian.

So perhaps the two universities are becoming more like each

---

[1] It should be remembered that this lecture was written in early 1988.

other, rather as old married couples, unless they go violently in the other direction, are sometimes said to get to look alike, or (which would be depressing) as modern cities become less individual, with the same hotels, the same shops, the same banks, the same traffic jams, the same food. I hope that will not go too far and that visually Cambridge will remain grander and Oxford more intimate, Cambridge more on show (even though the Oxford character is more exhibitionist), Oxford more hidden, Cambridge more like Paris, Oxford more like Rome amongst European capitals, Cambridge more like Venice, Oxford more like Florence amongst Italian cities.

We must not, however, become prisoners of our architecture, valuable a possession and formative an ambience though it is. Less physically we have in common the facts that we are both short of money, and that we are both still universities of the foremost world class, although neither of us can any longer take it for granted that this will continue effortlessly to be the case.

For seven centuries before 1922 we had both been privately funded universities – although private finance in the pre-capitalist era meant something very different from today – and remained substantially so until 1939. Then over the next thirty years we gradually became predominantly publicly funded institutions. I do not think that did us any harm. I speak here for Oxford, but I am not aware of a very different Cambridge experience. Over that period Oxford broadened its entry, improved its examination results, magnified its research capacity, maintained its *réclame* and preserved most of its framework of man-made beauty.

It is an over-austere – perhaps a doctrinaire – view that living off public money is enervating for an institution that knows how to spend it well. It is the cutting off of an adequate flow that is debilitating. But that has happened. There is no early prospect of a reversal, and if we are to maintain our reputations I see no alternative to major fund-raising efforts. I do not welcome the prospect. I think that there are considerable dangers in the idea of a university becoming increasingly that of extracting money from private benefactors, and skill in this task, which while important is not the greatest of the intellectual arts, becoming almost inevitably an important qualification for high academic office. I note with mild dismay that three-quarters of my conversation with the Vice-Chancellor of Oxford is devoted to this subject. I like to think that Curzon must have talked to Sir Herbert Warren about something more elevated. Yet I accept it as inevitable, made more so by the threat to university independence that is contained partly in the Education Reform Bill and partly in the proposal for contract funding which looms alongside it. Private money becomes necessary not only to preserve posts, to attract talent and to fund research, but also to maintain a hold on the independence of research and teaching judgement, without which no university can approach excellence.

University fund-raising, while it can be done from a platform of advantage by both Oxford and Cambridge, also presents them with certain special difficulties. In Oxford's case at least, the university's need for money is now greater than that of the colleges. This does not mean that the colleges, even the richer ones, have no needs of their own and still less does it mean that they could, if they were so minded, meet all the needs of the university. What it does mean is that the colleges, broadly speaking, need money for new buildings in order to accommodate undergraduates for a higher proportion of their time, which is a desirable improvement, provided it does not mean spattering the university areas with second-rate buildings. The universities need money to *maintain* posts and research facilities, to prevent a

184

damaging deterioration of performance. It is essential defensive need. The other is desirable and improving. But the colleges are much better placed for fund-raising. Their needs are more tangible and their contact with their old members is more intimate. There is a degree of mismatch.

In both our universities the need for money will in my view force some adjustment of relationships between colleges and the central core. We will no doubt continue – and desirably continue – strongly collegial. But even the strongest colleges could not be much more than conveniently sited liberal arts institutions without the university. Only the universities can discharge the knowledge guarding and the knowledge extending roles of Oxford and Cambridge, and they will not be able to do this without substantial sums of private money, which they will not be able to raise without a recognition by the colleges that they are essentially part of an archipelago and not isolated islands.

Glasgow's Place in the Cities
of the World

*A lecture given in April 1990 to the Royal Philosophical
Society of Glasgow to mark Glasgow's year as European City
of Culture.*

The two cities of which Glasgow never reminds me, whether
spontaneously or by design, are London and Edinburgh.
With many other great cities of the world it has some affinity,
with New York, perhaps with Chicago. I have also found echoes
of Glasgow in Barcelona, Boston, Lisbon and Naples. But I never
thought it had much to do with Paris (except for the Scottish
Colourists, and they, unusually for schools of painting, owe as
much to the east as to the west of Scotland) until in one brilliant
November sunset last year I stood on the Pont de la Concorde
and suddenly thought that the line of the Seine, while utterly
dissimilar to that of the Thames, was rather like that of the Clyde.
The Pont des Arts aroused a thought of the Suspension Bridge,
the Institut de France could be the Custom House, and looking
in the other direction the slopes above the Place de Chaillot rose
up in a passable imitation of the West End.

What does one mean by saying that one city reminds one of another? Not always a great deal could, I suppose, be a brutal answer. Sometimes there can be a certain logical basis for comparison, as when I suddenly realized that the reason brownstone New York, i.e. New York before skyscrapers or even large apartment blocks, seemed to me to have a considerable affinity with the less grandiose parts of Berlin was that, as great cities, they were contemporary with each other and with nowhere else. Both of them moved into the world league at almost exactly the same time, in the third quarter of the nineteenth century. Equally one could say that Lisbon is more like San Francisco than it is like Marseille or Genoa because although southern it is not Mediterranean but oceanic. More frequently, however, the thought of comparison comes suddenly and irrationally, although it can none the less be powerful and even productive as with the little dunked madeleine cake that set Proust off on the whole evocation of his childhood and the greatest novel of the twentieth century.

Thus if I take the Glasgow/New York connection, which I find stronger than the link of either with London, it has most vividly come to my mind in largely irrational ways. As each week of the first autumn after I ceased to be Member of Parliament for Hillhead went by, I found that I increasingly missed Glasgow. It is paradoxical that I should have felt more nostalgic as the Glasgow evenings got even darker than the London ones. But I have always found that the special metropolitan quality of the West End best expressed itself at the season of twilights soon after lunch. If I had to choose a single most evocative vignette it would be of an autumn or winter Saturday afternoon in the Kelvingrove Gallery with the organ playing, and then, as one came out, the light fading over the silhouettes of Gilmorehill and

187

the other hillocks of the West End.

In these circumstances I have several times experienced a stab of linking memory with coming out of the Frick Gallery on East 70th Street, in many ways the most attractive small museum in the world, and looking across at the setting of a December sun over the 1890s pinnacles of Central Park West. I cannot rationally say that Argyle Street is very like Fifth Avenue or Kelvingrove Park much like the granite outcrops of Central Park. It is not a direct physical resemblance that is at work. Few people if unblindfolded in the Byres Road would mistake it for Madison Avenue. It is more a common touch of metropolitan atmosphere and a feeling – that is why it being a Saturday is significant – that one is in both a city which in many ways is at its best at a weekend, and certainly not one which needs to be escaped from as soon as it has served its workaday purpose.

This leads on to the question of what gives a city metropolitan atmosphere, which Glasgow in my view indisputably has, and which, amongst English cities, Birmingham and Leeds for example, although both now bigger in population than Glasgow, do not. It is obviously not therefore a simple question of size, although a certain minimum is a necessary qualification. To stick to English examples for the moment, York and Bath, Salisbury and Winchester are all satisfactory and indeed distinguished little cities, but no one could possibly describe them as metropolitan.

Yet at the other end of the scale I do not think it is possible to deny metropolitan status to any of the really enormous cities of the world. Poverty and confusion by no means exclude it. Nowhere could be more pulsating with a metropolitan current that sparks well beyond the frontiers of the country of which it is the capital than is Cairo, with its seven million or so fairly wretched population and communications chaos. Nor can Calcutta, with ten million even more miserable inhabitants, be denied great city status. It is an artificial creation of the Raj, or at least of 'John Company' before that, and it is declining *vis à vis* Bombay and maybe Delhi too. But it has enough governmental, legal, commercial and journalistic tradition, expressed in its buildings and layout, to keep it in the metropolitan league. Shanghai, of approximately the same monstrous size as the other two, is another example like Calcutta of a city that has lost the purpose for which it was built. The early twentieth-century buildings of the Bund stand as an isolated and fossilized monument to Western commercial penetration. But as Shanghai remains the second city in political importance and the first in population of the biggest country in the world it too can hardly be pushed out of the league. Indeed it is Peking which, away from the contrasting authoritarianisms of the Forbidden City and the Great Hall of the People, looks unmetropolitan because of its unconcentrated layout.

'Spread-outness' is indeed in general the enemy of metropolitan quality. I cannot see Milton Keynes becoming a metropolis however large it grows. It is because New York is so far at the opposite pole that its position as the captain of the metropolises is not seriously in doubt. And it is a concept which provides a battlefield over which the metropolitan status of the other great American cities can be fought out.

Chicago does not suffer from 'spread-outness'. Fifty or sixty years ago it broke out of the constriction of the Loop which had previously held tight its downtown area. But it remains concentrated by its lakeside site, has the most striking high buildings in the world, and securely holds its position as America's second city, culturally and commercially. This is probably because the suburban sprawl of Los Angeles, Chicago's exact twin in population and the centre of a more rapidly growing area, is so scattered that it contains a peak significantly higher than Ben Nevis within the city limits. Its wealth, its size, its cultural resources, resulting partly from its position as world film capital, save it from being provincial, but its lack of a centre of animation means that it has never wholly vanquished the much smaller but superbly sited and highly concentrated San Francisco as the capital of the West Coast, let alone pushed Chicago out of national second place.

Philadelphia and Detroit, the fourth and the fifth United States cities, have dull sites and unexciting terrain. Philadelphia is redeemed by its history. It claims to have been the second largest English-speaking city in the world until the very precise date of 1794, and one wonders to what it then ceded this distinction: New York, Edinburgh, or perhaps Calcutta (if 'English speaking' is defined as loosely as in much of America today)? Detroit's start as a French fort does not give it a comparable historical redolence to William Penn's city and it remains a manufacturing town rather than a metropolitan city, no more a rival to Chicago than Leeds is to Glasgow.

Washington is the most intriguing example of a city that stands uneasily on the frontier of being a metropolis. It is also interesting as the oldest and the most important of the politically and artificially created capitals, and hence the one which has had the longest opportunity to grow into a real city. It is now large enough by any standards. With over three million in the metropolitan area it is bigger than any German city, and bigger than any other European one except for London, Paris, Madrid and Moscow. But for the first 130 years it remained a small town built on an often muddy brown marsh with remarkably few amenities. When Theodore Roosevelt, a fashionable New

Yorker, became President in 1901, he regarded Washington as a place of adventurous exile and life in the White House almost like being in an army camp. British diplomats there were paid an unhealthy living allowance until well into this century.

The city grew dramatically only when first Franklin Roosevelt's New Deal, then his wartime administration, and then the American captaincy of the West under Truman and Eisenhower led to an explosion in the size of the Federal Government. This growth took an essentially suburban form even quite close to the hub of government. Quintessential mid-twentieth-century Washington is made up of detached houses in dogwood-lined hilly streets. Not only are there virtually no even modestly high buildings, except across the Potomac in Alexandria, but there are hardly any carrefours which count as centres of animation and of which at least a hundred could be found in Paris. Nor is there any view that proclaims 'you are in the centre of a great city' with anything like the assurance that does, say, the approach to Central Station in Glasgow, either up from Broomielaw or across Gordon Street. The 1890s Central Hotel of uninspiring name but magnificent woodwork forms an important part of either view, and it is a minor tragedy that its decline should have left Glasgow, architecturally the finest Victorian city in the world, without a single good hotel of the epoch, whereas even Edinburgh has two. To have lost the St Enoch Station Hotel and the Grand at Charing Cross was, as Wilde might have made Lady Bracknell say, a misfortune, but effectively to lose the third points to carelessness, or at least to the disadvantages of breaking up and privatizing the old railway hotel chain.

I return for a moment to Washington where the suburban layout and the mono-cultural nature of the lifestyle (politics, politics all the way) make for provincialism, but are outweighed, although not by a wide margin, by the fact that the government of which it is the seat, and whose composition and doings are endlessly discussed, has been for the past fifty years the most powerful in the world. In Georgetown – the Kelvinside of Washington – the talk would be regarded by good West End standards as narrowly and unacceptably political, but it is at least conducted by the most famous journalists vying with the most favoured ambassadors to produce the most sophisticated witticisms about the most powerful cabinet officers to be found in any capital. And the talk is also perhaps less narrowly internal than political talk mostly is in London. That is one advantage of world leadership. Nevertheless, Washington remains essentially a one-purpose town.

The 'one-purpose town' aspect is repeated still more strongly in Bonn, which although a much more ancient city (2000 years old in 1989 so it was claimed, re-founded by the Emperor Julian in 359, and the birthplace of Beethoven 1411 years after that) is a much more recent and, it now again appears likely, a much more temporary capital. It has also been much more of a gimcrack capital, with most of the business of government of the world's third most powerful economy being carried on – and very successfully carried on – in a collection of thoroughly second-rate 1950s and 1960s buildings. For forty years there has been a remarkable contrast between the capitals of the two German-speaking countries. In Vienna the affairs of the little Austrian Republic have been conducted from what are by and large the grandest official buildings of any capital city. There is a touch of bathos about the Hofburg without the Habsburgs. In Bonn, on the other hand, the business of the Federal Republic of Germany, long the middle kingdom of the European Community, now the hinge power of the whole continent which recent events

192

again make the pivot of the world, is conducted in the most modest surroundings in Europe. Just as the Federal Republic of Germany has tried to exercise less political power than is commensurate with its economic strength, so on a diplomatic visit to Bonn one may look in vain for marble staircases, plumed guards of honour, screaming police escorts and glittering state banquets. Whether a move to Berlin will bring with it a return to Wilhelmine grandeur and a more assertive style of government is a fascinating and to some a worrying question.

On the whole I think not, although I do believe that the style of capital cities affects the style of the governments that operate within them. Thus I think it no accident that the three most centralized countries in Europe – Britain, France and Spain – are the three in which the governments operate from 'hub of the country' capitals – London, Paris and Madrid – which are the dominant cities, politically, socially, culturally, commercially. (It should be noted, however, that France and Spain are currently making strenuous efforts to decentralize themselves, whereas no such effort is visible in the British Government.) It is also noticeable that post-war Germany, when Berlin was split, operated with no city showing even a 'conurbation' population of two million, no city in other words amongst the first sixty or seventy in the world. The Federal Republic has been the most important and richest country but the one with the least big single city of the five big states of the European Community.

This fits in appropriately with the recent revaluation of fashion against excessive size in cities. And with the prestige of size so has its precision disappeared. An encyclopaedia published in the early 1920s, to the study of which I devoted many childhood hours, gave with complete confidence the exact population of every major city down to the last digit. I can still remember many of them. Glasgow then scored 1,111,428, as opposed, say, to 648,000 for Madrid, which now rates four and a half million, or 412,000 for São Paolo, Brazil, which now rates twelve and a half million. Modern editions of encyclopaedias are much more uncertain. They give alternatives – within the city limits and within the conurbations, and conurbations are rather vague concepts. But what is more significant is that nobody is now proud of being big. London and New York used to compete with each other for first place like two Atlantic liners passing and re-passing each other in bids for the blue riband of the fastest crossing. Now both competitions are as out of date as are the liners. New York and London have dropped far behind, being overtaken by Tokyo and Shanghai, and Calcutta and Bombay, and Seoul and Cairo, and Rio de Janeiro and São Paolo, and maybe Teheran, and above all Mexico City. But Mexico City, far from being proud of its pre-eminence, keeps its monstrous size and rate of growth as quiet as any ageing beauty used to do with her age, and hopes that it can escape too much obloquy for further engulfing the country and polluting the sky.

Glasgow has therefore chosen its time to shrink with great skill. The days when the claim to be 'the second city of the Empire' was a proud boast are as far past as is the Empire itself. And although the claim had a certain essential truth, as was symbolized by those great exhibitions of 1888, 1901, 1911 and 1938 in the parks of first Kelvingrove and then Bellahouston, I wonder how statistically accurate it was unless the population of Calcutta was calculated on the basis that you needed several Bengalis to count as the equivalent of one Scotsman.

In those days, however, it would have been a tragedy to have gone down in population from 1,100,000 to the present 750,000 (although of course the Clydeside conurbation remains much more like two and a half million). Now it does not matter in the least from a prestige point of view. Indeed, it is if anything an advantage, and excites the greater admiration that Glasgow's cultural impact, which I regard as comparable with that of Chicago, has been achieved on a population, city for city, of a fifth the size, and conurbation for conurbation, of a third the size.

There is only one word of warning that I must give to Glasgow. Glasgow has ridden high on a mounting wave of fashion in the 1980s. It amuses me to look back over the change in the outside perception of Glasgow during the period that I have been closely associated with the city. When I became Member of Parliament for Hillhead in 1982 I derived a lot of pleasure from surprising people all over the world with the wholly accurate information that my Glasgow constituency was, according to the census, the most highly educated in the whole of the United Kingdom. And I added for good measure that, while it was geographically only one-eleventh of the City of Glasgow, it contained at least fifteen institutions or monuments of major cultural, intellectual or architectural fame. That was all in the days before the Burrell Collection was open. The Burrell (not in Hillhead but three miles away on the South Side), while it is a fine heterogeneous collection, housed in perhaps the best building for a gallery created anywhere in the past quarter century, adds to what was previously in the Kelvinside Gallery and other Glasgow collections before but does not qualitatively change it. 1982 was also at the beginning of the 'Glasgow's miles better' slogan, and before there was much thought of Glasgow being either an important centre of aesthetic tourism or the European City of Culture.

What has changed since then has been that for three or four years everybody has come to accept these earlier facts without the previous surprise, while for me the sad fact amongst them is that Hillhead has ceased to be my constituency. (But if it no longer enables me to sit in the House of Commons it is at least now part of the name under which I sit in the House of Lords.) My warning is that fashion is a fickle jade. Glasgow has been tremendously *à la mode* for the past five years. But *la mode,* by its very nature, cannot remain constant. Last week, for the first time in my experience, someone said to me that he thought Glasgow had recently achieved an exaggerated reputation, and went on to add that he thought Edinburgh – admittedly he lived there – was the cultural as well as the political capital of Scotland. I rocked on my heels in amazement. No one had said such a thing to me for years.

I do not happen to believe that it is true. Edinburgh has of course great cultural assets, the Festival, the National Gallery of Scotland, the Portrait Gallery, and the copyright library, but they are none of them strictly indigenous. They come from outside or by virtue of capital city status rather than arise out of the life and work of the inhabitants of the city itself as is the case here. None the less, I think Glasgow must be prepared for the going to be a little harder in future. Having caught and mounted the horse of fashion in the early eighties and dashingly ridden it for seven years or so, Glasgow must be ready for its vagaries soon to take the horse veering off in another direction.

Glasgow can, I think, sustain this. It has almost indestructible advantages that should be immune to gusts of fashion. First the site, which is God-given in both the literal and the figurative senses of the phrase, and which helps to make Glasgow an exceptionally vivid city visually, and one to which a strong painting tradition is peculiarly appropriate. The city itself is finely placed with the hills rising on either side of the river in just the right places. Beyond that the estuary of the Clyde, with its associated inlets, islands and mountains, constitutes the most dramatic piece of seascape at the gates of a major city to be found anywhere in the world, with the possible exception of Vancouver Sounds and the Bosphorus. There are I believe equally memorable natural formations amongst the fjords of Norway, or on the western coast of Greenland or on the shores of Antarctica, but they are all wastelands so far as human population is concerned.

Glasgow's industry also had a peculiar vividness, which is retained by such of it as remains. The cranes of Govan, seen on the drive in from the airport, proclaim that this is Glasgow as emphatically as, and more authentically than, the Eiffel Tower identifies Paris, or the bridge and the opera house do Sydney.

Second, there is the solid base of Glasgow's educational strength. It is a remarkable double that a century after the narrow strips of flat land along the banks of the Clyde became the greatest industrial focus of the world, the hills behind the riverside on the north side should now have become, with the exception almost only of the banks of the Charles River between Boston and Cambridge, Massachusetts, one of the most concentrated educational areas: two universities, the 439-year-old eagle of Glasgow perched on its Gilmorehill eyrie and the enthusiastic young pouter pigeon of Strathclyde a couple of miles to the east and hatched only a quarter of a century ago out of a College of Technology; Jordanhill College of Education; four teaching hospitals; three units of the Medical Research Council; a number of specialized institutions of which the Glasgow School of Art is the most famous; all this, plus a clutch of four or five high schools or academies of note, is by any standards an extraordinary cluster and one which, as I believe the Massachusetts experience has shown, is of great economic value in the modern world.

197

Third, there is the quality of the human resources. Glasgow has its well-known warmth, but that is something on which in my view it is possible to talk a good deal of sententious nonsense. Glasgow people are capable of being very friendly, and they are almost invariably polite, but they are also capable, as are all people of discrimination, of being appropriately chilling when they think it is deserved. When in 1982 I first came to know Glasgow well, and in particular its West End, what most struck me was not so much the warmth as the quiet self-confidence. It was not a complacent or narrow or inward-looking self-confidence. It was not based on a desire to keep strangers out, or I would not have been made nearly so welcome. What it was based on was a consciousness of the contribution which this strip of river and hills had made to the advancement of civilization throughout and beyond Britain, and on a feeling that while it was desirable to go outside the West End from time to time it was as good a place to live as anywhere in the world. It was based neither on complacency nor on any sense of compensating for inferiority, but, as true self-confidence always is, on a desire to learn of outside things accompanied by a contentment within one's own skin. That is the dominant impression that I retain of Hillhead and of Glasgow as a whole.

So I have no hesitation about putting Glasgow amongst the great cities of the world, and far higher than population alone would entitle it to be. I do so upon grounds of site, metropolitan atmosphere, industrial history, visual impact, educational and cultural resources, and the self-confidence of its inhabitants, powerfully expressed in the architecture of its industrial heyday a hundred years ago, almost equally well exemplified by the City Chambers, the Kelvingrove Gallery and the Central Hotel, the self-confidence always there if sometimes as nearly hidden as the

River Kelvin is within its gorges, but strongly resurfacing within the last decade.

The renaissance of Glasgow has become a byword. The English city most like Glasgow is Liverpool, by virtue of its geography, the composition of its population, the historic nature of its trade, the eminence of its pre-1914 position ('Liverpool gentlemen and Manchester men' was the catchphrase) and the grandeur of its Victorian public buildings. The trough into which it descended was deeper than anything that has ever beset Glasgow. But when I went there two weeks ago I was struck by the fact that it seemed to have experienced an upturn in the past year or so. And the suggestion that aroused the greatest enthusiasm was that they might be following in Glasgow's path. At a time when cities as big as Calcutta, as rich as Cleveland, as beautiful as Florence, decline more easily than they revive, Glasgow's experience of the 1980s, admittedly building on a very good base, but after a period of foolish disregard, may stand out as the epitome of recovery through quality and effort.

High Victorian Trollope

An introduction to The Duke's Children

The last of the six political novels and the penultimate book of Trollope's life, *The Duke's Children* is a classical and perfectly matured example of his style and method. It is the apotheosis of his chronicles of the unending and fluctuating war between love and property. Although this is a campaign unmitigated by any hope of complete victory for either side, it is in general one in which, under Trollope's guidance, the strictest rules of civilized warfare apply.

There is no place for methods of barbarism in Trollope. And this is particularly true of *The Duke's Children*. The commanders on both sides are of the highest possible rank, Napoleon and Wellington, as it were, and do everything at the right time, in a predictable way, which leads to a satisfactory conclusion after eighty chapters of easy-flowing narrative that are also a compendious and reliable guide to the high Whig world (with a few Tories allowed in) of 125 years ago.

'The Duke', who combines an almost sacerdotal respect for aristocracy with firm attachment to moderate Liberalism, and great wealth with distaste for self-indulgence, is of course our old friend Plantagenet Palliser, who a million words and twenty years after grappling with decimal currency and marrying Lady Glencora MacCluskie, is Duke of Omnium and a former Prime Minister of a brief-lived coalition government. On the first page of this book Trollope kills off Duchess Glencora, a little cursorily considering how much spirit she had infused into the earlier political novels. I think his motive was probably the same as that which makes many writers of detective stories kill the corpse before the reader has a chance of identifying with it. Trollope, who always operated on tight emotional rations, wished to get on as quickly as possible to the Duke's problem of being left with three more-or-less grown-up children, for dealing with whom his combination of gruff affection and stubborn censoriousness was peculiarly inappropriate, without diverting the reader's sympathy on to a character who was inessential to this story.

The three were the twenty-two-year-old Earl of Silverbridge, the nineteen-year-old Lady Mary Palliser and the eighteen-year-old Lord Gerald Palliser. The third never presumes to attract more of the reader's attention than is appropriate to a younger son, and confines himself to a few horse-racing and card-playing scrapes which are suitable to anyone called Lord Gerald and sufficient to get him sent down from Trinity College, Cambridge. The story centres around the other two and their inappropriate if wholly uxoriously directed amours.

Lady Mary falls determinedly in love with another younger son who is more presumptuous than her brother Gerald, particularly as he is the younger son not of a Whig duke but of a Cornish Tory squire, and who is adequately in love with her. Frank Tregear is a little two-dimensional but he is neither an upstart nor an adventurer, unlike Burgo Fitzgerald who in the dim and distant past had excited the emotions, but not, fortunately, the matrimonial determination, of Lady Glencora MacCluskie. He is indisputably if almost too resolutely a gentleman, the closest friend of Lord Silverbridge (which is considered in no way inappropriate), with whom he was at Eton and Christ Church. His family is said to be more ancient than the Pallisers, but he is not considered by the Duke, nor indeed by Silverbridge, who is devoted to him in every other way, to have sufficient substance to aspire to the hand of Lady Mary. This is despite the fact that the one thing Lady Mary does not need is substance, for the Duke, who has far more money than he thinks it decent to spend on himself or than is good for Silverbridge and Gerald, could provide for them many times over.

This provokes some fine animadversions on gentlemanliness and who is and who is not appropriate to marry a duke's daughter:

'He is a gentleman, papa.'

'So is my private secretary. There is not a clerk in one of our public offices who does not consider himself to be a gentleman. The curate of the parish is a gentleman, and the medical man who comes here from Bradstock. The word is too vague to carry with it any meaning that ought to be serviceable to you in thinking of such a matter.'

'I do not know any other way of dividing people,' said she …

Tregear then somewhat improves his position in the Duke's eyes by becoming a Member of Parliament, even if as a Tory, a party which the Duke, rather ahead of his time in this respect, regarded as socially as well as ideologically inferior. This, it might have been thought, would make Tregear's financial position more not less precarious, but this was never the core of the objection, and is more than compensated for by an increase of status and by the fact that it gives him some claim to have an occupation even if not a profession (although what profession would the Duke have wished him to follow?). More important than Tregear's advancement, however, is the Duke's softening under the unrelenting determination of Lady Mary, accompanied by the unanimous advice of all the duennas in sight that the alternative to allowing her to marry Tregear is to see her grow into a sour old maid.

Meanwhile, Silverbridge's affairs, assisted by his much greater freedom than that of his sister ('How I do wish I were a man,' she said to him in his private hansom cab, '… I'd have a hansom of my own and go where I pleased'), developed in a more complicated way. He too was an MP for the wrong party although for the right place, the borough of Silverbridge (everything is almost too perfectly matched in *The Duke's Children*). He entered into a racing partnership with Major Tifto which led to his losing £70,000 on the St Leger, which was a lot of Victorian money even for the Omnium estates. (It was in fact exactly the sum which Trollope earned from his forty-seven novels.) He moved from one girl to another. The first was Lady Mabel Grex, the daughter of a Tory earl of impeccable lineage, strained resources and mildly reprobate tastes, who was just respectable enough to have acquired a Garter. Lady Mab was pretty (in a way that sounded healthy rather than romantic), pert, self-confident, and to begin with a good sort, thoroughly prepared to marry Silverbridge, although in love not with him but with her cousin, the ubiquitous although self-controlled heart-throb Tregear. In addition she was thoroughly acceptable to the Duke.

She made the mistake of treating Silverbridge as though he

203

were an immature boy, which he was. But that may well have made no difference, for he soon met the American Isabel Boncassen, whom Trollope comes very near to describing as the greatest beauty in the world. She was certainly a real girl of the golden west, or at least as far west as Fifth Avenue. She was on a long visit to Europe with her parents and seemed quite disposed to see it extended into permanence by a grand English marriage. The 1870s were the early days of the infusion of American blood and money into the upper ranks of the peerage, and Trollope was very *à la mode* in making this a central feature of the last of his political novels. In the earlier ones, around a decade earlier, 'foreigners' were more typically represented by Madam Max Goesler, the lady of Austrian property who became Mrs Phineas Finn, or Ferdinand Lopez, the dago adventurer who ended by throwing himself under a train at Willesden Junction.

Miss Boncassen's mother was 'homely' but her father Ezekiel Boncassen was given the appearance and dress of Lincoln, although he was rich with second-generation wealth, scholarly, and, in a homespun way, of refined manners. He was also spoken of as a possible President of the United States, which was odd, for no one of remotely his type got near the White House between John Quincy Adams fifty years before and Theodore Roosevelt twenty-five years afterwards.

The Duke of Omnium much enjoyed grave comparative political conversations with Mr Boncassen, found Mrs Boncassen inoffensive, Miss Boncassen decorative and ladylike, and invited them all to stay (together with Silverbridge, Lady Mary, Lady Mab and the Phineas Finns) for two weeks at his lesser but more agreeable country seat in Yorkshire. He hoped that the visit would result in the arrangement of a marriage between Silverbridge and Mabel Grex, and was as amazed as he was dismayed when it was the New York girl who emerged as the winner of the duchess stakes.

Trollope is one of the four novelists who have given me the greatest sum of pleasure – 'sum' indicating quantity as well as intensity. The other three are Proust, Waugh and Anthony Powell. This does not mean that I regard them as the four greatest. I have no doubt that Dickens, Balzac, Tolstoy, Dostoevsky, Jane Austen and George Eliot, to name only an almost random half dozen, are in some sense 'greater' than at least two, including Trollope, of my quartet. In the same way I accept that the cathedrals of Chartres and Bourges are 'greater' than those of Chichester and Exeter, but the sum of pleasure from the latter two is none the less more, if only because I have visited them more often, partly through opportunity and partly through choice. And there is also the factor of special affinity, which, for example, and switching to art galleries, the Frick, the Moritzhuis and the Kelvingrove Gallery in Glasgow possess for me and the Kunsthistorische and the Rijksmuseum do not. And as Trollope is the most prolific of my four authors he has a strong claim to the highest position on a graph that measures output along one axis and pleasure-giving quality along the other.

Like many of my generation, I first encountered Trollope during World War II. Between 1941 and 1945 I bought and read about twenty-five volumes in either the little Oxford World Classics or Dent's slightly bigger Everyman edition. They cost about three shillings each and have survived fifty years very well. Then, unconsciously following fashion, I never read another word of Trollope for a quarter of a century. The news that Harold Macmillan had found him as addictive during government crises as Asquith had found letter-writing to ladies of fashion did nothing to stir me to emulation. In the 1970s, however, long after Macmillan's reading patterns had ceased to preoccupy gossip writers, I suddenly took Trollope up again and plunged deep into the Barchester series, leavened with *Can You Forgive Her?* and *The Duke's Children* from the political novels.

In 1988 the invitation to write this introduction sent me back to a leisurely reading of the latter. I then made the mistake of postponing the execution of the writing task. This made me feel that I had to go back for yet a fourth time, although on this occasion reading quickly and under pressure. So this work is in the position, perhaps unique to a book not my own (in these frequency is dictated by the need for revision and proof-reading as well as by narcissism), of having been read four times. Even so, I found on the last go that the difficulty was not, as is often the case, that skimming led to aquaplaning so that I was soon hardly touching the surface, but that I could not bring myself to strike with sufficient ruthlessness from headland to headland but still wanted to re-explore, for the second time within little more than a year, every inlet of the convoluted coast.

What gives Trollope this strong if fluctuating attraction for me? Is it, as his detractors would have it, the comfortingly reliable pull of the second-rate? I do not think so. He was certainly not consistent, except in his output per hour. His quality varied enormously, both between books and within them, and the variation was accompanied by a remarkable lack of discrimination as a self-critic. He could write a novel as bad as *The Struggles of Brown, Jones and Robinson* and one as good as *Phineas Finn: The Irish Member* within a year of each other, and not be aware of the difference in quality between them.

Nor was he nearly as pedestrianly plodding as his critics and sometimes he himself liked to pretend. He was prolix, partly because it was the fashion and partly because he was over-fluent,

206

but in his better books, a few descriptive passages apart, he carried the reader over the ground with an easy momentum which belied his heavy frame and explained why he was so at home in the hunting field. His dialogue was always sure-footed.

This, however, is to some extent a defensive tribute, a refutation of those like Henry James who thought that Trollope was essentially a novelist for the unsubtle, even the stupid, in today's parlance a sort of chronicler for the saloon bar or the golf club-house. His positive strength for me lies principally in his command over both the physical and the social topography of mid-Victorian England. Some of his work is like that Canaletto picture of Whitehall in which the detail was so accurate that, nearly two hundred years after it had been painted, the Westminster City Council find it a useful chart for drainage repairs.

There never has been a writer who, thanks to his work as a postal surveyor, knew the geography of England (and Ireland) so well. And over it, with almost unparalleled logistic skill, he could marshal an army of characters. They may turn out to be a stage army that comes round and round for the second, third and fourth times, but we are always glad to see again.

His fictional imagination was not, however, bounded by his previous knowledge. He had great capacity to familiarize himself, as it were by order, with worlds he did not previously know but wished to write about. When he had already published *The Warden* and was deep in *Barchester Towers* he recorded: 'I never lived in any cathedral city – except London,[1] never knew anything of any close, never had any peculiar intimacy with any

---

[1] Not strictly true; he had lived briefly in Exeter.

clergymen, and had not then even spoken to an archdeacon.' But Trollope liked to make throwaway remarks about his own work, although not to sell it at throwaway prices. I wonder how seriously we should take such self-deprecation as: 'When I sit down to write a novel I do not at all know, and I do not very much care, how it will end.'? His journeyman's approach to writing, pretending it was no different from cobbling, was I suspect more designed to prick the illusions of uncomprehending interlocutors than to analyse his own methods and skills.

He was full of paradoxes: a man of boisterous, some said rather boorish, manners who loved social life, and who could write with delicacy about it and about more intimate human relations; a man who could satirize politics and politicians, but who regarded being a member of the British Parliament as the greatest honour that could possibly befall a man, and who in 1868 tried hard but unsuccessfully at Beverley in the East Riding of Yorkshire to get himself elected on a Liberal ticket.

He was perhaps lucky that he did not succeed, for I suspect that he would have meshed with the House of Commons no more happily than did, say, Hilaire Belloc nearly forty years later, and that the sourness of *The Way We Live Now* (1875) might have spilled over from its financial, literary and social milieu into the more political background of *The Duke's Children* (1880) and produced a more discontented culmination to the political novels. However, it did not happen, and *The Duke's Children* is essentially a good-tempered book. A few minor characters behave ludicrously, but only those who are created for villainy behave villainously, and even they, notably Major Tifto, do so rather pathetically.

Trollope was therefore able to remain relatively starry-eyed towards politics, much more like Harold Nicolson than like

Belloc. Nicolson, essayist of near genius, biographer of quality, novelist with too exiguous an output to be properly judged in this category, always attached more importance to being a third-rate politician than to being a first-rate writer. After he lost his seat he recorded that he could never pass near to the Palace of Westminster at night and see shining the light which indicated that the House of Commons was still sitting without feeling a twinge of dismay that he was no longer there. I have always experienced exactly the reverse. But Trollope would have been with Nicolson. He would have liked to be there.

Indeed, he always liked being *there*, in the gallery of the House of Commons if he could not be on the floor, in the Garrick Club, in the Reform Club, in a literary circle, at a publishers' evening party, at the kill in the hunting field. And this, combined with great technical skill, gives to his writing a gusto, a tolerance and an insight which puts him, after Dickens, Thackeray and George Eliot, on the fourth plinth in the pantheon of English mid-nine-teenth-century novelists. And nowhere are these qualities better used than in *The Duke's Children*.

Two Hundred Years of The Times

This was written for publication in a special Times *supplement
for the 200th anniversary of that newspaper in 1984*

Newspapers, perhaps because few of them achieve it, like longevity. As a result centenaries and bicentenaries are sometimes celebrated with a tenuous claim to continuity of identity. This is not true of *The Times*. It has throughout been a daily (always excluding Sundays), and its format, up to 1966, when news first appeared on the front page, bore a recognizable affinity to that of the first years.

The direct descendants of its founder, publisher and first editor, John Walter, remained as controlling proprietors until 1908, when Northcliffe moved in; and as partners in the enterprise for another fifty-eight years, until the arrival of Roy Thomson, when John Walter IV, aged ninety-three, relinquished his shareholding. (The Walters were almost unique among newspaper proprietors in spanning nearly two hundred years while hardly seeking and never acquiring a peerage.)

In addition the terms of editors, with a few exceptions, have been long. As a result there have been remarkably few of them.

Six covered the 124 years from 1817 to 1941. There was a little more instability at either end, but fifteen made up the whole of the apostolic succession for the first two hundred years, exactly the same as the number of Popes over the period, a few more than the number of British monarchs but less than half the number of British Prime Ministers and little more than a third the number of American Presidents. (In the nine subsequent years, however, there have been no less than four editors.)

Has the influence been commensurate with the longevity? First, it must be said that while there have certainly been journals that have from time to time exercised more political influence than *The Times* (the *Morning Chronicle* in the early years of the nineteenth century, perhaps the *Westminster Gazette* in its heyday, the *Daily Telegraph* at the time of the Abdication, arguably the *Daily Mirror* at its Cudlipp/King political peak), there has been no paper that has come within miles of rivalling *The Times* over the two-hundred-year stretch as a whole.

Apart from other considerations there are very few papers that have been there for any comparable period. The *Observer*, which has benefited from two notable editorships this century, was founded in 1791, but has never been a daily and went through many nineteenth-century mutations. The *Morning Post* was there before *The Times* and preserved a continuous high Tory identity until subsiding into the arms of the *Daily Telegraph* in 1937. The rest of *The Times*'s London contemporaries of 1785 are long since dead. Its contemporaries of today are relative upstarts: the oldest are the *Guardian*, founded in 1821, but only a daily since 1855, the *Daily Telegraph*, which began in 1855, and the *Daily Mail*, which inaugurated the era of mass circulation in 1896.

The influence of *The Times* must essentially be judged from the accession to the editorial chair of Thomas Barnes in 1817. Before then it was settling down. In the late eighteenth century it was an information sheet, the lesser offshoot of a printing business. By 1795 John Walter I was tired of his enterprise and handed over first to his elder son, William, who had more literary taste than journalistic flair, and then in 1803 to his second son, John Walter II, who made the paper but fractured his relations with his father. John Walter I wanted to be a printer to the government and to the aristocracy. John Walter II wanted to run something approaching a modern newspaper. The circulation when he took over was about 1700 copies, having been up to nearly 3000 in the 1790s. The circulation of all others, including the influential *Morning Chronicle*, was still lower, however. Newspaper prices were formidable. *The Times* opened at 2½d and quickly went to 3d, the equivalent of nearly £1 today. By the time of the death of John Walter II in 1847 its circulation was nearly 50,000. In mid-century, just before the full repeal of newspaper taxes, *The Times* was the nearest paper to approach a mass daily. The *Daily Telegraph*, within a few days of its own launch, paid it a somewhat convoluted tribute: 'The circulation of the *Daily Telegraph*', it announced, 'exceeds that of any London morning newspaper, with the exception of *The Times.*'

More important, however, was that John Walter II first rejected political subsidies and lived successfully without them both during his own editorship from 1803 to 1810 and during his joint editorship of the next five years with John Stoddart, a barrister and Hazlitt's brother-in-law; and that he then got bored with exercising control from the proprietor's chair and withdrew to Wokingham to become a Berkshire country gentleman, and subsequently MP for the county, leaving Thomas Barnes with the elbow room to become the first independent editor.

Barnes was only thirty-two when he was appointed. It was not his youth that made him exceptional. *Times* editors have often been young when they started. Of his notable successors Delane and Buckle started at twenty-three and twenty-nine, and Dawson and Rees-Mogg at thirty-eight. (They have also shown a regrettable tendency to die young, mostly while still in office.)

Barnes was the son of a Kent solicitor, educated at Christ's Hospital and Pembroke College, Cambridge, of high intellectual gifts, who as a young man lived in the literary society of Leigh Hunt, Lamb and Hazlitt. He came to editorship by way of theatre criticism and parliamentary sketch writing.

He was considered a very advanced liberal at this time, and always wrote, and encouraged others to write, in a fairly rough tone. 'Put a little devil into it' was one of his prescripts for his own and other people's writing. He was a full editor not merely by virtue of his independence of his proprietor but also because he orchestrated the whole paper. Leigh Hunt considered him to have placed it 'beyond the range of competition not more by the ability of his own articles than by the unity of tone and sentiment which he knew how to impart to the publication as a whole'.

Barnes supported Catholic emancipation and the great Reform Bill, was generally favourable to the Grey administration, and was particularly close to the Lord Chancellor, Brougham. In 1834 he did a great switch of sides, and in so doing gave a most remarkable demonstration of the power of the instrument he had partly created. He quarrelled with the Whigs and provoked the Chancellor of the Exchequer (Althorp) into writing to Brougham a subsequently notorious letter requesting an urgent meeting to discuss 'whether we should declare open war with *The Times* or attempt to make peace'.

Months later, when William IV in effect dismissed Melbourne, and Peel was being hurriedly summoned back from Rome (still taking almost exactly as long as Caesar would have done), Barnes attempted to lay down with Lyndhurst, the new Lord Chancellor, and (of all people) the Duke of Wellington, who were temporarily in charge in London, the terms on which he would support a Conservative government. They were: no going back on the Reform Bill or on other measures, such as the Tithe Act and the Corporations Act, already voted by the House of Commons, and a continuity of foreign policy. What is still more remarkable is that they were substantially accepted. The brief first Peel Government came into being, the Tamworth Manifesto was issued, and the way was paved for the creation of a Conservatism that could live with the railway age and the nineteenth-century middle-class. 'Why,' Lyndhurst reportedly said to Greville, 'Barnes is the most powerful man in the country.'

Lyndhurst further endorsed Barnes's importance by giving him a dinner party. This was regarded as being almost the most remarkable of this entire series of events, for Barnes rarely went into society and Lord Chancellors or other great officers of state did not habitually entertain journalists. Fortunately, perhaps, ladies were not included, for Barnes remained faithful to his early bohemianism by not being married to his 'wife', who looked to Disraeli like 'a lady in a pantomime'.

However, he maintained a considerable style of life, first in Great Surrey Street, over Blackfriars Bridge, and then, after his salary had been raised to the considerable sum of £2000 (augmented by a one-sixteenth share in what he had made a very profitable enterprise), in a fine house in Soho Square. There he indulged his high taste for wine and food, was much called upon by politicians, and died in May 1841. 'The Thunderer' had achieved its soubriquet under his reign.

John Thadeus Delane, the son of W. F. A. Delane, manager of *The Times*, had been with the paper for about a year, mainly on parliamentary reports, when he succeeded Barnes. He was appointed what can perhaps best be described as 'lieutenant editor'. John Walter II moved back to take substantial responsibility and Delane did not assume Barnes's full authority until that chief proprietor's death in 1847.

Delane was more of an operator, less of a scholar than Barnes. He was more social, dined out a good deal with the grand, instead of waiting for them to call upon him, and quite often stayed with them in the country, where he could indulge his passion for hunting. In London, however, he worked immensely hard, never lived more than a mile away from Printing House Square, and habitually stayed in the office until five in the morning. *The Times* was the whole of his life in a way that it was not with Barnes. The *Dictionary of National Biography* offers some pointed and not wholly expected comments: 'Though never erudite, Delane was very quick in mastering anything which he took in hand ... He was not a finished scholar; he was not as brilliant as Barnes; he hardly ever wrote anything except reports and letters, both of which he wrote very well ... He saw 13 administrations rise and fall ... he met all statesmen on equal terms ... Lord Palmerston, whom he resembled in temperament, was the statesman he liked best, Lord Aberdeen was the one he most respected.'

In the Barchester novels Trollope portrays Delane under the name of Tom Towers, editor of the *Jupiter*, in terms that are more a tribute to his influence and grandeur than to his judgement or humanity. In *The Warden* (1855) Towers played some considerable part in driving the good Mr Harding out of his somewhat archaic benefice. In *Barchester Towers* (1857) he is an occasionally of the oleaginous and scheming Reverend Obadiah Slope. But it is in *Framley Parsonage* (1861) that he reaches his apogee. He appears at an evening party given by Miss Dunstable, the patent medicine heiress, who was none the less in the centre of fashionable society and a lady who combined astringent comment with a heart of gold: That the two great ones of the earth were Tom Towers and the Duke of Omnium need hardly be expressed in words,' Trollope wrote.

The paper was tolerably disposed towards the great Peel Government and particularly towards its foreign policy, because it was conducted by Aberdeen, but was uncharacteristically detached on the great mid-century issue of the Corn Laws. Lord John Russell was a man Delane could never abide and his 1846–52 administration was therefore treated coolly, even while Palmerston was Foreign Secretary, for Delane's love affair with his alter ego (if the *DNB* is to be believed) did not begin until about 1857. When the Russell Government fell in early 1852 as a result of Palmerston's 'tit-for-tat with Johnnie Russell' and the first of the several brief Derby-Disraeli administrations came in, Delane was much courted by Disraeli. But the courtship was not very successful. When Disraeli led his government to defeat in the House of Commons by proclaiming in a phrase more memorable than sensible, that 'England does not love coalitions', *The Times* answered that 'Nothing suits the people to be governed and the measures to be passed so well as a good coalition.' It quickly got what it wanted, in the form of one headed by Aberdeen. And it received its reward by being able to publish exclusively on Christmas Day, 1852, a full list of the unannounced Cabinet appointments, a tribute as much to the regularity of *The Times's* nineteenth-century publication as to the quality of its sources.

Its influence, however, was set immensely high. Cobden claimed it never entered his house, but Clarendon in 1853, while complaining that 'I can't understand why it should be considered the organ of the Government' and expostulating that 'The ways of *The Times* are inscrutable', nevertheless reluctantly recorded that 'As its circulation is enormous and its influence abroad is very great a Government must take its support on the terms it chooses to put it.' Abraham Lincoln's tribute was still more fulsome but was not reciprocated, for *The Times* thought the Gettysburg Address made the dedication ceremony 'ludicrous'.

In the years that followed, *The Times* became disillusioned with Aberdeen because of his lack of bellicosity in the approach to the Crimean War, and lack of vigour in its conduct. The war correspondent William Howard Russell, who there made his reputation, denounced the inefficiencies of supply and generalship and played a significant role in the replacement of Aberdeen by Palmerston in 1855. *The Times*, however, took a year or two to adjust to its new loyalty. Delane did not become an habitué of Broadlands or Cambridge House until the end of the decade, and amongst the first acts of the new government was one which was thought to be highly inimical to the interests of *The Times*. This was the abolition of the newspaper tax.

The change meant much cheaper newspapers, and in the possibly exaggerated language of John Bright set *The Times* 'howling, and splashing about like a harpooned whale'. It was assumed that the move would damage the oligopoly, with *The Times* as clear market leader, which a few established journals enjoyed. This was true to the extent that *The Times* fairly quickly lost, and never regained, its position as the paper of greatest circulation. By 1861 the *Daily Telegraph* was selling about 140,000

217

against *The Times's* regular 65,000. The abolition of the tax also led to a substantial, but not permanent, shift in the balance between the London and the provincial press. Before it there was little of substance published in England outside the capital. By 1864 the circulation of the provincials was nearly twice that of the London papers.

But the change did not damage the influence of *The Times,* or its profitability, and increased its circulation in absolute terms. Its 1861 figure was about a third up on that of a few years before and concealed occasional surges: 89,000 on the day after the Prince Consort's death and 86,000 when it published a nine-column obituary of Palmerston.

The gain in circulation was far from being worth the loss of Palmerston. *The Times* had not been his client, but Delane had certainly done well out of the connection. Palmerston had supplied him with information and given him a government and a statesman he could mostly support with a good conscience. He had even offered him the permanent under-secretaryship of the War Office in 1861 when he heard that his eyes were failing through too much night work. Now Delane was left without a lodestar. Lord John Russell, who succeeded, was as unattractive to him as he had been twenty years before. Gladstone had not hitherto been much of a favourite in Printing House Square. And the efforts of the third and last short Derby-Disraeli Government to get Delane on their side proved as abortive as on the previous occasions. The paper, largely due to the influence of Robert Lowe, MP for Calne, and a *Times* leader writer for fifteen years, was also cool in its approach to the second Reform Bill, in marked contrast to its 'thundering' in 1831, and some-what to the annoyance of John Walter III.

The Times soon reconciled itself both to reform and to

218

Gladstone. It supported him with an unwonted partisanship, both in 1868, when he won, and in 1874, when he lost. Delane, who always had exceptional gifts of seeing what was likely to happen, correctly and exceptionally foresaw the result of the Franco-Prussian War. Yet throughout the twelve years from Palmerston's death in 1865 to Delane's retirement there is a distinct sense of a slowly declining sun. Even the circulation, often the last index to respond to a decline of quality, dropped below 60,000 by the turn of the decade. Despite the offer of a pension of £2000, munificent by the standards of the age, Walter had to assert himself in 1877 to get Delane out and Thomas Chenery in. 'But who will look after the social side of the business?' Disraeli asked when he heard of the change.

Chenery was the least successful of *The Times's* nineteenth-century editors. He was, however, the first of a series of gentlemen scholars to occupy the editorial chair. He was the first editor to be an Etonian (there have been two subsequent ones). He was a graduate of Gonville and Caius College, Cambridge, and since 1868 had been Professor of Arabic at Oxford while continuing his long-standing leader-writing role on the paper. He was fifty-four when appointed, but this long period of waiting did not give him longevity. True in this respect to the tradition of Barnes and Delane, he was burnt out before he was sixty. His years were notable mainly for the employment of the remarkable Blowitz to cover the Congress of Berlin in 1878, and for swinging the paper, which had been critical of the demagoguery of the Midlothian campaign, into a mildly pro-Gladstone position for the beginning of his second administration in 1880.

George Buckle, with two or three years' experience in Printing House Square, succeeded in 1884 at the age of twenty-nine. He was the son of a cathedral-close clergyman with strong academic

219

connections. He went to Winchester and New College, and was a Fellow of All Souls, thus beginning a link between *The Times* and that peculiar Oxford institution which was to last, with a short break, until Geoffrey Dawson's retirement as editor nearly sixty years later.

Buckle's good fortune were his fine late nineteenth-century intellectual good looks (he was the first handsome editor of *The Times*), and his health, which enabled him again to break another pattern, by surviving for twenty-two years after a twenty-eight-year editorship – to write the last three and a half volumes of the six-volume biography of Disraeli (which Moneypenny had begun) and to edit Queen Victoria's letters. His misfortune was that he presided over a paper with falling circulation and falling profitability which met a journalistic disaster early in his editorship and a drastic change of proprietorship near its end.

The circulation loss was not huge, but enough to be mildly depressing. The journalistic disaster, which was much worse, was the publication of forged letters allegedly written by the Irish Nationalist leader Charles Stewart Parnell.

The débâcle did *The Times* great damage, both material and moral. Buckle and MacDonald, the manager, who was dead within the year, offered their resignations, but John Walter III, whose own responsibility was equally great, refused them. The costs, falling upon the newspaper and the Walter family, of the 129-day Special Commission of inquiry exceeded £200,000 (the equivalent of £6 million or £7 million at today's values), and the blow to its prestige was at least as great. 'Something of the awe of holy writ, which from the days of Barnes had clung about its columns, now faded away' is the judgement of the official *History of The Times.*

Oddly perhaps, the principal whose equanimity best survived

the Parnell case was Buckle. He was never an editor of the force of Barnes or Delane but there was no question of his spending a quarter of a century as a lame duck. There was a considerable, and perhaps necessary, touch of self-righteousness about him. Not long after the débâcle he was rebuking the Leader of the House of Commons (W. H. Smith) for criticism of *The Times*, and he continued to exercise substantial influence throughout the long years of Conservative hegemony. He supported both the imperialism and protectionism of Joseph Chamberlain, provided he was not too disruptive within the Unionist Party, while carrying on a mild flirtation with Rosebery and his Liberal Imperialist associates. He was hostile to Campbell-Bannerman and not much more enthusiastic about Asquith. He kept up a good, self-confident right-of-centre 'non-partisanship'. His humiliations were that by 1908, when Lord Northcliffe's *Daily Mail* was selling nearly two million, an unheard-of circulation for any newspaper when Buckle became editor, *The Times* was down to 38,000 and that, partly as a result, the paper was sold, to Northcliffe, so completely over his head that he was dependent on *Observer* paragraphs for news of what was going on.

Alfred Harmsworth, made a baronet one year and a baron the next by the self-consciously fastidious Balfour, twelve years before being made a viscount by the less fastidious Lloyd George, was a bizarre man even by the high standards set by generations of newspaper proprietors. He was the eldest of fourteen children of an Irish barrister and compensated for this profusion of siblings by producing no heirs: he was the only Northcliffe.

His father omitted to educate him. At the age of seventeen he was a reporter in Coventry. Throughout his life he regretted that he had not been at Oxford 'for one year'. A year, he thought, would have given him 'poise'; longer would have been a waste of time. He was at least half a genius and he was at least half not a vulgarian. More important, he was the greatest journalistic innovator of the past hundred years. He was, of course, a megalomaniac who, unlike most people to whom that label is loosely applied, did literally go mad before he died at the age of fifty-seven.

He was a character of operatic quality and his methods of acquiring control of *The Times,* to which role a few decades earlier a man of his stamp would have been considered as likely an aspirant as Bradlaugh to become Archbishop of Canterbury, were rich in farce and melodrama. His rival was C. Arthur Pearson (no connection of the Pearsons who became Cowdray), the owner of the *Daily Express* and the *Standard,* and at stages in the battle Northcliffe sent him telegrams of false congratulation like a tenor singing one message across the stage and another to the audience. He embellished the farce by retiring for most of the period of negotiation to a hotel in Boulogne, to and from which communications passed in code, he himself having assumed the rather grand name of Atlantic, while his chief man of business, who had the unreassuring real name of Kennedy Jones, was Alberta. Walter was Manitoba. Buckle did not qualify even for a town, let alone an ocean or a province.

Whatever the methods, Northcliffe had secured control of *The Times* by March 1908, although this fact did not become public knowledge until several months later. There was an element of apprehension as well as fascination and impatience in his proprietorial approach to the queen of British journalism. There were jibes that it was going to be merely the threepenny edition of the *Daily Mail.* In time, however, Northcliffe scotched that by reducing its price to Id (and even playing with ½d), so that *The Times* became as cheap as its new stablemate.

But it was not as popular. The *Daily Mail* sold fifty times as many copies as *The Times*. If he had had to send one to the abattoir there is no doubt which Northcliffe would have chosen. But he did not have to choose. He lived on the *Daily Mail*. He half admired and half despised *The Times*. How could a newspaper be regarded as a serious enterprise when most of its senior staff never used the telephone, and the editor opened all letters submitted for publication with his own thumb? Before Northcliffe had thought of reducing the price the former chief proprietor suddenly asked him what he would do with the paper. 'I should make it worth threepence, Mr Walter,' was his rather good reply.

Buckle was not Northcliffe's man. He did, however, survive for more than four years before being replaced by Geoffrey Robinson (the only man to occupy the editorial chair twice and who made the story more complicated by doing so under different names, changing from Robinson to Dawson in order to inherit from an aunt a substantial landed property in Yorkshire). Although Buckle's going, partly because it closely followed the deaths of Moberly Bell, the long-serving manager, and Valentine Chirol, head of the foreign department, marked a considerable clearing out of the old gang, Robinson came from a roughly similar stable. He was, indeed, not only Northcliffe's but also Buckle's choice as successor, although Buckle did not welcome the speed with which he achieved the chair.

He had been at Eton and Magdalen College, Oxford, was a fellow of All Souls, and had been Lord Milner's private secretary in South Africa. He was thirty-eight when be became editor and had been on the staff of *The Times* for eighteen months. His first stint as editor lasted six and a half years until he in turn, having had a moderately rough ride, fell foul of Northcliffe. It embraced the whole of World War I, a period of great press influence, partly because the House of Commons, then as now almost totally geared to a two-party system, was thrown into limbo by coalition government.

The Times was central to this period of journalistic politics, but to an extent that had not been seen since the advent of Barnes it was *The Times* of the proprietor rather than *The Times* of the editor which called the game. This was largely because of the extraordinary symbiotic relationship between Northcliffe and Lloyd George. Their periods of high power almost exactly coincided. Lloyd George became Chancellor of the Exchequer in April 1908, and was driven out of the premiership in October 1922. Northcliffe acquired *The Times* in March 1908, and died in August 1922. They both had daemonic energy, rootlessness, and inner irresponsibility.

This did not mean that they liked each other. Lloyd George told Beaverbrook in November 1916 that he would 'as soon go for a sunny evening stroll around Walton Heath with a grasshopper as try and work with Northcliffe', and Northcliffe had little sooner helped to make Lloyd George Prime Minister than he was talking about destroying him. Each deserved the other, and there was considerable mutual fascination.

The Times, through its military correspondent's reporting of the shell shortage in France, played a substantial role in the forcing of the 1915 Coalition. But the apogee of its influence in wartime political intrigue was reached during the manoeuvrings of December 1916, which led to the replacement of Asquith by Lloyd George. Its main leader of Monday, 4 December made it publicly clear to Asquith that the concordat he had reached with Lloyd George was, and would be interpreted as being, a humiliation of himself. Accordingly he withdrew from it, overplayed his hand, and ejected himself from 10 Downing Street after eight and a half years' tenancy. The article was thought to be Lloyd George-inspired. To some extent it was. Northcliffe had been flitting heavily between the pillars of the Whitehall scenery. It had, however, been written by Robinson, mostly at Cliveden, but titivated after a Sunday evening dinner with Northcliffe.

This was the high point of their collaboration. Their relationship was sometimes eased by Northcliffe's absences in America, but otherwise they grew increasingly incompatible. Dawson (as he had then become) was sacked three months after the armistice and replaced by Henry Wickham Steed. In contrast with Dawson, an Empire-orientated, conventional English scholar-squire, there was a touch of the continental adventurer about Steed, which made him more acceptable to Northcliffe. He had been on the foreign staff of *The Times* for twenty years, but the combination of his education (Sudbury Grammar School and the Universities of Jena, Berlin and Paris), his elegant beard, and his involvement with the intricacies of Balkan politics, set him a little apart. His greatest qualification, however, was that he shared what had become Northcliffe's detestation of Lloyd George. The paper survived the next three and a half years under this unstable partnership better than might have been expected. J. L. Garvin of the *Observer* at this time considered it 'far and away the best morning paper'.

The death of Northcliffe was a relief to almost everybody, including Steed, who fell soon after him. *The Times* moved curiously but not causally in step with British politics. This provides perhaps the best evidence of its position as a national journal. In Lloyd George's time it was febrile. Coincidentally with his fall it moved into a period of Baldwinesque calm. The ownership gap left by Northcliffe was filled by the junior branch of the Astor

225

family, Major (later Colonel) J. J. Astor, later still Lord Astor of Hever, providing most of the money and moving into a partnership with a revived John Walter IV. Dawson was brought back as editor and stayed for another nineteen years, until 1941. Together with John Reith of the BBC and Archbishop Lang of Canterbury, Dawson of *The Times* formed a tripod of slightly self-righteous respectability which sustained the British establishment of the inter-war years.

The Times's semi-official position, never exactly sought, sometimes embarrassing both to the government and to the paper, but sometimes valuable too, particularly for the prestige that it gave its correspondents abroad, was strengthened during this period. So was the pre-eminence of some of its features, most notably the correspondence columns. In 1917 it had rejected (by decision of Dawson, not, as was commonly thought, Northcliffe) one of the most resonant, if to some eyes infamous, letters to the editor in British political history. The Lansdowne 'peace letter' went to the *Daily Telegraph* instead. In 1919 this was compensated for by Baldwin's 'FST letter' (he was Financial Secretary to the Treasury at the time and used the initials to achieve at least the appearance of anonymity), in which he announced that he was giving a fifth of his fortune to help reduce the national debt, and by two extraordinary effusions from Bonar Law. In one he sounded the death-knell of Lloyd George's Coalition. In the other, written during his brief period as Prime Minister, he castigated under the curious pseudonym of 'Colonial' the American debt settlement his Chancellor had just negotiated.

Dawson was always an appeaser, in the better as well as the worse sense of the word. Therefore he liked Baldwin's general approach to politics, and Baldwin in turn was always close to

226

him. On a crucial morning in August 1931, having reluctantly returned to London from Aix-les-Bains to deal with the crisis that led to the formation of the National Government, Baldwin was 'lost' for several hours. He had, in fact, slipped away to consult his trusted friend Dawson. As a result he missed a summons to see the King before Herbert Samuel did so, and plans for a coalition gathered almost irresistible momentum. By the time he had his own audience, Baldwin, against his better judgement, could only acquiesce. British politics were distorted for a decade, and the new balance which Baldwin had devoted the twenties to achieving was seriously upset. The incident was a tribute to the drawing power of Dawson, but not an indication that a politician is always best employed in calling on the editor of *The Times*.

The paper was far from being alone in its support of Neville Chamberlain's foreign policy. It did, however, carry its enthusiasm beyond the call of duty. For Christmas 1938 it offered its readers the opportunity to buy cards showing the Prime Minister waving from the balcony of Buckingham Palace on his return from Munich. It opposed Churchill's inclusion in the government as late as July 1939. And it had the power, unlike most of its contemporaries, to help make policy as well as merely to comment upon it. The most famous (or notorious) example was the leader of 7 September 1938, which first advocated the handing over of the Sudetenland to Germany. The Foreign Office disowned it to the Czech government, but there is evidence that the article had been inspired by Halifax, the Foreign Secretary. His contact with Dawson was intimate and continuous.

As appeasement collapsed war came, and the Chamberlain Government tottered towards its fall. *The Times* inevitably suffered somewhat for its over-commitment. Stephen Koss in his *Rise and Fall of the Political Press in Britain* makes a fine distinction: 'Its influence had declined but not yet its reputation.' The period of *The Times's* being almost a great Department of State and its editor almost an honorary member of the Cabinet was over, and not merely for Dawson's day.

His long day came to an end on 1 October 1941. The *History's* 'obituary' says: 'He gave lifelong adherence to his chosen leaders, above all Milner, Baldwin, Chamberlain and Halifax.' It was not an eclectic choice of friends. In particular it left his successor, who had been his co-adjudicator for the previous fourteen years, somewhat isolated from the War Coalition, and indeed the Churchillian Conservative Party.

This successor was R. M. Barrington-Ward. He was the son of a clergyman, educated at Westminster and Balliol. He was part of the warp and woof of *The Times*. He had first joined its staff in 1913 at the age of twenty-two. He spent eight years away at the *Observer*. That and World War I apart, the paper had been his whole life. He had refused the director-generalship of the BBC in 1938. Yet, although very much an inside appointment, he was an editor of note. Some thought that had he succeeded ten years earlier he would have avoided the excesses of the late Dawson period. He never sought to detach himself from them, but as editor he moved the paper firmly to the left.

He was enthusiastic about the Beveridge Report and other plans for post-war reconstruction. He believed in 1942 that Cripps might easily become Prime Minister within a short time. He employed E. H. Carr to write leaders advocating the closest postwar Anglo-Russian partnership. True to this view he opposed the British Government's resistance to the Greek left-wing revolutionary movement at the end of 1944, and infuriated Churchill by so doing. To loud Conservative cheers, the Prime Minister, with the editor sitting prominently in the gallery, delivered a virulent parliamentary attack upon *The Times* in January 1945. Barrington-Ward was shaken but undeflected. His proprietors, Astor, then MP for Dover, and Walter, were embarrassed but gentlemanly. He was denounced by a less gentlemanly Conservative MP (Sir Herbert Williams) for producing 'the threepenny edition', this time not of the *Daily Mail* but 'of the *Daily Worker*'.

When the Attlee government came in, *The Times* under Barrington-Ward accepted it as a natural government for Britain in the epoch. His criticism was sometimes sharp but basically friendly. His reward was scant. He was excoriated by many Conservatives, and called in and denounced by Ernest Bevin for the 'spineless' and 'jellyfish' attitude of *The Times* towards Russia. It was neither for him nor against him, Bevin typically complained. 'Why should it be?' Barrington-Ward very reasonably retorted, but to his diary, not to Bevin. Again he was shocked rather than influenced. Those who saw him when he returned to Printing House Square thought that he looked as though he had been in a nasty traffic accident. Bevin could be a fairly roughly driven articulated lorry. And Barrington-Ward was a natural St Sebastian of journalism. He carried the arrows without much complaint. But they hurt a great deal. And they may even have helped to kill him in 1948 at the typically early *Times* age of fifty-six.

His successor, William Casey, was both the oldest and the most obvious stop-gap to be appointed to the *Times* chair. He was Anglo-Irish and from a background not dissimilar to that of Northcliffe. But he had been to Trinity College, Dublin, and he was a calm man. At first it was thought that he might merely be there for a year. In fact he lasted five, and was rather a good editor in a quiet way.

Then came Sir William Haley, the first editor to be born (just) in the twentieth century, the first since 1803 not to have been to a university, the only one to arrive with a title and perhaps the last to believe intermittently that he commanded the thunderbolts of Zeus. His most famous leader was entitled 'It *is* a Moral Issue', and was a rather holier-than-thou lecture on the Profumo scandal of 1963 and the climate out of which it had sprung. Previously he had been critical of the Suez adventure, although not as vehemently so as the *Observer*, the *Manchester Guardian* or the *Daily Mirror*, had presided very uneasily over the successful but unappetizing 'Top People Take *The Times*' advertising campaign, had been affronted by the Lady Chatterley verdict, had urged a Conservative victory but an upsurge of Liberal votes in the general election of 1964, and had put news on the front page in May 1966. He was a successful but reluctant editor of transition.

His reign of fourteen years came to a voluntary end in 1967 together with the withdrawal of the Astors from principal proprietorship. A successful new proprietor (from the point of view of the paper if not of his family fortune) was found in the shape of Lord Thomson of Fleet, and William Rees-Mogg became editor and the best editorial leader-writer since Barnes. Thomson's disadvantage was that he provided no dynasty of loss-absorbers. He and his son lasted barely as long as Northcliffe. Of the paper since then it is impossible to write with perspective or objectivity. Harold Evans has written his own *pièce justificative* after the briefest editorship in the history of the paper. Rupert Murdoch and Charles Douglas-Home (editor from 1982 to 1985) are too contemporary to appraise, at any rate in their own columns.

They are the heirs to a long but fluctuating tradition, which mostly worked best when editors were strong and proprietors were quiescent. This is not an invariable rule. Buckle, left entirely to himself, might have run the paper quietly into the sand. Dawson might have benefited from some proprietorial arm-jogging. *The Times* has no record of impeccability. Other newspapers have quite frequently been better. But none has on average been so good for so long.

Bologna's Birthday

This was an article in Oxford, *the dons' periodical, written shortly after the Bologna celebrations.*

The university of Bologna, which has a well-authenticated claim to be the oldest in the world, celebrated its 900th anniversary in the autumn of 1988. The festivities, while not perhaps quite up to the 800th when Giuseppe Verdi was chairman of the organizing committee and Giosuè Carducci delivered the principal oration, were none the less splendid. Nearly four hundred *rettori,* which was the generic term under which all of us, chancellors, vice-chancellors, presidents, principals, and genuine rectors, were lumped, were assembled for the main open-air ceremony in the Piazza Maggiore in front of the great basilica of San Petronio in which the Emperor Charles V was crowned in 1530 and Rossini's *Stabat Mater* was first performed in 1839.

A wide variety of academic dress was favoured by this throng. Some, mainly from Eastern Europe and down through the Caucasus to the borders of India, looked more like judges than academics, and judges of a tribunal which had been engaged for many centuries in handing out cruel and unusual punishments to students and teachers alike. One British chancellor was bedecked in his gold regalia and the vice-chancellor of Cambridge was impressive in fur. I decided, however, influenced by the combination of the reluctance of the Oxford authorities ever to allow the cancellarian robe to go more than half a mile from Carfax, the problems of luggage, and the likely heat of an Italian September sun, that the University of Oxford could afford to dress down. I made do with white tie, bands and the cool silk of a DCL black gown, and felt rather like a notary in an elaborately costumed Mozart opera. The status of Oxford was however preserved, and Cinderella asked to the ball (to vary the operatic metaphor), when the President of the Italian Republic arrived and paused in his procession across the square to exclaim to me *'il mio cancellario'*, thereby illustrating the value which those in authority abroad place upon having been honoured in the Sheldonian.

In general, however, I had the rare experience for a representative of Oxford of not being pre-eminent at a festival of age. 'The University of Oxford is not used', I began my short speech, 'to saluting institutions of greater venerability than itself, but when it has to recognize an indisputable claim does so with the greater enthusiasm and respect.' Having made that obeisance I then felt able to point out that we had far more remaining mediaeval academic buildings than either Bologna, although they are very splendid from about 1550, or the Sorbonne, which achieved second place to our third, and that in Merton we have the fount of collegiate living, where people had slept, eaten, read, taught, and prayed together in an entity with clear continuity since the very early fourteenth century.

There had to be a certain finessing to enable me to make that speech at all. Obviously all four hundred could not speak without the proceedings lasting some considerable way towards the millennial celebrations. So it was decided that there should be an oration of greeting from the head of the senior university in each continent. This was interpreted sufficiently rigidly that the Americas were not split and Harvard was relegated to a silent role behind Lima.

It should also have had the effect of leaving Oxford to be represented by Paris and hearing Sydney speak as the representative of the venerability of Australian academic life. Oxford's reputation as a talking rather than a listening university was judged by the Bolognese authorities to be too strong for this to be possible and my European position (which Bologna was anxious to stress because of their leading role in the Erasmus scheme and consequent close relationship with the European Commission) was amalgamated with our semi-seniority to create a special slot. This sleight of hand passed off without hostile demonstrations from Paris, Coimbra, Salamanca, Prague, Cambridge and St Andrews and other near competitors. Cambridge and St Andrews had more reason to complain the next morning when Paris and Oxford headed a column of twenty European 'venerabili' and they were relegated to the kindergarten, although the 1592 upstart of Trinity College, Dublin, got in because it was from a separate and sovereign state.

As with all grand celebrations there were elements of theatre about the occasion. But it was also a moving and genuinely splendid event. The notes of the slaves' chorus from *Nabucco* swelling into the great square was a suitable accompaniment to the signing by us all (including the Rector of Leningrad) of a ringing declaration of the independence of universities which had certainly not been drafted in the Department of Education

234

and Science – nor even in Mr Gorbachev's Kremlin, for that matter.

There are also always experiences and problems in common between universities. As the large, ebullient, and resplendently besashed Communist Mayor of Bologna, a serious commercial (and gastronomic) city which looks after its art treasures but does not allow itself to be dominated by tourism, said to me as he drove me back to my hotel from the Prefect's lunch for President Cossiga: 'There is a tradition of hostility between town and university here, but we have recently decided that, as a substantial part of our reputation seems to come from the university, we had better strengthen our links with it.' I have noted with pleasure that, in my short experience, the Lord Mayor of Oxford has never missed an Encaenia. I doubt, however, if he (or recently more frequently she) would have emulated the Bolognese Sindaco's feat of responding with pride to my remark that his city was famous for its large pedestrian zones by proceeding to drive me through them at approximately 60 m.p.h.

Anniversaries in Pall Mall

*This essay is based on parts of two talks: one a lecture given
in 1986 for the 150th anniversary of the founding of the Reform
Club and the other a dinner speech in 1992 for the twentieth
anniversary of the amalgamation of the Oxford and
Cambridge and the United Universities Clubs.*

The pall mall clubs were born in a different century from the
St James's Street ones and were to some extent a reaction
against them. Those who founded them saw themselves as part
of an age of improvement and not of imitation. They were unim-
pressed by the fashionable rakishness of Brooks's, White's and
Boodle's, and wanted to create something newer, grander, more
wholesome, with less gambling, less debauchery, and perhaps
fewer cockroaches as well. The bourgeois palaces of Pall Mall
were to outshine the louche if aristocratic stews of St James's
Street. To paraphrase what W. S. Gilbert was to write in *Iolanthe*
half a century later:

> Hearts for more pure and fair
> May beat down Pall Mall way

Than in the squalid air
Of rich St James's.

The origins of the Reform Club, which eventually achieved the
greatest of all the palaces, epitomized this approach. The first
Reform Bill and the new politics that flowed from it obviously
provided the first strand of inspiration. Paradoxically, however, it
was the Tories who reacted first to the new need for political
organization and in 1832 established the Carlton Club only a
few yards from what became the site of the Reform Club. There
it remained until it was severely bombed in December 1940.

The Liberals were three and a half years behind. This was
partly due to the Radical/Whig dichotomy, and partly due to
the complication of relations with Brooks's. The Whigs did not
much want the Radicals in Brooks's, but were even less keen on
their forming a club of their own. The Radicals, notably
Molesworth, Parkes and Hume, determinedly wanted a club
and did not want to be in Brooks's anyway, despite or maybe
because of the fact that it provided every single member of
Melbourne's 1834 Cabinet. They were in a semi-Groucho Marx
position. Eventually the Whigs, notably Edward Ellice, Lord
Grey's brother-in-law and his Chief Whip at the time of the
Reform Bill, later Secretary of State for War, decided that unless
they wished the Radicals to go off on their own, they had little
choice but to join with them in forming a new model club. And
out of that decision the Reform Club emerged, as an entity in
1836, as a complete and splendid edifice by 1843.

The 'reformers', however, although they did not want to
imitate the old, aristocratic, proprietary gaming clubs, were not
looking for the simple life. 'The family motto is service,' said a

237

recent Lord Rothschild, 'and by God we get it.' The 'reformers' were looking for the best, and by God they got it. The names most naturally associated with the first twenty years of the Club are neither Ellice nor Molesworth, nor even Russell or Palmerston, but Charles Barry, the architect, and Alexis Soyer, the cook. And what remarkable jobs they both made of their confections, Barry's happily the longer lasting. It makes his neighbouring creations, the Travellers Club and Bridgewater House, look inferior, the first too cautious, the second too imitative, and his most massive monument the Palace of Westminster too undisciplined.

Soyer could not create quite so permanently, although he did pretty well by chef-ly standards. It is interesting to note that the financial relations of neither with the Club were wholly smooth. The 'reformers' believed in the best, but they did not believe in paying more for it than the going rate. Barry and the General Committee went to arbitration before his total fee of £3934 (I suppose about the equivalent of £150,000 today) was agreed. Soyer had many disputes on issues from butchers' bills to insolence to members before he finally resigned in 1850.

In architecture, gastronomy, membership and purpose, the Reform Club was very much a creation of its age. It would be impossible to imagine its foundation twenty or thirty years earlier. Even its name is, I suppose, the most contemporary – and the most ideological – ever given to a major and lasting London club. The early membership was also symbolic of the period. The franchise had been significantly extended and made more rational in 1832, but it had certainly not been democratized. The Reform Club matched the franchise. It did not turn its back on the landed aristocracy any more than did the Liberal Party of Russell, Palmerston or Hartington. But it was in no way based upon aristocratic connection. Its members were prosperous, established, confident. There were few poor men amongst them. But its doors were more open to new men and to new categories – merchants, solicitors, surgeons, architects, professional men of letters and journalists, all categories alleged to be excluded from the generality of the clubs of the period. The position of the Club was thus assured throughout the three decades and a little more between the first and the second Reform Bills.

During its first half century the Reform Club was intensely political. The stated qualification for membership – or even for being introduced as a guest – was that of being a 'reformer', which may be thought not to be a very precise category. But it was interpreted sufficiently rigidly, and partisanly, that as late as the general election of 1880 a member was expelled for the offence of having publicly voted for a Conservative candidate.

Throughout this period the Club was essentially parliamentary as well as political. This did not mean that anything like a majority of its members were MPs. Despite a more 'serious' approach, it never rivalled Brooks's record of having as a good half of its early members men who at some time in their lives were members of one House or the other (or both). But the nineteenth-century Reform Club probably contained more members who *wanted* to be MPs and were therefore happy that the tone should be taken from the Liberal benches at Westminster.

This showed itself in the library with its remarkable collection of parliamentary papers. It showed itself in the fact that Members of Parliament were admitted as members outside the quota and almost without question, provided they did not sit on the wrong side of the House. And, most clearly of all, it showed itself in the gearing of club hours to parliamentary habits. The hours were generous enough in any event. There was no question of weekend closing and refuge having to be sought in lesser establishments. On each day of the seven the clubhouse was open from eight in the morning until two the following morning, unless either House of Parliament should sit later, in which case the club was to remain open until an hour after the adjournment. To some substantial extent the clubhouse was run as an annexe to the Palace of Westminster, which I suppose their common architect, even though he gave them no common architectural style, made appropriate. Whether or not supper was laid out in the Coffee Room depended upon whether the House was sitting after 10 p.m.

The political if not the parliamentary emphasis was brought to an end by the Liberal Unionist Home Rule split of 1886. It was not as visceral for the Reform Club as for Brooks's which was based more on family tradition and where there followed a fine outbreak of mutual blackballing of the sons of prominent members. In the Reform, perhaps because it was less tightly knit, there was less bitterness. If the Club was not to be destroyed they had to live together in an approach to mutual tolerance, as is epitomized in the 1890 drawing of members which now hangs in the Audience Room. Of the nine most visible, seated in unnatural proximity, three were Unionists, six were Gladstonians. It was like the Opposition front bench in the House of Commons, where they also sat cheek by jowl, one occasionally advancing to the despatch box to excoriate half the others.

However, there could no longer be any question of the Club applying Liberal political tests. By 1898, three of the five trustees were serving in a predominantly Conservative government. In the following year, nevertheless, the meeting to confirm the choice of Campbell-Bannerman as Liberal leader was held in the Club, the new leader himself having resisted abandoning

240

'our hold on so excellent a property'. Asquith was also elected there in 1908, and eight and three-quarter years after that summoned the last general Liberal Party meeting ever to be held in the Club in order to explain why he could not serve in the Lloyd George coalition. It was an appropriate *terminus ad quem*. For thirty years, by that time, the Reform as a Liberal club had been a chicken running round with its head cut off. As a general club, however, it had a secure hold on life, which it has more than since maintained. It has continued to be in many ways a club of government, much involved with the public affairs of the nation, but not one to which even the loosest sort of political test could be applied. Its 1880 rule, exercised at either of the 1980s general elections, would probably have halved the membership.

The two university clubs of Pall Mall came a little, but not much, before the Reform Club. They were like it in looking to a limited and defined catchment area (members of the two ancient universities) for members, although supplying general social club facilities. They none the less managed to achieve a subtle but considerable difference of spirit between themselves, and existed independently and within about six hundred yards of each other for nearly 150 years. They stood like two gatehouses, the one the most easterly and the other the most westerly of the Pall Mall clubs.

The United University Club was the easterly one and was also the earliest of the Pall Mall clubhouses. It was designed by William Wilkins and completed in 1823. Wilkins was a prolific and distinguished early-nineteenth-century architect. He had already designed Haileybury School and Downing College, Cambridge, as well as substantially embellishing King's College, and in particular adding the screen which fronts on to King's Parade, in that university. Subsequently he was to do the

241

National Gallery and the central building of University College, London.

Next in Pall Mall came Nash's United Services Club (now the Institute of Directors) in 1827, then Decimus Burton's Athenaeum in 1830, then Barry's relatively modest and tentative Travellers Club in 1832, and Smirke's now demolished Carlton completed in 1833, and then the westerly gatehouse of the Oxford and Cambridge Club in 1838. This was also by Smirke, whose other London works were the Royal Opera House, the old General Post Office in St Martin's-le-Grand, and the British Museum. No one could say that the new clubs did not employ the most notable and fashionable of architects. The group was crowned with the completion in 1843 of the Reform clubhouse, Barry having gained greatly in confidence and flamboyance over the eleven years since the Travellers. The Junior Carlton, by Brandon, since gone, was added on the north side of the street, in the 1860s. And in 1911 came the last great clubhouse to be built in London. Mewès and Davis gave the Royal Automobile Club the external appearance of a Beaux-Arts American railroad station and the internal feel of a Cunard liner.

Long before amalgamation there were two other developments in the university club field. In 1864, waiting lists being long at both the others, the New University Club was set up, and in 1867–8 Alfred Waterhouse built it a gothic clubhouse on the upper west side of St James's Street. Betjeman described Waterhouse as the greatest English architect since Wren, but, whether or not this was true, photographs do not suggest that his New University Club was his greatest success. It was more comparable with the Broad Street front of Balliol College, Oxford, than with his Manchester Town Hall, or the Natural History Museum in South Kensington or St Paul's School in

242

Hammersmith (also, alas, demolished) or his second and unforgettable London club building, the National Liberal Club, completed in 1886.

Even if inferior to those pinnacled Liberal glories in Whitehall Gardens, the New University Club did not suffer from F. E. Smith's pretence that he had mistaken it for a public lavatory, perhaps only because it was less conveniently placed for his walk from the Temple to the House of Commons. It did, however, suffer from declining fortunes, demolition, and amalgamation with the United University Club in 1938. In the meantime, that club had decided it needed a more opulent and modern, even if less distinguished, façade than that with which Wilkins had provided it. Accordingly, in 1906–7 it commissioned Reginald Blomfield to re-model the clubhouse in what Pevsner disparagingly described as his Champs Elysées style. At the Oxford and Cambridge Club Blomfield was also set loose to design the entrance and the staircase as well as, after an interval, adding the bedroom floor. But Smirke's framework, unlike that of Wilkins, was allowed to survive. It was therefore desirable that, when the amalgamation of 1972 took place, the Oxford and Cambridge Club was allowed to provide the clubhouse even though the United University Club provided most of the officers.

The combined club has since prospered. But, unlike the Reform, which had no particular obligation to do so, it has not accepted women as full members. This is an anomaly for a club called the United Oxford and Cambridge University Club, for both those universities are now 40 per cent female.

Ten Pieces of Wine Nonsense

This is based on a not very serious talk delivered to the Wine Guild in March 1988.

My reputation both as a wine drinker and as a wine expert has long been exaggerated. While this has I think done me some harm politically, it carries with it the partly compensating advantage that some (but not all) hosts tend to give me better wine than they might otherwise do. Occasionally indeed they are misled by my alleged partiality for claret by providing such sustenance at all times and in all circumstances, as for example before or after a speech, when I would much rather have a stimulating or reviving whisky. However, they are right to the extent that, in so far as I know anything about wine, my knowledge is confined to the red wines of Bordeaux. It is not that I do not like Burgundy. It is simply that I do not know how to choose it.

So you must expect a certain amount of bias in the following bits of wine gossip, anecdotes or old wives' tales that I have randomly put together in no particular framework or order except for making them add up to ten.

(1) Why is it that the greatest wines come from the very limits at which you can effectively produce wine of any sort. If you draw an arc from the mouth of the Gironde, looping around the Loire (not much *great* wine there) to, say Autun at the eastern end of Burgundy, then turning north to skirt Epernay and Reims in Champagne before turning east to take in the Mosel and the Rheingau, you will find with a minor exception to which I will come in a moment that there is nothing produced to the north or the west of it. It is the frontier of the European empire of Bacchus. The exception is southern England. As yet that produces no red wine, so I am essentially unqualified to judge, although remaining in this respect a little sceptical about the glories or the value for money of Hampshire. But does this pattern of *Ultima Thule* being the best suggest that if there were a climatic change, as was strongly prophesied a few years ago, the frontier would move north? Would the Bordelais become a more robust and less delicate region like the slopes of the Ebro, and the Weald and the Thames Valley become the difficult but fine new frontier region? Not, I think, in under a hundred years or so. I cannot see Château Moulsford replacing Château Mouton in less time than that.

(2) How does New World wine compare with Old? I recently had to make two Australian bicentenary speeches and have aroused marked lack of enthusiasm by giving them what I thought was the relative accolade of being the third-best producer of red wine in the world. (My unspoken premise was that the second place should go to California, although maybe Spain ought to have been next, giving Australia only the fourth plinth.) More important than this, however, is

how the 'steady climate' New World wines come out compared with the meteorological vagaries of Bordeaux and Burgundy. They always do very well on blindfold tastings. But that is a doubtful concours. It is, in my view, always better to know what you are tasting. It gives much more authority to your pronouncements. I also think that removing the variation of years from the equation (which the Californian or Australian climate effectively does) takes about a third of the fun out of wine. In addition, for my money, Bordeaux gives if not a bigger bang as least a subtler taste for a buck than California does. I therefore remain a strong and prejudiced Old World partisan.

(3) What is the best rule for dealing with an unfamiliar restaurant wine list of moderate quality when parsimony makes one loath to go above the châteaux that are as unknown as is the list itself? The answer in my view is in such circumstances always go for the Graves. There is hardly such a thing as a bad red Graves. In any event it is of course very foolish ever to order wine of more than a modest quality in a restaurant. To pay 100 per cent (at least) mark-up on expensive wine is more akin to lunacy than to generosity. The *sommelier* of a distinguished Oxfordshire hotel/restaurant once won my heart by flatteringly rejecting my tentative order of about the fourth cheapest claret and saying, 'Oh, Mr Jenkins, don't waste your money. You'll have much better wine than that at home. I'd have the house red if I were you.'

(4) I once amused myself when I was President of the European Commission by arranging the main countries of the Community according to different categories of quality

in their governments' attributes, some of them frivolous as well as specialized to an official visitor. Thus for the ruthless brio of their motor-cycle escorts I put the French easily first, with the Italians second and the British and the Germans third and fourth. (It should be added that had the test been the performance of the economy the Germans, although not the British, would have moved markedly up.) On the quality of government entertaining, however, I without hesitation give the accolade to the British, with the Italians second, the French only third and the Germans again fourth. This was based entirely on the quality of the wine. The Elysée could not begin to rival the 1945 and 1961 first growths which, when I was last a minister, still lurked in the cellars of the Whitehall Hospitality Department.

(5) Do I believe that I can perform precise feats of wine recognition? Alas, no, except purely by accident or by lucky cheating. I think it is a gift like 'perfect pitch' and I do not have it. My best recipe for recognizing is to get a quick look at the label. The second best is to know approximately what your host has in his cellar, and then decide at what grade in his stock he is most likely to rate you and his other guests.

(6) What is the greatest wine feast I have ever had? In 1975 I attended a dinner for eight at which seven different bottles were provided. They were, believe it or not, Lafite 1953, Margaux 1929, Cheval Blanc 1934, Lafite 1961, Margaux 1900, Haut Brion 1929 and Haut Brion 1934. The host was, as the *Sunday Times* would now call him, Lord Victor Rothschild. He had probably acquired most of them for little more than £2 or £3 a bottle, and the replacement cost, while already considerable, would in 1975 have been

247

barely a tenth of what it is today. The then Governor of the Bank of England, who was also present, might have found the bottles a more appreciating addition to his reserves than gold or dollars, let alone sterling.

(7) What is the most spectacular wine present I have ever received? I have two candidates. In 1966 at a Bristol banquet I paid tribute to a great Bristol wine merchant, with whom I had long had dealings. He responded by sending me a single bottle of Lafite 1897. When we drank it about a decade later I managed what with shrinkage and ullage to get from it only about two-thirds of a decanter. It had a strange, haunting taste.

Then in 1979 I sat next to a French minister at a Council of Ministers lunch. His constituency was centred on Libourne in the Gironde. I expressed some interest in certain areas of his domaine, most notably Pomerol. Two weeks later he sent me a case of Pétrus 1970. Two months after that he committed suicide. I do not know what the moral of that is.

(8) What is my best example of a throwaway wine remark? 'We always drink the bad years *frappé* with the fish,' I was once told at Château Lafite, as the unmistakable label with a little 1968 on it was brought in from the refrigerator.

(9) Can you make too much fuss about wine? Yes certainly, in at least three ways. First by believing that if the wine is sufficiently splendid you do not need enough of it. Excessive reverence to about the equivalent of half an egg-cup is no way of enjoying oneself or of entertaining one's guests. Second, by putting the bottle in horrible and pointless

baskets or silver trolleys, a bogus and inconvenient piece of Edwardian vulgarity which has lingered on. Third, if you get too excited about what wine you drink with what food. I have always found red wine perfectly good with chicken, or with sole or halibut or turbot.

(10) What is the most meaningless wine question? To my mind it makes no more sense to ask what is your favourite wine than to ask what is your favourite thread in a great tapestry that dominates a room, or to suggest that if you like a book you ought to go on reading it over and over again to the exclusion of all others. The occasional drinking of great wines needs a background of ordinary everyday drinking against which to stand out, and even amongst the stars it is the comparison with their peers that provides half the enjoyment.

Should Politicians Know History?

This essay is based on a talk given in the Library of Congress, Washington, DC, in June 1988.

The question to which I address myself today is whether or not a lively awareness of history is going the way of a classical education and becoming a discarded attribute for the leaders of the Western world? And second, if it is does it matter? And third, are there any great differences in this respect between the main states of the Atlantic basin?

First, has there in fact been a significant and secular decline in historical knowledge and interest? Cromwell said when laying down a prescription for the education of his third son Richard: 'I would have him learn a little history'; and it has been written of Thomas Jefferson and his contemporaries that compared with modern statesmen 'they thought more about the future and knew more about the past'. But I am by no means sure how consistent was the historical erudition of nineteenth-century Presidents or Prime Ministers. I would not put Andrew Jackson in the 1830s – or indeed Andrew Johnson in the 1860s – very high in this respect, less so indeed than Lyndon Johnson a hundred years later, even though he would not be thought of as one of the most sophisticated intellectuals amongst American Presidents. British mid-nineteenth-century Prime Ministers were probably somewhat more informed, although I do not think that the historical knowledge of the Duke of Wellington or of Lord Grey or even of William Lamb, Viscount Melbourne, was very meticulous.

What is certainly the case, however, is that for nearly twenty-five years from 1940 British governments were led by a series of men whose minds were to an exceptional extent moulded, refreshed and stimulated by their historical knowledge. Churchill (1940–5 and 1951–5) was of course the outstanding example. Although he had no formal training, he wrote history with a verve unequalled by any other British statesman and with a professionalism that could be rivalled in this category only by John Morley or James Bryce. Beyond that, his imagination was constantly seized by the tides of historical events and an epic view of how great men could divert them. He was undoubtedly much motivated by an awareness of his own historical destiny.

Clement Attlee (1945–51) saw himself and events less grandiloquently. He had no gift of narrative prose. But his training was historical, as were his continuing intellectual interests. He had an acute instinct for balance between change and continuity, and his laconic sense of proportion, which cut men and events down to size, owed much to his knowledge of the past.

Anthony Eden (1955–7) knew a lot about Persian and Arab history and came to acquire an encyclopaedic knowledge of the minutiae of diplomatic exchanges of the first half of this century. But his interests were more aesthetic than intellectual, and of this quartet his mind was probably the least conditioned by history, just as his term of office was much the shortest.

251

Its fourth member was Harold Macmillan (1957–63). He, like Attlee, had little of Churchill's command over written English, and he could not therefore compete as a chronicler. But his knowledge was at least as great as Churchill's, and indeed covered a wider span. He knew Greek and Roman history in a way that Churchill, whose interests were always concentrated on the past three hundred years, never did. Harold Macmillan was not a great writer of history (his six volumes of memoirs, unlike his wartime *Mediterranean Diary*, were pretty dull stuff). But his most characteristic speeches moved easily from the Peloponnesian War to the Battle of the Somme.

Since Harold Macmillan's resignation in 1963 it has in Britain been gradually downhill nearly all the way so far as historical knowledge and interest are concerned. Alec Douglas Home (1963–4) has a history degree, but has maintained the amateur status of a gentleman commoner of Christ Church, Oxford; the knowledge of Harold Wilson (1964–70 and 1974–6) while by no means negligible is somewhat over-concentrated upon the American Civil War. Edward Heath (1970–4), although he thinks in broad and generous terms, has never much illuminated his speeches or writings with historical parallels going back beyond his own, now long, experience.

James Callaghan (1976–9) does not break the pattern, even though he, too, now likes to think broad. Margaret Thatcher (1979–90), while her own impact upon history will be great, is curiously bounded by her own period of office, and that of the previous Labour government. She is fond of argument by historical comparison, but it is almost invariably done in a scale of two, and her history does not often go back before 1974, the date of the beginning of the second Wilson Government. Nor does John Major (1990–?) or any likely alternative British Prime Minister show much sign of ability to reverse the trend.

The case could therefore be regarded as superficially proved: twenty-three years from 1940 to 1963 producing four Prime Ministers, of whom at least three were impregnated with historical sense; and thirty years from 1963 to 1993 with six Prime Ministers on an incline of descent towards indifference or ignorance. History appears to be in retreat.

Yet might it not have been the first rather than the second period that was exceptional? If we consider the eight preceding Prime Ministers who took office since 1900, this looks quite plausible. Arthur James Balfour (1902–5) brooded on the likelihood of cosmic doom when 'the energies of our system will decay, the glory of the sun will be dimmed, and the earth, tideless and inert, will no longer tolerate the race which has for a moment disturbed its solitude', but this grand pessimism did not encourage much detailed historical application, even though one of his dominant political thoughts was that he was determined not to be like Robert Peel in 1846 and 'betray his party'. Sir Henry Campbell-Bannerman (1905–8) was an indolent Cambridge classicist who preferred French novels to English political biography, and managed more on a mixture of shrewdness and niceness than on historical thought or erudition.

H. H. Asquith (1908–16) had absorbed a lot of history, as his smoothly purring brain absorbed almost everything, and could have easily held a historical conversational candle to Attlee or Macmillan, as he frequently did to Churchill who was a young minister in his government. But he was no writer – except of personal letters to ladies, frequently penned with great fluency during Cabinet meetings over which he was presiding. Lloyd George (1916–22) made a lot of history, but he was always too much a man of the moment to be greatly influenced by historical lessons. In his oratory he preferred topographical imagery – 'the great peaks ... of honour, duty, patriotism and ... sacrifice' contrasted with 'the enervating valley' of selfishness – to historical analogy.

Bonar Law (1922–3) knew the works of Thomas Carlyle inside out, and his historical reading beyond the works of that 'sage of Chelsea', eclectic though these were, was remarkably thorough and wide for a commercially educated accountant of rather rigid views. Stanley Baldwin (1923, 1924–9 and 1935–7) loved the rhythms of the English countryside and had a strong sense of continuity, but although he claimed (not wholly plausibly) to have been most influenced by the writings of Sir Henry Maine, his favourite historical author was probably the somewhat more middle-brow Arthur Bryant.

Ramsay MacDonald (1924 and 1929–35) attached considerable importance to political theory, but found more parallels in biological evolution than historical precedent for the form of socialism that he wished to introduce. Neville Chamberlain's (1937–40) practical and somewhat intolerant mind did not much require the support or the recreation of history.

Nevertheless, I think that on balance this group of early twentieth-century Prime Ministers knew more history than do their successors of the last decade or so, and they were certainly buttressed by other ministers – Lloyd George by Curzon, Milner and H. A. L. Fisher, MacDonald by Haldane and Sydney Webb, the early Baldwin by Churchill and L. S. Amery, the later Baldwin and Neville Chamberlain by Halifax and Duff Cooper, to take some random examples – who knew incomparably more than do those who are ministers or likely ministers today. The case for secular decline can therefore be regarded as substantially if not overwhelmingly proved for Britain. And the early

254

part of the twentieth century was already a significant decline from the habits which had prevailed in the nineteenth century.

What about other countries? First the United States. The American pattern of decline is much less clear. The early Virginian and Massachusetts Presidents are naturally thought of as gentlemen of eighteenth-century squirearchical culture, as at home amongst their books as in the saddle and the open air. And of Jefferson, the two Adams, Madison and probably Washington, this must be allowed, although with the exception of John Quincy Adams's diary their literary output was exiguous, even if, in the cases of Jefferson and Madison at least, its constitutional impact was vast. Their minds were set in a constitutional and historical mould by the objective circumstances of creative flux in which they lived. James Monroe does not seem to me to be in the same category of library culture, although his doctrine has echoed down a century or more.

Nor were the mid-century Presidents between Andrew Jackson and Abraham Lincoln. Lincoln acquired his considerable historical knowledge rather in the way that Harry Truman did seventy years later: through solitary, sometimes unselective reading more than through structured teaching or the interplay of ideas with members of a group of equals who were interested and informed. But as a composer of memorable prose and an importer of the sweep of history into oratory he was clearly in a different category from Truman. Truman's 'the buck stops here' and 'if you can't stand the heat get out of the kitchen' are good adages but not exactly of the quality of 'four score and seven years ago our fathers called forth upon this continent a new nation ...'

After Lincoln we have to wait until the turn of the century before we get back into significant historical hills let alone into the commanding peaks of knowledge. I suppose the twentieth century might be very crudely categorized by saying that Woodrow Wilson knew a vast amount, that Theodore Roosevelt (in a not very applied way), Truman (in a plodding way), and Kennedy (perhaps more through associates than by detailed study) knew quite a lot; that Taft, Hoover, Lyndon Johnson, Nixon and perhaps Carter knew some, Coolidge and Ford a little, and that Harding, Eisenhower and Reagan have practised a very rigid economy of historical reading. Bush ought to have picked up some at Phillips' Andover Academy and at Yale, but I do not think it was very profound, and he certainly cannot be counted a master of structured historical or any other sort of prose.

In Europe I have mostly found the French to be more interested and better informed than the Germans and most others, although with the Belgians and some Italians inclining more to the French category. Both President Giscard and President Mitterrand combine knowledge and interest, although the former has more detail and the latter, like de Gaulle in this respect, more sweep. De Gaulle indeed was as dominated by a sense of historical sweep and destiny as was Churchill. Helmut Kohl looks likely as the Chancellor of German unity to make a lot of history, but has no great interest in it as a study. But nor did Helmut Schmidt, who was the most constructive statesman of my time as President of the European Commission. I think that for someone of Schmidt's generation the immediate past constituted a noxious barrier which discouraged him from retrospective peering. Adenauer almost was history. He was first Mayor of Cologne in 1917, forty-six years before he ceased to be Chancellor. He was first mooted as Reichskanzler in 1921. Even so I do not think he was a great amateur of history.

Does this catalogue tell us much about how desirable a qualification for statesmanship is historical knowledge? On the whole, and surprisingly cautiously, I think it can be said that those with knowledge and interest performed better than those without, with, on the European side of the Atlantic, Lloyd George and Schmidt providing notable exceptions one way, and Eden a less certain one the other. On America I am more hesitant to pronounce.

Why should this be so? The most obvious explanation is that history helps to lengthen perspective and by so doing discourages excessive partisanship. This must, however, be qualified by saying that it applies to a reasonably detached study of history and not to living in its shadow with an obsessive concentration. No communities are more difficult to bring together – Northern Ireland, Cyprus – than those where the contemplation of ancient wrongs is a way of life. It could also be cited in contrary evidence that few politicians have been more short-sighted than the elegant biographer Harold Nicolson, with his five switches of party, or more partisan than were the great constitutional historians A. V. Dicey and William Anson at the time of the Parliament Act of 1911. I suspect it is more that historical knowledge stems from a mixture of curiosity and a generally well-stocked mind, and that those with these attributes are better equipped than those without.

There has been another recent development of possible beneficial importance: this is the enormous growth of memoir writing. It applies on both sides of the Atlantic. Of the eleven British Prime Ministers between 1880 and 1940 none of them wrote anything approaching full-scale memoirs. Balfour wrote a fragment of autobiography and Lloyd George a major *pièce justificative* about his stewardship of World War I, but not an autobiography. Of the nine Prime Ministers since 1940, only Edward Heath and Mrs Thatcher, both said to be busy writing or in the latter case being written for, have been silent.

In the United States there were twelve Presidents between 1880 and 1945. Three of them (Theodore Roosevelt, Coolidge and Hoover) did write memoirs. But since 1945, of the eight who have gone from the highest office, no one has remained silent except for John Kennedy who obviously had no choice. Even George Bush has already produced an interim volume of autobiography, memorable, if for nothing else, for its sole reference to Britain, which was a statement that 'Barbara and I met with Prime Minister Margaret Thatcher and her husband, Norman.'

The inevitability of the political memoir has become a fact of political life. This may not produce much good literature, or even in some cases satisfactory narrative reading, but it does, I believe, make the prospective authors a little more aware of how their actions may look in longer perspective and of their comparative performance *vis-à-vis* others who will be working at the memoir face alongside them. And the effects of this are more likely to be good than bad.

I therefore give my vote in favour of history and memoir writing rather than in favour of Henry Ford's dictum that history is bunk, but I do so with suitable caution and reservation. What I really believe is that those with curiosity, whatever their educational and occupational backgrounds, are bound to have interest in and acquire some knowledge about the past; and that those without it are likely to be dull men and uncomprehending rulers.

Oxford's Appeal to Americans

This is based on an article written for The American
Oxonian *magazine in March 1989.*

I am writing this article on the evening of Easter Sunday, 1989,
twenty-four hours after attending my first University Boat
Race for thirty years. On the previous occasion in 1959 I watched
from the Hammersmith riverside house of A. P. Herbert, author,
musical comedy librettist, and the last MP for Oxford until the
abolition of the university seats in the House of Commons in
1950. He and I were currently engaged in a joint enterprise to
liberalize the law relating to literary censorship.

The three-decade interval makes it clear that I was not and
am not a rowing man. But this year I gladly accepted an invitation to go on the Oxford launch and follow a few yards behind
the umpire's craft, which was itself accused of being too close
behind the Cambridge boat – the Oxford boat, after the first
half-mile, being happily outside its reach. The pressure for my
presence arose out of the attendance for the first time of the
Cambridge Chancellor, Prince Philip. I could hardly be expected
to balance him in rank (Oxford, despite its more royalist history,

has been consistently faithful to political, non-princely and elected Chancellors since the eighteenth century), but at least I would have prevented the Oxford crew being bereft of any official support in the event of defeat, and in victory was able to commiserate with Prince Philip (who had elided gracefully from Cambridge partisan to independent royal personage) for his having to present the Beefeater Gin Trophy (sponsorship seems unavoidable these days) to the rival crew.

Oxford on this occasion slipped through to victory rather against the expectations. But as it was the fourteenth Oxford victory over the past fifteen years it could hardly be regarded as an underdog's triumph. Underdoggery is certainly not one of Oxford's characteristics, although it must be said that in this specialized sport of propelling boats through the water, Oxford, in spite of the triumphs of the 1970s and 1980s, has never since the beginning of the event in 1829 been ahead of Cambridge. It has, however, been consistently ahead in other concours, such as producing Prime Ministers, Archbishops of Canterbury and Lord Chancellors.

Our traditional role as a repository and guardian of humanistic learning set in an almost unique framework of man-made beauty remains intact. The Bodleian Library, judged by a mix of the three criteria of range of contents, interest of buildings and intensity of use, has no earthly rival. Together with its outstation, Gibbs's domed Radcliffe Camera, which is the centrepiece of the Oxford skyline, the Sheldonian Theatre, which was Wren's first architectural design, the Theatre's near contemporary the Old Ashmo-lean, the Clarendon Building which Hawksmoor did fifty years afterwards, and the late mediaeval Divinity School, it constitutes the most remarkable group of university buildings in the world (the glory of Cambridge is almost all in the individual colleges), and is less spoilt than it was a generation ago because of the substantial exclusion of motor cars from Radcliffe Square.

To set out this list of unmatched physical assets (buttressed of course by all the individual quality of the colleges) sometimes arouses in my mind the fear that we might cease to live up to them and become a British version of a Hofburg without the Habsburgs. That has certainly not happened up to the present. The fame of Oxford alumni has survived at least as well as the fabric of its buildings. In the past hundred years out of a total of twenty-one home Prime Ministers, eleven (from Gladstone to Mrs Thatcher) have been Oxonians, as well as a clutch of over-seas ones, including Indira Gandhi, Benazir Bhutto, and the last two Australians (the second surprisingly buttressed in that almost aggressively independent country by a third of his Cabinet), as well as the King of Norway and the President of the Federal Republic of Germany. There is as yet no American President, but with five current US Senators, including one or two who are distinctly *papabile,* there is always hope.[1]

Nor, strong though is Oxford's tradition as a nursery of government, need those who dislike politicians feel oppressively isolated at a reassembly of their university. Amongst my electing body of Convocation I could feel as at home in my rather unde-served capacity of President of the Royal Society of Literature as in that of a former government minister. Even with Evelyn Waugh (for my money the greatest English novelist of the mid-twentieth century) several decades dead, the current Oxonian

---

[1] Writing in 1989, I did not include Governors, which limits the degree of prescience that I can claim.

literary roll of Graham Greene, Anthony Powell, Iris Murdoch, Kingsley Amis, William Golding and Vidia Naipaul is not bad.

Alumni are of course necessarily products of the past, and the more distinguished they are, unless athletes, mathematicians or pop singers, the more likely is that past to be fairly remote. What shape is the university in today? Is it a substantially different place from that which most Rhodes scholars, whether of the 1930s, 1950s, 1970s or intervening decades, have known? In so far as it is, are the changes for good or ill? And if for good, how is this reconcilable with the fact that Oxford has suddenly had to throw itself much more than ever before upon the generosity of its old members and others who are well disposed?

Compared with the time that I and others up to fifteen years younger were undergraduates, there are three major changes. First, Oxford in the post-war decades created a major new scientific university, alongside yet integrated with the traditional university. Before World War II, while Oxford was a more successful seminary for the young who wished to become famous, Cambridge undoubtedly conducted more vigorous probes on and beyond the frontier of knowledge. That latter difference is no longer so.

Second, there has been the injection of over 3000 graduate students into the Oxford firmament. In my days the University was made up of undergraduates and dons. When they ceased to be undergraduates a small number of the academically inclined became fellows, a handful at All Souls, rather more of their own colleges, a few elsewhere. The rest went away from Oxford to make their way in the world. To become a graduate student was almost unheard of. Now a D. Phil. is virtually a *sine qua non* for an academic job, and many who are not academically directed take this or a lesser second degree while they are

262

thinking what else to do.

This change has brought at least one substantial benefit to Oxford. It has made it a more international university. Graduate students are frequently not indigenous plants. When I addressed the Christ Church graduate common-room last term I discovered that only a small minority had been undergraduates at the House. Some were from elsewhere in Oxford, a sizeable group were from Cambridge, and a bigger one from overseas, including a number of the 770 Americans currently enrolled in the university.

Nevertheless, Oxford, so far as its student body is concerned, remains predominantly an undergraduate university. One of the things it does best is instil into the young during a first degree course a critical articulateness that makes them outstandingly employable inside or outside the disciplines they have been taught.

The composition of the said 'young' has of course undergone some considerable change over this span of thirty or so years, but certainly not a greater change, indeed arguably less, than has been the case with the foremost American universities. Women have become 40 per cent of the undergraduate body, although they account for a very much smaller proportion of the dons. None of the former male colleges remains single sex. Oriel, in 1986, was the last to change. Amongst the women's colleges Somerville and St Hilda's have remained exclusively female. One of their arguments, which undoubtedly has some force, is that this helps to keep open channels through which women can become dons. It is the case that in now mixed Lady Margaret Hall, for example, the rush to balance for a time almost closed up female teaching recruitment. In any event there is a widespread view that a university of thirty-five colleges ought to have

263

room for a little variety.[2]

In addition, both the standards demanded for entry and the final examination performance have become higher. At the top end there has not been much change, but the intellectual passengers have, I suppose, been largely eliminated. This applies, I discovered rather to my surprise yesterday, even to the Oxford boat. In the ten years from 1976 to 1985, when Oxford won all ten races and beat the all-time record in 1984, five of its crew members got firsts and two-thirds of the rest got seconds. There were also five who later became D. Phils. The pass-degree blue is a dying species. On the other hand the school (and hence the social) provenance of undergraduates has not changed as much as might have been expected, or as perhaps ought to have happened. The independent (i.e. prep) school proportion in the university as a whole is now at about the same 50 per cent level as it was in Balliol (which was different from the average, but not uniquely or overwhelmingly so) in my day fifty years ago.

How does this picture, which is substantially that of a self-confident and successful university evolving quite fast but without breaking the shell of the more desirable parts of its ancient heritage, square with Oxford's present urgent need for money? I will try to deal with this by answering three questions. First, from and for what does the need arise? Second, cannot the wealth of the colleges solve the problem? Third, what will the money, when raised, pay for, and what guarantee is there that it will not just be

---

[2] Since this passage was written the Somerville governing body has decided it wishes to become mixed. Lady Margaret Hall has achieved marked success in its mixed status. The number of colleges has increased from thirty-five to thirty-six. And the problems of being a single-sex college in a mixed university have perhaps become more acute.

a form of concealed subsidy to the British Treasury?

Oxford, which was a wholly privately financed university until 1919 and largely so until 1939, had become by the mid-seventies like other British (and European) universities, overwhelmingly publicly financed. The University, as such, has very little endowment. In the past ten years the government grant in real terms has been steadily squeezed so that it is now down by over 10 per cent. As a result posts (including some of the most famous ones) have to be left temporarily unfilled, research facilities, the cost of which inevitably escalate much faster than the rate of inflation, become inadequate to attract and retain the best people; and the great collections of the Bodleian, the Ashmolean and the other University museums cannot be maintained in the state they deserve. Oxford, if it is to remain amongst the handful of world-class universities (almost all the rest are American) needs to supplement its government income with an endowment which, while modest by the standards of Harvard or Stanford, is large by traditional European standards.

The thirty-five colleges vary greatly in their assets. Seven or eight are comparatively rich, although none of these has wealth comparable with that of Trinity College, Cambridge. These richer ones already subsidize to some quite considerable extent the poorer colleges. They are also currently helping the university and it is hoped will do more in response to the appeal. The colleges are responsible for housing their students and for much of their teaching, as well as for the often very expensive upkeep of their irreplaceable buildings. They have a great deal more to do than just maintaining their High Tables. It is a complete illusion that they could, if they were so minded, carry the needs of the University on their backs.

It is important to get the balance right. The colleges necessarily have more intimate contact with their members and therefore easier access to their generosity, but for the moment the needs of the University are still more urgent. Furthermore the University is essential to the colleges. It was there before them, and it provides an essential framework for their existence and justification. No college is an island. But nor in relation to the responsibilities are they treasure islands selfishly harbouring their wealth.

Oxford has received the most specific assurances from the government that success in fund-raising will not be used as a reason for providing less public money in the future. This is enshrined not merely in the promises of Cabinet ministers but in the statutory language of the Education Reform Act of 1988. Any alternative government is committed to a policy of somewhat greater generosity towards universities, although not sufficiently so, in my view, as to render the current appeal in any way unnecessary. The Labour Party has not traditionally been hostile to Oxford's needs and private assets. Too many of its ministers have been educated there.

Whatever the political future, it therefore seems overwhelmingly likely that Oxford will both need the money and be free to spend it for the high purposes of maintaining and developing a university which belongs to the world and not merely to Britain, whose research is of the highest quality, whose alumni leave their mark in as many different countries as in different fields of human endeavour, and which does it around an architectural core which rarely fails to hold a place in the memories and affections of those who have once experienced it.

The British University Pattern

This piece began life as the Open University's Annual Lecture for 1988, but has been substantially changed over the past five years.

During the past decade I have become more closely engaged with British universities than I ever previously thought likely. I enjoyed my undergraduate time starting nearly fifty-five years ago, but even without the war I do not think it would have occurred to me to do a post-graduate degree. In this I was like most of my contemporaries. After the war I played with the idea of becoming a university teacher but not very seriously, and never did.

I then passed thirty years during which my main contact with universities was to address political meetings in them. Then in the 1970s, I began to collect honorary degrees, partly, I think, because Senates, Vice-Chancellors and Principals thought that when I was President of the European Commission I could unlock the door to Brussels grants and research contracts. But I comfort myself that it cannot have been entirely that, for some of the doctorates came before and some of them came afterwards. But whatever the motives, I found the honours agreeable and

267

the practical result a series of day-long (or sometimes twenty-four hour) excursions to a large number of universities in England, Scotland, Ireland, Wales, America and the continent of Europe. This honorary degree phase produced a wide but highly superficial perspective of universities.

It was only in the 1980s that I began to replace this with a less bird's eye view. In 1982 I returned to the House of Commons as MP for the Hillhead division of Glasgow, which has a strong claim to be the most higher-education-dominated constituency in the United Kingdom. Apart from the major and ancient University of Glasgow, Hillhead contains several important teaching hospitals, three units of the Medical Research Council, the biggest College of Education in Scotland, and a number of important specialized institutions, of which the Charles Rennie Mackintosh-designed Glasgow School of Art is the most famous, with the University of Strathclyde immediately on its eastern border. The socio-geographical shape of Glasgow, or put less pompously the attraction of its West End, is also such that a high proportion of both universities' staff live close to the campuses in a way that is not true of, for example, the universities of Manchester and Salford. The net result was that the Hillhead constituency of 1982 (since then diluted by enlargement) had by the somewhat mechanistic measuring rods of the census the most highly educated population in Britain.

The more relevant result for the purposes of this lecture is that my five years there greatly concentrated my mind upon the problems of universities. This was compounded by my being elected Chancellor of Oxford in March 1987. The Chancellor of Oxford has traditionally been more a supernumerary great officer of state – from Cromwell through Wellington, Salisbury and Curzon to Macmillan – than a bearer of a banner

268

of educational knowledge and reform. Even so, it gave me a remarkable brace of university vantage points to be Chancellor of the 'dreaming spires' and MP for the West End of Glasgow.

It was too good to last. In the strictest sense I never occupied them both at the same time. There was an overlap of three months between victory on the banks of the Thames and defeat on the banks of the Clyde. But Oxford installation takes place on a leisurely time-scale. In 1925 Lord Milner died in the interval. I merely suffered the lesser fate of being defeated in Hillhead by Mr George Galloway. Twelve days before I was given the statutes, keys and seal of Oxford, I had lost the Glasgow travel warrants and rights of admission to the House of Commons. It was a good lesson in the even-handedness of fate. Nevertheless, the juxtaposition gave me an exceptional opportunity to see the problems of British universities in the 1980s from north to south of the Scottish border, through the eyes of what some would regard as the proud peacock of Oxford strutting on its over manicured lawns, past the 441-year-old eagle of Glasgow sitting in its Gilmorehill eyrie, to the enthusiastic young pouter pigeon of Strathclyde, hatched thirty years ago out of a college of science and technology.

They are as different as any three universities to be found within the British university spectrum, but they all suffered in the 1980s from a decade of debilitating financial restriction, with cut imposed upon cut and squeeze upon squeeze. The government policies of the 1980s towards universities were, I believe, the most shortsighted that Britain has had the misfortune to encounter. Nearly every previous administration of whatever party had been responsible for some major advance – some creative act – in our academic framework. That one alone was distinguished for creating nothing and for inflicting great damage on teaching, research, morale and students.

The charitable view is that it simply stemmed from penny-pinching and an inability to grasp how much long-term damage may be done by the short-term saving of very limited sums of money. But the determination never to let the patient recover from a squeeze before inflicting a fresh one, the willingness to impose redundancies in the way that cost as much money as they saved, and the accompaniment of financial restrictions with increased control from the centre for its own sake, made one fear that there was an admixture of less material and more ideologi-cal motives: an anti-intellectualism; a disapproval of the universities as not being willing to embrace every excess of the enterprise culture; and a dislike of them as bastions of indepen-dent thought and potential allies of such dangerously radical institutions as the Church and the BBC and even the House of Lords.

For the moment, however, I shall not pursue such subversive thoughts, but merely abstract from them the conclusion that the restriction of public money made a major impact on all our universities during the 1980s, and that this is unlikely to be suffi-ciently or quickly reversed for these not to be major considerations in any view of the position and prospect of British universities today.

Before dealing with that prospect, however, I turn for a time to the past. In England, although not of course in Scotland, the Oxford and Cambridge duopoly was complete until *circa* 1830, when University College, London, King's College, London, and Durham were all established within four years. Oxford and Cambridge had been there in some form since the twelfth century, and were unchallenged in Britain until the eighteenth century when they began to slip badly down the European league for knowledge and enquiry. At the end of the eighteenth century Edinburgh University, founded in 1583, was of higher intellectual repute. Edinburgh, although it had become a fashionable magnet by the end of the eighteenth century, attracting such metropolitan Whigs as Palmerston and Lord John Russell, and was the main centre of the Scottish Enlightenment, was the youngest of the Scottish universities until the twentieth-century wave of Dundee, Stirling, Strathclyde and Heriot-Watt. St Andrews (founded in 1411), Glasgow (1451) and Aberdeen (1494) were all earlier. And Glasgow could claim at least a share of the Scottish Enlightenment. It was in the cloisters there, and not in Edinburgh, that Adam Smith, even though he had been an East of Scotland boy, paced up and down when evolving the theory of the division of labour for *The Wealth of Nations*. Trinity College, Dublin, founded in 1592, completed the pre-Victorian Britannic university constellation. There had nearly been a third English university at Stamford in the fourteenth century and at Warrington, of all surprising places, in the eighteenth century, but they did not quite come off.

In the nineteenth century Oxford and Cambridge recovered their British pre-eminence, even if it took them substantially longer to remount the European intellectual ladder. Meanwhile, and particularly between 1870 and 1914, the English university scene was being modified, although not exactly transformed, by the modest beginning of the civic universities, the majority in the northern half of the country. Before 1870 the most significant developments were the decision of London University in 1858 to make eligible for its degrees those who were not members of its affiliated colleges, and the foundation of Owen's College, Manchester, in 1851. The first event made possible the gradual proliferation throughout the country of university colleges (almost all of which are now full universities), whose students were able to obtain degrees even though the institutions themselves could not grant them.

The second provided the nucleus out of which sprang Manchester University, the senior and still in many ways the preeminent English provincial one. The evolution here was a little complicated. In 1880 Victoria University was created. It was in Manchester but it over-arched colleges in Leeds and Liverpool. In 1903 this empire split up, Liverpool and Leeds became independent universities, and Manchester, retaining the title of the Victoria University was reconstituted. By 1914 they each had about 1000 students, Manchester rather more.

Another typical evolution was that at Birmingham, where Mason College was founded in 1870 and became a university in 1900. This was very much the creation of Joseph Chamberlain, the father of both Austen and Neville Chamberlain but a more striking politician than either, one of the great destructive geniuses of British politics (he first put the Liberal Party out of effective power for twenty years and then the Conservative Party out for seventeen years), who became its first Chancellor and very firmly appointed its first Principal. He gave Birmingham a workaday 'Brummagem' approach, by which it has not subsequently been bound, concentrating on science, particularly engineering and mining, as well as brewing and commerce. It too had about 1000 students by World War I.

Bristol had a university college from 1876 and became a university in 1909. It was intellectually more widely based and pre-1914 had rather more students than Birmingham. Sheffield evolved from Firth College, founded in 1879, to a university in 1905. The University of Wales was created in 1902, a federation of the University Colleges of Aberystwyth (1872), Cardiff (1883)

272

and Bangor (1885); Swansea was added in 1920. Lampeter, although an Anglican seminary from 1822, and UWIST, which is the only university institution to have brought off a take-over bid for another, came after the last war. The pattern of dates is a remarkably regular one: a college created by local endeavour and subscription in the high period of civic pride and industrial prosperity which burgeoned forth in the brighter plumage of a university when Victorian self-help gave way to more opulent Edwardian display. But of course the numerical impact of this string of seven new universities was very limited. Their total intake in 1914 was barely more than 2000 a year – perhaps a quarter of 1 per cent of the population of relevant age.

There was a second wave of civic universities, which mostly remained as university colleges under the aegis of London University until after World War II: Southampton (which grew out of the Hartley Institute and became a University in 1952), Nottingham, Leicester, Exeter, Hull. Reading was half in this category, but a double exception because it was sponsored by Oxford not London, and because it became a full university in 1929, the only institution to receive such a charter between the wars. Newcastle, whose Armstrong College had been part of the University of Durham following its foundation in 1871, split from its older (but not ancient, contrary to frequent popular supposition) parent in 1963 and became an independent university, as did Dundee from St Andrews in 1966. By this time, however, the second wave of civic universities, and the fifth wave of British universities as a whole (the first wave being Oxford and Cambridge, the second the four old Scottish universities, the third Durham and London, and the fourth the Manchester, Birmingham, Bristol group plus Wales) was being overtaken by the sixth and post-the 1963 Robbins Report wave, which was half made up of Colleges of Advanced Technology turned from pumpkins into coaches by a touch of the Secretary of State's wand and half of 'green field' universities mostly established outside historic cities.

To recapitulate the late pre-Robbins position, however, there were then twenty-two universities in Great Britain (or twenty-three with Northern Ireland), of which the only one not so far mentioned is Keele, which was set up as an Oxford-inspired liberal arts college in North Staffordshire in 1947, with the then Master of Balliol becoming the first Principal, and which became a university on the eve of Robbins in 1962.

The 1960s took the number of universities up from twenty-three to forty-six, the proportion of admissions to 7.5 per cent of the population of relevant age, and provided a decade and more of vastly expanding employment and promotion prospects for the university teacher. This period now seems almost infinitely remote from the restrictive financial climate in which all British universities have lived for the past ten years.

Apart from the major broadening of the gate of entry to which this period of expansion led, it also produced a desirable loosening of the British university hierarchy. Oxford and Cambridge in their differing ways maintained their near duopoly of assumed English excellence for the first half of this century. There was of course major work done elsewhere, particularly perhaps in London, with its specialized schools of which the London School of Economics on the arts side was matched by a number of others in science and medicine. But, broadly speaking, the civic, provincial or red-brick universities were then seen by themselves and others alike as no more than subsidiary hills in a mountain complex of which the twin peaks were Oxford and Cambridge. Most undergraduates, certainly on the arts side, would have preferred to go to these latter two had not lack of money, or connection, or confidence, without exceptional scholarship-winning ability, put these institutions just outside their reach. And there followed from this limitation of reach a subsequent exclusion, with very few exceptions, from the highest ranks in the law, the public service, the Church, and perhaps less strongly a range of other occupations. There were notable professorial spans at Manchester, at Birmingham, in London and elsewhere. But a high proportion of those who achieved them either came from Oxford or Cambridge and went back to them, or went on to them, or both.

The American position (admittedly in a much bigger country) where the general pre-eminence of a few great universities existed alongside a patchwork made up of differing clusters of particular quality, seemed to me to be much better balanced. Over the twenty-five years, from, say, 1955, the English experience moved to some quite considerable extent in this direction, with apart from the continuing independent tradition of the Scottish constellation, universities like Manchester and Bristol, Warwick and Newcastle achieving very distinct styles, qualities, and pulls of their own, with no degradation of Oxford and Cambridge but a consequent and healthy dilution of their monopoly. But that era is, I fear, over. I at once accept and half regret that the beginning of my Chancellorship should have coincided almost exactly with the return of Oxford to major fund-raising. I accept it because there is no other way in which we can keep Oxford as one of the handful of world-class universities. Neither the present government (and maybe no future government) is going to enable us to compete with the vast and continuing endowments of Harvard and Stanford. And in our case we have the additional burden of keeping up matchless collections of books and manuscripts as well as expensive but irreplaceable buildings.

If Oxford were to fail to stay in that league I do not think that any other British university would do so. It is now the biggest British university except for the federated ones of London and Wales. While more may not be worse, bigness is clearly not in itself excellence, but it is nevertheless remarkable that Oxford, which pre-war was barely two-thirds the size of Cambridge, should now be marginally bigger. It is largely the result of the grafting on of what is virtually a new scientific university in the past fifty years. I do not think that any other European university would do so either, in spite of the ancient fame of Bologna, or the central intellectual position of Paris, or the traditional teutonic authority of Heidelberg, Göttingen or Tübingen: maybe Tokyo, maybe Toronto, maybe more doubtfully Sydney might compete, but if Oxford were to withdraw I doubt if there would be anywhere outside the United States that could claim to be in the first six or eight. I think that would be bad not merely for Oxford, but for Britain and indeed for the whole world balance.

I am therefore a resolute fund-raiser. But I am not a wholly joyous one for three reasons: it over-elevates the position of the rich. They have been far more courted and cultivated – this is no doubt part of the purpose of the enterprise – in Thatcherite Britain than they were in Churchillian or Wilsonite or Heathite Britain. There is also a danger of making universities and colleges too money-centred with fund-raising ability too much of a qualification for appointment to high academic office. There is the additional danger that it may reverse the highly desirable trend towards competing and more dispersed poles of excellence which I noted earlier. Ths concept of making universities more dependent on private fund-raising is certainly not a radical or an

276

iconoclastic one. It is a deeply conservative (with a small 'c') one for it underpins the existing hierarchy. The competitive ability of universities and/or colleges to raise money from their alumni is an almost direct function of the rich undergraduate-attracting status of the various institutions a generation or two ago.

I therefore have no doubt about my duty in relation to fund-raising as Chancellor of the University of Oxford. But I have a certain amount of general caution, I do not want 'the idea of a university', to use Cardinal John Henry Newman's famous phrase, to become that of locating the nearest potential benefactor and squeezing him until the pips squeak.

A Selection of Political Biographies

A Daily Telegraph *article of 1988.*

G ood biography as a general rule dates much more quickly than does good fiction. Perhaps this is simply because it is a lower art form, and therefore, like perfectly decent but undistinguished wine, suffers rather than benefits from age.

In any event I am convinced that it is so. No one who has ever liked Dickens or Dostoevsky, Jane Austen or George Eliot is likely to find them dated on a return visit. Yet the general run of good-quality pre-1914 biography is not much read or appreciated today. Maybe the highest peaks survive intact. In this category of outstanding Victorian biography there would, I suppose, be strong support for Froude's *Carlyle,* G. O. Trevelyan's *Macaulay* and Morley's *Gladstone.* Yet I do not think that either Trevelyan or Froude survive as well as the subjects' own non-biographical writing, and Morley's smooth-flowing three-volume narrative does not capture the Grand Old Man's massive inner turbulence, which made him so quintessential a figure of his age, nearly as well as do Gladstone's own *Diaries*.

If we step down a rank, however, which means that we are still dealing with works that were greeted as highly competent and comprehensive portraits when they appeared, we are into a pace and style of treatment that seems as remote today as a hansom cab in a pea soup fog. When over forty years ago I first read books like A. G. Gardiner's *Sir William Harcourt* and J. A. Spender's *Campbell-Bannerman* I found them useful and enjoyable. Now, however, I would much rather re-read a chapter (in the course of looking up an incident) in the present Lord Moran's *C.B.* (1973) just as I prefer Robert Blake's *Disraeli* to Moneypenny and Buckle's six volumes. On Harcourt, who was an engaging and rumbustious figure sometimes known as 'the great gladiator', there is nothing much to switch to, which makes him one of the rare undeveloped sites available to a young biographer in the overcrowded world of today.

Despite the Disraeli example the difference is not just a question of length. It is much more one of angle of view. The old tombstone lives, in Lytton Strachey's words 'those two fat volumes with which it is our custom to commemorate the dead', mostly unrolled the career of the commemorated one with political respect and personal discretion. An occasional short chapter on his literary taste or country pursuits was about the nearest one got to inquisitive dissection of character. It is as impossible to imagine Alistair Home's *Macmillan* being published fifty or sixty years ago, as it would be to imagine the *Life of Sir Michael Hicks Beach* by his daughter being published today.

Was it Strachey himself who was most responsible for the change? He was certainly contemptuous of the prevailing style, tried to miniaturize it as much as any Japanese woman ever did to constrict the size of her feet, and believed that in achieving this by a preference for aphorism over fact he could make each small picture into an iconoclastic work of art. In a sense he was as sterile as he was brilliant. He had remarkably few imitators. And, with a short pause for breath, the bland multi-volume portraits resumed their sway. Clustered around 1932, the year of Strachey's death, were Ronaldshay's *Curzon*, Spender and Cyril Asquith's *Asquith,* and Mrs Dugdale's *Balfour,* all of them in the strict tradition of the *genre.*

Yet Strachey had shot a destructive arrow into the established school, the poison of which spread slowly but surely. Eventually, when assisted by the wartime and post-war paper shortage, it did so fatally. In the 1940s and early 1950s the tombstones got much smaller (G. M. Young's *Stanley Baldwin,* Keith Feiling's *Neville Chamberlain,* even Harold Nicolson's *George V* managed to do it in single not over-gross volumes). And when later a taste for books of 300,000 words and more was re-imported from America, where there has been a foolish trend to value biographies, as though they were fat cattle, by dead weight on the hoof, they were of a very different format and content. Simultaneous multi-volume publication was out and a mixture of scandalous revelation and psychological analysis was in.

Far less, therefore, than in the case not merely of fiction but of most other literary forms, do unchanging standards apply to political biography. I consequently think it best to confine my choice to the 'moderns' – mostly post-1945 with only a brief glance back to illustrate the change of habit.

First, J. L. Garvin's *Joseph Chamberlain* as a good illustration of the tradition: spacious, sympathetic, even adulatory, but well written by a professional (much better than by a relation, which was only too frequent at that period), with even a touch of pace. The only trouble was that he never finished it and left the last two volumes (of five) to be done by Julian Amery over twenty years later.

Next, in view of what I have said about Strachey, *Eminent Victorians* must be included. None of the four subjects were politicians, of course, but they all, soldier, headmaster, worldly prelate, lady with the lamp, were sufficiently wily public figures to qualify for inclusion in the category. From the 1930s I chose Churchill's *Great Contemporaries*. It wears remarkably well. The style is a bit florid, and he is much better on British politicians than on either foreigners or Bernard Shaw and T. E. Lawrence. The essays on Asquith, Balfour and Curzon each contain phrases that are as illuminating as they are memorable.

Moving on into the 1950s, I regard Philip Magnus's *Gladstone* as a very good book, in no way definitive, but the work of a sensitive architect pulling together into a compact shape what had become a house almost submerged in a sprawl of outbuildings. Although substantially longer, Blake's *Disraeli* deserves to be put in the same category, even though he had far less sympathy with Disraeli as a character that Magnus did with Gladstone.

John Grigg's *magnus opus* opened in 1973 with the promise of being the long missing (but not for want of other people trying) great biography of *Lloyd George*. Now twenty years later he is showing signs of emulating Garvin on Chamberlain (or, from across the Atlantic, Schlesinger on Roosevelt) and leaving us stranded half-way across the river, three fine arches of the bridge built but not much early prospect of reaching dry land. He has been particularly good on what one would expect to elude him most; the socio-topographical background of Lloyd George's North Wales life.

I end with two books which, although not in the least malevolently written, have greatly enhanced the reputations of the authors while putting their subjects through all the (fortunately posthumous) rigours of having their portrait painted in the style of Sutherland. John Campbell's *F. E. Smith* (1983) and Ben Pimlott's *Hugh Dalton* (also 1983, although supplemented by two volumes of his diaries in 1985 and 1986), are both memorable and definitive. They skilfully extract the treasures and seal up the tombs, probably never to be opened again.

The Maxim Gun of the
English Language

*This essay is based on a combination of a speech at an OUP
lunch for the publication of the new edition of the* Oxford
English Dictionary *and of an article in the* Independent
Magazine.

A hundred and ten years ago James Murray started serious
work on the first edition of the *Oxford English Dictionary.* It
was part of a great late-Victorian wave of collating information
in a much more systematic way than had hitherto been done.
Leslie Stephen began producing the *Dictionary of National Biography*
in 1888. *Who's Who* first appeared in something approaching its
modern form in 1897.

Murray's work took longer to mature. He began publication
in 1884, but it was 1928 and thirteen years after his own death
before the project was complete. There was a substantial supplement published in 1972, and in 1989 a complete new edition
with 5000 new words and a total of over 21,000 pages in twenty
separate volumes was launched upon the world at the modest
price of £1500.

The period since Murray began has to a remarkable extent coincided with two superficially contradicting developments. The first has been the decline of British power in the world. The second has been the advance of the English language.

In 1879 the Empire was approaching its zenith, Queen Victoria, to whom the first edition was dedicated, had recently been made an empress by Disraeli, on top of being a queen. Hardly another empire was proclaimed until Jean Bédel Bokassa rather overreached himself in the Central African Republic a hundred years later. The Zulu War, the epitome of an imperialist adventure, was also being fought in 1879 and Rorke's Drift and Isandhlwana engraved themselves on the history of British bravery and incompetence. More significantly, Britain was still just ahead of Germany and the United States as an industrial power and the leading exporter in the world. Within a decade or so, however, the apogee was past, and it soon became downhill all the way for British imperial and industrial refulgence.

The language, on the other hand, supported by the *Oxford English Dictionary*, has gone from strength to strength. If the agents of the old imperialism sometimes advanced with a Bible in one hand and a bottle of whisky in the other, their descendants have replaced these insignia with the OED and a glass of British Council wine. Of course we have been lucky in this linguistic context in having the United States as an immensely powerful ally. Like Blücher at the battle of Waterloo, it may have arrived on the scene a little late in the day but its intervention has been even more decisive than was that of the Prussians in 1815.

The French were in both cases the victims of afternoon reinforcements, and I always felt a good deal of sympathy when I observed close up, and suffered some inconvenience from, their determined rearguard action to hold the European Community as the last international organization that was a Francophone bastion. With Britain alone they might at least have hoped to draw a linguistic war. But against Britain and North America, not to mention Australasia, most of Africa, and the curious influence of India – which is at once a great reservoir of English-speaking millions and the potential breeding ground of a new language that has some but by no means all of the characteristics of metropolitan English – the French, allied with the Québecois, the Maghreb, most of the Sahara, and hardly anybody else, are sadly outgunned.

How sullenly resentful the British would have been had it been the other way round: if Creole influence had crept up from New Orleans and that of New France down from Detroit and the heartland of the United States had become Francophone, and that as a result French became the twentieth-century international language of commerce and summits and airlines as well as the nineteenth-century language of diplomacy and gastronomy and sleeping cars.

This emphatically did not happen. An Air France pilot landing a Concorde at Charles de Gaulle airport is supposed to talk to ground control in English. And a former French Ambassador to the United Nations is alleged to have lost his place as chairman of the late 1980s-instituted weekly lunch of the five permanent Security Council members at least partly because he took his rules too much *au pied de la lettre* and tried to talk to his colleagues in French. The British Ambassador, who got the job in his place, did not mind, but the American, the Russian and the Chinese Ambassadors did.

But whatever had happened in America we would have had in the OED a priceless weapon of attack or defence. As Belloc wrote:

> Whatever happens, we have got
> The Maxim gun, and they have not.

which, modified to adjust to the new imperialism, I render (with some sacrifice of the not very poetic original rhythm) as:

> For we have got
> The OED, and they have not.

And as from 1989, moreover, we have got the OED Mark II, which modern weapon is not only formidable against our linguistic enemies, but more surprisingly is not rivalled by the intellectual armaments industry of our principal ally. The production of the Dictionary must be almost the only field of university endeavour (except for living amongst mediaeval and baroque buildings, which is not exactly a field of endeavour) where Oxford is not challenged by Harvard or any other of the great American universities.

The price paid is perhaps that when the name Oxford is mentioned throughout the educated English-speaking world it is the Dictionary that comes to mind at least as quickly as the University. If a poll were conducted from Seattle to Singapore and from Auckland to Accra as to which was the more indispensable cultural asset to the world, I would be a little uneasy during the compilation of the results. But, of course, the question would be even more meaningless than most opinion poll questions, for the Dictionary would not exist without the Oxford University Press, and the Press would not exist without the University.

Croquet Taken Too Seriously

This slight essay was first published as a Spectator *review of* The Queen of Games *by Nicky Smith (Weidenfeld and Nicolson).*

Ionce had a long audience with the late Emperor of Japan. We had obviously both been concerned to find subjects to keep us going. I had been told that he had written thirteen books, mainly on marine biology. I endeavoured to 'show awareness' as editors encourage political writers to do, but he deflected my compliments, at once modestly and grandly. 'No, no,' he said, 'I do not write them myself. I employ scholars to do that.'

He, in return, seemed to have been told that my main private occupation was playing croquet, and with immense politeness had absorbed a good deal about the game. Ms Nicky Smith's current work was not available to him, although he, or his Court Chamberlain, had become as well informed as if they had followed closely her regular contributions to *Country Life* under the appropriate pseudonym of Arthur Mallet. The only trouble was that he appeared to think that I was a world-class croquet player. I could not tell him that I employed professionals to win championships, and I felt it would have been an anti-climax to say that my experience was mostly confined to post-prandial foursomes, often on roughish ground, which was best compensated for by making the hoops a little wider than regulation, after weekend country lunch parties. So both our subjects were founded on elements of misapprehension.

Nevertheless, I did spend a considerable amount of time in the 1960s and 1970s – more so than I do now – on the croquet lawn. This was partly because I often played on my own, having discovered that it was a good form of patience. These solitary sessions could take the form of seeing in how few strokes one could get round the long course of ten hoops and the stick, and sometimes, if everything went right, achieving it in under twenty. This was quite good practice discipline, although I always disliked being made to play with others the bastard game of golf croquet with its one stroke a go as opposed to the full game of roquets, croquets and the possibility of long breaks.

More frequently, however, I made my patience take the form of the full game but playing all four balls myself, which at least avoided the tedium of waiting for others. The disadvantages were the difficulty of remembering what point in the course they had each reached, the curious fact that one's loyalties became attached to red and yellow, or less frequently to black and blue, which made it difficult to try equally hard with the unfavoured pair of balls, and at the end of the session the very limited satisfaction to be gained from victory over oneself. However, I suppose it provided good practice as well as fresh air, and improved one's performance for more competitive but still strictly informal encounters.

At least since the 'foot on one's own ball and opponent into the bushes' form of play went out *circa* 1890, I have never been able to understand the theory of croquet being a peculiarly vicious and bad-temper-producing game, as compared with, say, tennis. It is not exhausting, it has a certain gentle rhythm, and its billiards in the open-air aspect, with the verdure of country lawns substituted for the smoke-filled saloon bar traditions of billiards itself, ought surely to produce calm and benignity. Yet in practice I do recall the most epoch-making row with Anthony Crosland at Ann Fleming's on what was an otherwise perfect spring day. I also recall that his wife urged him on with loyalty whereas mine merely commented on the ludicrousness of two allegedly grownup Cabinet Ministers quarrelling over the position of a ball. I also recall a disputatious game, played in a summer twilight, with Teddy Kennedy who was partnered by Senator Tunney, the son of the old boxer. But I think that was entirely due to my irritation as the prospect of victory over a Kennedy, always a good thing to achieve, slipped needlessly away under the incompetence of my partner (who was Kennedy's brother-in-law so perhaps there was collusion). Happily my games with the literary editor of the *Spectator*, mostly on that same lawn which produced the eruption with Crosland, have never ended quarrelsomely. Otherwise I might not be writing this piece today.

Nicky Smith is very informative about the history and current state of the game, and mostly writes clearly and tautly. She is, however, muddling about dates. Having convinced me that croquet, imported from Ireland, had first become a serious 'garden game' in England in the 1860s, she then announces that it was exported to Australia by settlers of the 1850s, 'whose personal baggage often contained a boxed set of croquet equipment – a standard part of the paraphernalia of the Victorian middle-class family'.

Nor can I decide, fluctuating one way and the other, whether or not she has a sense of humour about her game. At times she assumes a sort of Jennifer's Diary inconsequential glossiness. Thus of the World Singles Champion of 1989: 'He is a cheerful character whose most singular characteristic is his relentless control of his game. A trained carpenter who also studied for a career in the priesthood, Joe Hogan is a great exponent of adopting the "right psychology". Like most of the New Zealand players, this seems to consist of an undemonstrative but unyielding determination to win.'

At other times she adopts the moral uplift tone of an old-style preparatory school headmaster whose school is not quite worthy of him. 'Five years later they [the United States] have already made great strides towards this goal [of "strength in depth"] and in the meantime have invested croquet with an enthusiasm which has been sadly lacking in the British game.' My reaction to this is to paraphrase King George V's response to H. G. Wells's 1917 complaint about an alien and uninspiring court. 'I may be uninspiring,' he said, 'but I'll be damned if I am an alien.' I feel that I may lack 'strength in depth', but I'll be damned if I am unenthusiastic. I once played in three inches of snow when grooves had to be constructed between the hoops. Once made, the balls ran in them remarkably truly.

Leopold Amery

The Amery Diaries 1929–45 *(Hutchinson) were reviewed in the* Observer *in 1988*. In the Name of God, Go! *by W. R. Louis, was published by W. W. Norton in 1992.*

Leo Amery was born in India in 1873, the son of a member of the Indian Forest Department, and died in 1955. He was educated at Harrow, where he was a year senior to Churchill, who none the less exploited Amery's smallness to push him fully clothed into the swimming pool, and at Balliol, where he got a fine first in Greats before becoming a prize fellow of All Souls. He was very clever, perhaps in a slightly pedantic way. He had a varying degree of command over German, French, Italian, Russian, Turkish, Magyar, Serbo-Croat and Bulgarian, as well as Latin, Greek and Sanskrit. He wished his life to be dedicated to public service in the cause of British imperialism. He was also very short, never more than 5 feet and 4 inches. It was said that he might have been Prime Minister had he been half a head taller and his speeches half an hour shorter.

He published three volumes of moderately interesting autobiography in the last years of his life, and two volumes of his diaries have since been edited and published. In the second of these, dealing with 1929–45, the prolix editors got totally out of hand and wrote the equivalent of a four-hundred-page book of their own under the guise of explaining the context of the relatively sparse diary entries, which were in consequence buried under a mass of other people's verbiage.

It is therefore just as well as desirable that Amery should have been rescued, like a man retrieved from underneath the rubble after a bomb attack, by a significantly taut and penetrating little book by William Roger Louis, Professor of English History and Culture at the University of Texas, and the pre-eminent living historian of the British Empire, certainly on the other side of the Atlantic, and maybe on this side too.

Amery thoroughly deserves the attentions of a rescue expedition, for he was an unusual and interesting man, as high in courage as in erudition. He was an effective Colonial Secretary from 1924 to 1929 but was left out of the National Government in 1931 and of all subsequent Baldwin/Chamberlain reconstructions. He half minded and he half did not. Whenever a reshuffle became imminent he began to quiver with anticipation, but then some mixture of integrity and over-excitement made him constantly blot his copybook with some unfortunately timed piece of over-vigorous criticism. So he went away half sorrowing and half enjoying his hair-shirt. In May 1940 he more than had his revenge, although I do not think this was his motive for he was singularly honest, when he made what was probably the decisive speech in the Norway Debate which brought about the fall of Chamberlain.

The quotation from Cromwell with which he concluded and which has since rumbled down the decades was alighted upon in a way that well illustrates the element of haphazardness in nearly all memorable speeches: 'Some correspondence and spent the rest of the morning on my speech for the Norway Debate ... I looked up my favourite quotation of Cromwell's about his selection of the Ironsides and then remembered his other quotation when he dismissed the Long Parliament. ["You have sat too long here for any good that you have been doing. Depart, I say, and let us have done with you. In the name of God, go!"] I doubted whether this was not too strong meat and only kept it by me in case the spirit should move me to use it as the climax to my speech, otherwise preparing a somewhat milder finish.'

Churchill then made him Secretary of State for India, which was in a sense generous for although he had lately been a determined opponent of appeasement he had been an equally determined and very effective opponent of Churchill's obscurantism on India and had generally slightly patronized his future chief from the superiority of one year in age and a confidence in his own better judgement. Amery then served at the India Office until he was swept out of the House of Commons in 1945 at the age of seventy-two. In his last decade he endured the appalling personal tragedy of the hanging of his elder son as a traitor, but rallied to meld his British imperialism with enthusiasm for a united Europe in a vision of a Euro-Commonwealth bloc.

His personal qualities and interest exceeded the range of his middle-rank political career. He was a very small man of wide vision. He was probably the most authentic political heir to Alfred Milner: intellectual, imperialist, a votary of the temple of public service, agreeably vain yet never besotted by his own self-interest, either material or careerist, a little over-serious. He was thought of as right-wing, but he was affronted by Neville Chamberlain's narrow partisanship, he cared deeply for social reform and little for business values except in so far as he could

293

harness them to his imperial cause, and he had more Labour Party contacts than did most Conservatives of that deeply divided decade of the 1930s. He was a rather Bismarckian figure, but unlike that prince of the German Empire he was untouched by aristocratic connections or aspirations. He occupied an impressive London house – 112 Eaton Square – in which undivided vastness his younger son Julian, now Lord Amery, still lives, but he never sought a country estate. There was more of Buddenbrooks than of Bismarck about this. He was a man not so much of government as of ideas and public concern. He would be ill at ease in any party today and he was altogether rather admirable.

David Astor and the Observer

Newspaper anniversaries are tricky events. Even the celebrations of personal birthdays can have their problems, although there can be reasonable assurance that the person concerned has lived for the seventy or eighty years or whatever is being celebrated under a single continuous identity. Most old newspapers on the other hand have been changelings in infancy. This was true of the *Glasgow Herald* (the *Glasgow* has since been dropped), which celebrated its 200th birthday eight years ago, but which had to get over the fact that it began by appearing on Mondays and Fridays and was called the *Glasgow Advertiser and Evening Intelligencer* for its first twenty years. And *The Times*, the *Observer's* other rival in venerability, spent its first three years from 1785 under the even more unrecognizable guise of the *Daily Universal Register,* and only settled down into its 'Thunderer' role when Thomas Barnes became editor in 1817.

The *Observer,* however, has always been the *Observer* and has throughout been a Sunday newspaper, although it would be difficult to deny that it has experienced several changes of role and style amounting almost to a change of identity even if not of title, during the past two hundred years. It has, however, had a remarkable stability of editorship: only eight since the first decade of the nineteenth century. And the twentieth century has been memorably marked by the long and disparate reigns of J. L. Garvin from 1908 to 1942 and of David Astor from 1948 to 1975. Astor was the proprietor as well, but it was his editorial role that was in my view the more important, although the confluence gave a stability of purpose and prospect of continuity. I wrote for the paper a lot from the middle of his period onwards and also at about this time, from, say, 1955 to 1975, first came to know well the upper reaches of Fleet Street in general. There were then three other interesting editorial and/or proprietorial combinations. There was the Newton/Drogheda *Financial Times*, there was the King/Cudlipp *Mirror*, and there was the Hamilton/Evans *Sunday Times*.

Each of them, as did the David Astor *Observer*, produced higher quality journalism than is to be easily found today, although they did so through utterly different methods and personalities. Cecil King eventually succumbed to the megalomania that he may have inherited from his uncle Northcliffe, but in his heyday he made a wonderful partnership with Hugh Cudlipp, who had the rare quality of being a popularizer of genius and a responsible and civilized man. At the *Financial Times* Garrett Drogheda as manager was feline and Gordon Newton as editor seemed an uninspiring individual, although he had some touch of talent which enabled him to preside over the widening of the paper from a stockbroker's sheet to more or less its present form.

Denis Hamilton revitalized the *Sunday Times* with the quiet efficiency of a staff officer, using to do it the serialized memoirs of some of the generals and air marshals he might have served so well, but also the agency of Harold Evans, who was half a crusader against scandals and half a radical liberal who liked sophisticated politics. Evans had in him something of a young Cudlipp, who happened to be operating at the other end of the market.

The newspaper world in which David Astor had to operate was not therefore an easy or uncompetitive one. And, unlike the others, he had no partner. He had of course a number of distinguished writing collaborators. Indeed, his fostering of them was one of his outstanding achievements. Rather in the way that General de Gaulle's leading adjutants were known as the barons of Gaullism, not because they thought of imposing a Magna Carta upon the King or because they were a fawning court, but because they combined loyalty with some independent position of their own, so there developed a group of *Observer* barons. When they started they had mostly not been brought up with the taste of newsprint in their mother's milk, or served heroic stints on the Glasgow *Daily Record* or the *Manchester Evening News*. They were men of letters or 'intellectuals' in the continental sense, and indeed several of them came from the mainland of Europe. They contributed greatly to the unique quality of the paper, but they did not take any of the central responsibility off Astor.

There was therefore a position in which one man, still relatively young, without much training or academic or other achievement behind him at that stage, had undiluted ultimate responsibility for the financial and editorial direction of a newspaper with a long history, but without, at the end of the Garvin era, much drive or high circulation. The scene might so easily have been set for a rich man's dilettantism, leading soon to boredom for the proprietor and to decline for the paper. On the contrary, it led to thirty years of inspiring editorship as well as proprietorship. It made the *Observer* for me, and I believe for many others, the paper with which, across the whole spectrum of

British journalism, daily, Sunday and weekly, they most identified and were most proud to be associated. I may be prejudiced, for I know how much David Astor's *Observer* contributed both to developing me as a writer and to sustaining the causes for which I cared in politics, but I regard his civic service as being the most outstanding amongst the distinguished company which I previously mentioned.

In my autobiography I wrote of Astor as being 'the greatest non-writing editor/proprietor of the thirty post-war years'. To describe him as 'non-writing' is not perhaps entirely fair, although he was even better at inspiring other people's pens than using his own. But he did rewrite the crucial opening sentences of the 1956 leader on Suez, which both helped to turn the issue into the most divisive national controversy since Irish Home Rule and cost the *Observer* heavily in circulation and advertising, although not in repute. Probably the most damaging and resented of these sentences was the simple 'We had not realised that our Government was capable of such folly and such crookedness.'

The commemorative volume for the *Observer's* bicentenary was good at bringing out the vicissitudes as well as the achievements in the paper's history. It was also skilfully selected so as to give a fine ride through the landscape of changing styles as well as providing a lot of information of inherent interest and a lot of writing of inherent quality, as well as very good pictures. What emerged was that the well-turned essay of a thousand words or more has been much more a feature of the post-1945 *Observer* than it ever was in the nineteenth century or even in Garvin's day.

The items from the first hundred years of the paper's life were much more news snippets, often interspersed with good laconic comment. I found the following few lines on the death of George IV coolly penetrating, particularly as they were written at, as it were, the heat of the moment: 'Although a scholar, a gentleman and a patron of arts, our Sovereign, however worthy of being regretted, was neither a great King, an enlightened statesman, nor a national benefactor.'

I also thought that considerable prescience was shown both by: 'The wide-spread habit of smoking has not yet had due medical attention paid to its consequences' (1846); and the demand for an underpass to relieve the weight of traffic at Hyde Park Corner (1877). I was less impressed by the *Observer's* championing of the right of every newspaper to be represented at prison executions (1879). Any sensationalist sin here was, however, more than expiated by the paper's leading role against the death penalty eighty years later, when a series of mind-jerking articles from Arthur Koestler operated with the uncomfortable efficacy of a dentist's drill.

Looking at the collective evidence I am persuaded that there was something of an *Observer* house style in the post-1945 quarter century. There were inevitable variations in how it was executed, but it encouraged the normally tight-lipped Lord Attlee to be quite expansive on King George VI, and even the Central Europeans such as Sebastian Haffner, Isaac Deutscher, Lajos Lederer, who were a great post-war feature, were persuaded by it to write remarkably unheavy English. (Koestler needed no such persuasion, for hardly anyone, unless it be Joseph Conrad, has written so well in a language not his own.)

The *Observer* stylist who stood out, however, was Patrick O'Donovan (1919–81). His piece on Churchill's funeral was as near to a perfect example of gossamer writing as it is possible to imagine. It was not written to convey any great message. Nor was it written to express deep emotion. As O'Donovan frankly said: 'We were not sad ... And we did not weep – that is not fitting for great old men – but we saw him off and because he was us at our best, we gave him a requiem that rejected death and was almost a rejoicing.' What it was written for was to fill an 800-word space, and to do so elegantly, grippingly, with occasional fresh insights, and without striking any false notes. And the simultaneous achievement of these objectives is a good part of the art of high-class journalism.

O'Donovan was buttressed by striking pieces from John Gale, William Millinship (on de Gaulle), Cyril Dunn and Kenneth Tynan, while Edward Crankshaw's farewell piece (1968) on the future of the Soviet Empire was of the same quality of writing with more of a message. Anthony Sampson and Colin Legum were two of the knights of the de-colonization crusade, in which the *Observer* played as notable a role as *L'Express* did in France.

The regular *Observer* contributor of this period who is somewhat under-represented in the collection is Hugh Massingham. He was not taut enough to be a great stylist, but he did invent a new form of political journalism. While his opposite number on the *Sunday Times*, shrewd and respected though he was, was still playing out the last act of the old forelock-touching, hat metaphorically on the back of his head, cigarette-in-mouth, pencil-poised-above-notebook style of deferential relations with politicians, Massingham was developing the funny iconoclastic style, which no quality paper would now dream of being without. The *Observer* owes much to him for innovation just as it does to Patrick O'Donovan for style and to David Astor for direction and inspiration.

Beaverbrook

This is based on a 1992 Observer *review of* Beaverbrook:
A Life *by Anne Chisholm and Michael Davie (Hutchinson).*

William Maxwell Aitken, first Lord Beaverbrook from the age of thirty-seven to his death at eighty-five in 1964, was a figure of wealth, glamour and would-be influence (the wish occasionally turning into reality) over five decades. As a multiple newspaper proprietor he was never on the scale of Rothermere or Kemsley, let alone Murdoch, but the three horses (the two Expresses and the *Evening Standard)* to which he confined his stable, were to an unparalleled extent his personal creatures, reflecting his whims from social gossip to political causes.

He was a spider at the centre of a somewhat rackety web, who held his insects in place by a mixture of charm (which could be dazzling, particularly as it was mostly accompanied by great courtesy), bribery and ruthlessness. His primary purpose in life was probably to combat boredom and to still the mounting fear of his own extinction. As a result, there was a rootlessness about him which irresistibly recalled Keynes's immortal description of Lloyd George: 'One catches in his company that flavour of final purposelessness, inner irresponsibility, existence outside or away from our Saxon good or evil.'

Nevertheless, he was a serious Minister of Aircraft Production at a crucial time in Britain's history; he was a fluctuating but often sought-after friend of the two most exciting Prime Ministers of this century (Lloyd George and Churchill); he was the subject of Graham Sutherland's best portrait, and provided the central character for novels by Arnold Bennett and William Gerhardie, as well as being a somewhat more peripheral model in books by H. G. Wells and Evelyn Waugh. He employed a galaxy of disparate journalistic talent such as has rarely been assembled.

In addition, through five books of his own, particularly the two written in his late seventies and early eighties, he showed himself to be a narrative historian of compelling power even if of somewhat partial interpretation. On top of this he had a string of lady friends ranging from Diana Cooper and Barbara Cartland (to me a new and amusing revelation) to Tallulah Bankhead, Rebecca West and the pianist Harriet Cohen, which would have kept any modern gossip columnist in copy for months at a time. Needless to say, these friendships did not appear in the columns of his own papers. But nor did those of other people, for he was not prurient in print and respected the privacy of private lives in a way that is unimaginable today.

He liked to convey the impression of great manipulative power, but was saved from the megalomania of a Citizen Kane by the fact that he had genuine wit, and was a considerable provoker of laughter, both intentionally and unintentionally. It was well summed up by the claim of a mutual friend (probably apocryphal) that when after his death she had sent condolences to his second wife (of only a year's standing, and known as Christofor), she had received in reply a cable transmitted through a possibly slapdash West Indian telegraph office, which said 'Your sympathy is much appreciated. (Signed) Christ for Beaverbrook'.

It was thus not surprising that he attracted a number of books about him (as well as by him) in his later years. The most troublesome was a 1956 biography by Tom Driberg, who was deeply indebted to Beaverbrook for journalistic opportunities, legal protection and direct subventions when in financial trouble, but was a good biter of the hand that fed him. The most hagiographic was a posthumous one by A. J. P. Taylor, which for that reason, as well as for some others, could not be accused of being calculatingly sycophantic. Taylor became spontaneously besotted in the last five years or so of Beaverbrook's life, although he had written of him with dismissive disapproval in a review of Driberg's book. (And, to round the circle of paradox, Taylor is on record as having thought Driberg one of the few really good men he had known, which is, to say the least, an unusual judgement.)

Since Taylor in 1972, however, Beaverbrook has fallen into the crevice of disregard which is an almost invariable fate in the second and third decades after death. He is indeed now lucky to have interest in him revived by such a fair and substantial biography as has been written by Michael Davie and his wife Anne Chisholm. It opens with a brilliant *pas seul* by Davie. This is a riveting and funny contemporary 4000-word account of Davie (then a member of the *Observer* staff) being summoned in 1956 to Beaverbrook's villa in the South of France in order that he might be poached as *Evening Standard* New York correspondent. For the rest the spousely couple seem to have performed the difficult feat of joint authorship without undue marital strain or it ever being obvious which had written which particular passage. They manage to combine journalists' eyes for what is interesting with scholars' respect for what is accurate. They write with

303

geographical sensitivity both about Canada and England, and indeed re-create Beaverbrook's restlessly changing physical surroundings with great vividness.

This is important in a life of Beaverbrook. In the introduction to his *Men and Power* he sets the tone by writing: 'It may be asked "Were you there? I was there!"' 'The authors enable us to feel 'there' with him, whether on the deck of the *Queen Mary* or on the terrace of Cherkley, his ugly house with a fine view in the Surrey hills. But they paint the unfolding landscape of Beaverbrook's long life somewhat flatter than the landscape looking south from that terrace. The many events are treated too equally.

Yet the authors capture the conflict between his relentless energy and his sense of ultimate futility. When Arnold Bennett died Beaverbrook uttered one of the sadder, most self-deprecating remarks of his life. 'How I loved my Arnold, and how he loved my champagne.' (Bennett probably liked him more for himself than he realized.)

He was equally uneasy with the great chunks of twentieth-century history (in the form of private papers) that he had bought. Having bought history, what do you do with it? Exhibit it freely or keep it under wraps? This dilemma he failed to solve. To escape from a dour manse background in a remote part of the Canadian Maritimes into commanding the most brittle aspects of café society of the early and mid-twentieth century is not perhaps the best recipe for philosophical calm or moral certainty. Although these desirable states conspicuously eluded him he compensated with an exceptional vitality and magnetism which persisted throughout his long if unadmirable life.

Richard Crossman

This essay is based on an Observer *review of Dick*
Crossman: A Portrait, *by Tam Dalyell (Weidenfeld and*
Nicolson, 1989), and of Crossman: The Pursuit of Power,
by Anthony Howard (Jonathan Cape, 1990).

R. H. S. Crossman and C. A. R. Crosland, like multi-initialled amateur cricketers, were two great middle-order batsmen of the last years of Labour in government, and the last years too of amateur cricketers. They were sometimes (but not often) confused with each other, and each of them at least once expressed envy of what they saw as my own more monosyllabic and mnemonic name.

For most of his life Crossman was the better known. Indeed I once heard Field Marshal Montgomery do a put-down of Crosland on this ground. In 1951 a dozen or so MPs, including these two, paid a visit to SHAPE. Eisenhower, Supreme Commander, received us with bland goodwill. Montgomery, who was deputy, treated us like a lot of slack subalterns. 'Give your names clearly and keep your questions short,' he commanded. 'Crosland, not to be confused with Crossman,' the later author of *The Future of Socialism* began in an even more disdainful drawl than usual. Montgomery said: 'I would not dream of confusing you. I have heard of Crossman.'

Nevertheless, Anthony Crosland ended up with more lasting fame for what he himself had done, both as a political theorist and as the (brief) holder of the Foreign Secretaryship, the great office of state which Richard Crossman, then two years dead, had most desired. Crossman's chief monument was *Diaries of a Cabinet Minister*, mainly a recording of the words and behaviour of others. It was also what he increasingly came to care most about, even when he was still a minister, and overwhelmingly so between 1970 and his death in early 1974. It was not exactly for the sake of the truth, to which even his most devoted fan could not say he was peculiarly addicted. In argument he regarded 'facts' as dialectical weapons to be forged as one needed them rather than as objective entities to be respected for their own validity. Yet his *Diaries* are in my view remarkably accurate. Harold Wilson, of whom Crossman had been a considerable friend and ally, used to claim that they were all imaginative fiction, stuffed with nonexistent meetings and encounters which never took place. I did not find this so. I often disagreed with Crossman's judgements and sometimes with his descriptive angle, but I could always recognize the events he was talking about if I had participated in them, and thought that they never diverged more from my version of accuracy than might the accounts of a motor accident seen by two men of different temperaments standing on opposite sides of the road.

Yet Crossman, although unlike Crosland he was never even in his own eyes a serious competitor for the party leadership, was a more dominant figure in Cabinet, more central for thirty years to the life of the Labour Party, and a more striking speaker both

306

in Parliament and on a political platform. As a Cabinet member it was more the tone than the outcome of discussions that he influenced for he did not have a high reputation for wisdom and often changed his mind in the middle of the argument. He specialized in rumbustious iconoclasm. He asked questions that nobody else would. Although he dropped off to sleep in the Cabinet more frequently than anyone I ever saw, whenever he himself was awake he was very good at keeping others so too. I sat next to him in 1967–70 and greatly missed him in the dull Cabinet of 1974–6.

His party activity I mostly disapproved of. We belonged to different tribes. He was always a Bevanite, although a surprising one because he was neither particularly left-wing nor a natural hero-worshipper, either in general or of Aneurin Bevan in particular. I fear it stemmed from the facts that he could not get over having rather despised Gaitskell both at Winchester and at New College, and that Attlee (a family neighbour in Essex suburbia) so deeply disapproved of his behaviour as a young man towards both his dry Chancery judge of a father and his more outgoing mother that he would not contemplate giving him a government job. Palestine and the 'Keep Left' revolt he might have forgiven him, but not his bullying around the tennis court in the Buckhurst Hill garden.

As a speaker Crossman imported his Oxford teaching methods into politics. Yet his style was the antithesis of the austerely academic. His central desire was to grip the attention of his audience, almost to seize them intellectually by the throat, and to this end he would always prefer a slightly shocking generalization, whether or not well founded in the facts, to platitudinous verities. He was also a master of the art of keeping his audience on tenterhooks. I remember once comparing his speaking method

307

with that of a trick motor cyclist who rode as hard as he could at the end of a cliff. Everyone in sight was held fascinated, waiting to see how on earth he was going to turn round before going over the edge. I was sufficiently impressed as a young MP that he was the only parliamentarian I ever consciously tried to emulate. I am not sure I had much success in this.

Why, with all his verve and talents, did Crossman as a politician never get into the league of Wilson or Callaghan? There were two major reasons. First, he really was the classic example of being his own worst enemy. Ernest Bevin never applied his famous 'not while I'm alive, he ain't' to Crossman, bitterly though he accused him of the 'stab in the back', perhaps because he recognized that Crossman's self-destructiveness needed no assistance. Crossman had an extraordinary penchant for gaffes. The major ones were well spaced: 1952, 1957, 1969. But they were buttressed by a host of minor ones which bespattered almost every year. 'I have measured out my life in howling gaffes,' he could have written towards the end, paraphrasing Eliot.

Second, penetratingly though he wrote about it both in his *Diaries* and in his 1963 preface to Bagehot, Crossman was remarkably bad at operating the Whitehall machine. He believed civil servants were instinctively disloyal, which they are not, and as a result, despite his sparkle and exceptional intelligence, succeeded in making them almost uniquely so towards himself. I will never forget a pensions meeting which as Chancellor I had with Cross-man as Social Security Minister accompanied by a galaxy of his officials in 1969. It was a pushover. He was jumping about from one intellectual position to another, and his officials wanted to see him lose. I never saw a departmental minister so badly supported. It almost made me rally to the side of his expenditure claims.

Yet, in spite of the weaknesses, Crossman was by no means wholly a bad minister. He was vigorous and innovating. It was merely that he was not as good as he ought to have been in relation to his talents. He was always a commentator first and an executant second. He was frequently more interested in the argument than in the result. But his *sotto voce* remarks made him an irreplaceable companion.

Part of his desire to shock, out of which he never grew, may have stemmed from a persistence of his adolescent bullying. But there was also a much more amiable side to it. He was as natural a teacher as he was a commentator. An aggressively conducted seminar, with himself in the chair, was his idea of paradise. And his early and continuing conviction was that the best way to open closed minds and to keep open minds engaged was to shock them. Of the time when I first met Crossman (fifty-six years ago) I wrote in my autobiography: 'The visitor [to my parent's house in South Wales] who most dazzled me was without doubt Richard Crossman. His brand of verve and paradox I found very exciting at sixteen.' In later life I did not exactly admire him, but I enjoyed his company to an extent matched by that of only three or four other politicians.

Garret FitzGerald

This piece started life as a 1991 Observer *review of Garret FitzGerald's autobiography* All In a Life *(Macmillan).*

I have long found Irish politics both fascinating and mystifying. From the Phoenix Park assassination of Lord Frederick Cavendish in 1882 to the Easter Rising in 1916 they provided a crucial and mostly unhelpful background to the careers of my main biographical subjects, Dilke and Asquith. In my second period as Home Secretary (1974–6) terrorism of Irish origin was obtrusive, and I provided a *locus classicus* for the permanence of the provisional by introducing the Prevention of Terrorism (Temporary Provisions) Act, which is still on the Statute Book nineteen years later.

As President of the European Commission three years later I had dealings with three Taoiseachs, paid a dozen or more visits to Ireland, and leant over backwards, as any British President should have done, to cultivate my Dublin relationships and to encourage and enjoy the Irish pleasure at leap-frogging over Britain's semi-detachment into the mainstream of full European commitment. I did not find this difficult, for my natural prejudices, such as they are, are much more green than orange. I am a poor unionist, believing intuitively that even Paisley and Haughey are better at dealing with each other than the English are with either.

This does not stem from any condescending view that the Irish should be left to work off their perverse provincialism on each other. Indeed, on the early occasions when I met Garret FitzGerald it was his cosmopolitanism which, together with his charm, most struck me. It was he who made me feel provincial. I remember a day in Strasbourg for the opening by Valéry Giscard d'Estaing of the new European Parliament building, which in fact belonged to the Council of Europe and was merely graciously loaned to the Parliament. FitzGerald, as Irish Foreign Minister, was currently president of the Council of Europe's ministerial group. After a Strasbourg civic banquet he responded to Mayor Pflimlin's somewhat florid oratory with an elegance of French diction that matched the style of the eighteenth-century Hôtel de Ville. At the afternoon ceremony, again in French, he was the only speaker who was neither too long (like Giscard) nor too fractured (like me). There, I thought, spoke the Ireland of Joyce and Synge and the Countess Markiewicz.

Nevertheless, the Dublin political and official world is one that is very close-knit and interbred, and FitzGerald was born and brought up at the centre of it, even though his mother was an Ulster Protestant, but one so dedicated to the Nationalist cause that she took the anti-Treaty side in the great Irish split of 1922 and deprecated her husband's participation in the first govern-ment of the Irish Free State under W. T. Cosgrave. Desmond FitzGerald, the husband and father, was half poet and half poli-tician, with a cast of feature and cut of hair somewhat reminiscent of a less forceful Hugh Gaitskell, who as Minister of External

Affairs presented the Free State's application to join the League of Nations in 1923, but who subsequently faded as a leading politician.

He brought up Garret FitzGerald (who was the youngest of a large family) in a large but socially indeterminate house on the southern edge of Dublin, sent him to a good Jesuit school and on to University College, Dublin, which as part of the National University was by the 1940s as much the core of Dublin's future intellectual and political life as the relatively alien Trinity College, Dublin, was its topographical core. Indeed my impression throughout these memoirs is that UCD was as effective in putting FitzGerald in the middle of a magic circle as ever Eton was in Harold Macmillan's heyday. It was FitzGerald's peculiar strength that while he was completely at home within this circle he never allowed himself to be bounded by it or to absorb too much of its values.

His first job was good training for not being narrowly bounded. He joined Aer Lingus and worked out the first schedules of the nascent airline. This gave him a continuing familiarity with timetables which enabled him to confound his Russian hosts on a first visit as Foreign Minister during a logistical discussion of his provincial tour by pointing out that the 4.15 for Baku would just make it possible to catch the 7.30 to Irkutsk. In the interval, however, his twelve years with Aer Lingus had been followed by a sixteen-year abstention from flying. This should not be damagingly attributed to the inside knowledge he has acquired. It was in deference to the dislike for flying machines of his wife, to whose wishes and wisdom he constantly pays deserved regard.

When he became Foreign Minister in 1973 both FitzGeralds had to change their habits. The time when Ernest Bevin could be a sea-travel-only Foreign Secretary was twenty years past,

312

apart from the fact that it would have been particularly irritating for an Irish minister to have to go everywhere through London. The sacrifice was well worthwhile, for FitzGerald's four years as Foreign Minister stand equal in my view to his two periods (one of nine months, the other of four years) as Taoiseach. In the higher office he tried to lay to rest more of the ghosts of Irish history than anyone for three hundred years, showed imaginative cross-border sympathy, moved the South away from the limitations of a confessional state, and after infinite patience got the limited achievement of the Anglo-Irish Agreement of 1985. But as Foreign Minister he made Ireland not merely an official but an integral part of the European Community, an honorary member of the somewhat exclusive club of the original six. His conduct of the Irish Presidency, which came within two years of joining, was a model example of triumphing over the limitations of small-power resources to exercise skilled and authoritative diplomacy. This was not the motive, but FitzGerald succeeded in making London look peripheral to Europe, while Dublin was metropolitan.

These two chapters of his life add up to major achievements of statesmanship, not seriously marred by an engaging tactical ineptitude in domestic politics. FitzGerald as Taoiseach was manifestly a goldfish of international class forced to swim in a fairly small bowl. But whereas most people in these circumstances ineffectively bang their fins against the glass, it was his peculiar achievement that he seemed to make the bowl bigger, certainly temporarily for himself and to some extent permanently by his broadening of the horizons of Ireland and his strengthening of its international position.

John Kenneth Galbraith

This was a speech delivered at the eightieth birthday party of Professor Galbraith in the Century Club, New York, on 13 October 1988.

George Ball was ironically eloquent about Kenneth Galbraith's humility. But I do not think that he has ever emulated the feat of an English friend of mine, an earl, a socialist, the father of a notable brood of writers, who produced a quasi-religious book which was actually entitled *Humility*, who walked down Piccadilly, looked at the display in Hatchard's bookshop, went in, sent for the manager, and demanded, 'Why have you not got my book on *Humility* in the window?'

Thirty-five years ago last month, on my first visit to the United States, I took a plane from Detroit to Newark. For the first hour it bumped a great deal as was frequent in those pre-jet days. When the bumping ceased my silent neighbours all suddenly became very loquacious. It turned out they were mostly economists, returning from some gathering of the American Economic Association. The chief among them, or at least the one I remember best, was Seymour Harris, I suppose the most devoted of

Keynes's United States disciples. He invited me to Cambridge for three days and installed me in the Dana-Palmer House. There he performed a function which for me was much more significant than his introduction of Keynes to the American public. He introduced me to Galbraith – and indeed to Schlesinger. Having performed this function, he then fell away rather like the first stage booster in a rocket launch. I am not sure I ever saw him again. But he had transformed my life, or at least its American dimension. For more than half of it John Kenneth Galbraith (and Arthur Schlesinger, his historical adviser and junior by nine years) has been an unfailing source of wit, friendship, vicarious repute, and hospitality to me. I count that 1953 Detroit flight the luckiest journey I have ever made.

At this stage of course Ken was only a semi-fledged sage of the Western world. He had published *American Capitalism: the Concept of Countervailing Power*, but I think nothing else – between hard backs at least. He was still half thought of as an agricultural economist. Although he might talk of the Office of Price Administration, I think that by far the most important thing that he had done until then was to marry Kitty, thereby demonstrating the concept of countervailing height as well as underpinning his life and enriching ours.

In 1955 came *The Great Crash* and I took Kitty on to the roof of Milan Cathedral where she was overcome with vertigo and I was very glad that it was her end of the theory of countervailing height and not Ken's that I had to manoeuvre back between the minarets and gargoyles.

In 1960, soon after *The Affluent Society,* I took two friends to stay at the Galbraith house in New Fane, Vermont. 'Well, we have certainly seen the public squalor on the way here,' one of them said as we bounced up the rough and long dirt road. 'I only hope we see the private affluence when we arrive.' So, I suppose, we did, but only up to a point. For while Ken would never dream of not staying at the Carlyle in this city or the Ritz in London, neither he nor Kitty has ever believed in changing their domestic lifestyle to keep up with the royalties. That of course is a tribute to their supreme, unaffected and therefore wholly splendid self-confidence. Thirty Francis Avenue in Cambridge, Massachusetts, is fast qualifying as a house in a time warp. Happily, practically nothing changes. It ought to become a national shrine eventually acquired by Mrs Wrightsman, moved to a new extension of the Metropolitan Museum – and entitled *New England Academic Interior, circa 1950.*

From that New Fane visit I retain another memory of Ken's imperturbable self-confidence. He took us to see the beaver dams about half a mile from the house. Suddenly there was a great clanging of wires overhead. 'That's my private telephone alarm,' he said, adding, 'It will be the Senator' (and there was no doubt which Senator that meant in that autumn of the Kennedy election), before loping off through the undergrowth. When we got back we asked him what the Senator wanted. 'No,' he said, 'it was the plumber from Brattleboro', but the Senator will be through soon.'

However, my final proof of the indestructibility of Ken's self-assurance came nearly a decade later, when he and I ran into a former British Prime Minister. It became apparent to me after about ten seconds of casual conversation that, unbelievable and discreditable though it was, the former Prime Minister did not really know who John Kenneth Galbraith was. It became apparent to Ken a moment or two later. He was in no way disconcerted. As soon as we separated he turned to me and said: 'Who was that man? I thought he was Alec Home.' The logic was

316

impeccable. If he did not know Galbraith, he could not be an ex-Prime Minister. The dismissal was complete.

I have left myself no time to talk about the eighteen or so books I haven't mentioned, including at least three major pieces of innovative socio-academic analysis, or the volumes of autobiography, or the travel books, or such reassuring titles as *Annals of an Abiding Liberal,* or Ken and Kitty in India, or Ken as an inimitable and iconoclastic lecturer, or Ken stealing the show at a Harvard Commencement Day, or Ken as a Fellow of Trinity College, Cambridge, the jewel in the crown of that junior university, or Ken the television presenter, or Ken the connoisseur of Indian art, or Ken the *littérateur,* the writer of reviews of Waugh and forewords to Trollope. I stop while my catalogue is still illustrative and not exhaustive: and merely ask you to drink to a man who has put more phrases into the language than the rest of us put together; whose great gifts have always been used in unselfish causes; whose friendship has given us all both pride and pleasure; and whose life if it exceeds the norm as much as do his other qualities, will, I calculate, extend to the age of ninety-seven (after which Kitty can be the Pamela Harriman of the 2008 campaign), so that we all look forward to meeting again for the ninetieth and the ninety-fifth birthdays. In the meantime I give you the toast of Kenneth and Kitty Galbraith.

Valéry Giscard d'Estaing

This miniature is based on a 1991 European *review of*
Giscard's Le Pouvoir et la Vie, Vol II: L'Affrontement
(Cie 12).

This second volume of President Giscard's memoirs covers
roughly the second half of the seventies – although chrono-
logical order is not its strong point – and, therefore, the bulk of
his *septennat* as head of state (and of government) of the French
Republic. It is very well written, revealing in a somewhat self-
conscious way, like a boy letting off a firework and then standing
back to judge the effect before deciding when the next one can
be ignited, and wholly compulsive reading.

Giscard's main objective I would judge to be the straightfor-
ward one of writing a good book, even a striking piece of
literature, which enables him to express a view of life and himself
which has been bottled up within him. But there was probably a
subsidiary motive of making himself a less remote and condescending figure to the public, which he had been slowly persuaded
was a factor in his shattering 1981 defeat, against the odds at the
time, by François Mitterrand: perhaps, put bluntly, simply to

make himself more likeable.

Happily this second objective produces no falseness of tone. The Giscard that he presents to the public is the Giscard that he believes he is, and not a bogus creation designed to make people like him because he is so like them. What he brings out to an astonishing extent is his vulnerability, which some might regard as closely allied to vanity. The most striking image from his first volume was that of his having to walk ceremonially and alone across the vast *pavé* of the Place de la Bastille on his first 14 July as President, and becoming terrified of losing his balance or fainting.

Even this did not prepare me for the revelation that, from 1979 to 1988, he could not bring himself to read a French newspaper or to watch an RTF news bulletin. It was not merely the fear of an attack. He had become neurotic about even a neutral mention of his name. After a time he found that he could keep up with events through the international and foreign press because, as he rather engagingly says, these journals had ceased to be much interested in him.

Equally he tells us that when walking in a street he is tormented by the risk of catching his image reflected in a shop window, for he dislikes both his shape and his baldness. Both of these reactions I find extreme, but not incomprehensible, having always avoided watching myself on television and even being reluctant to read my own printed words. Even so, I find Giscard's cunicular terror in front of the headlights of *Le Figaro* or even *Antenne II* a bit over the odds.

This neurosis, however, neither kills his sense of wit nor prevents his casting an immensely observant and critical eye over those with whom he has direct dealings. I agree with most of his judgements on the statesmen or would-be statesmen who were his contemporaries in office, not least with those on Mrs Thatcher.

319

He may betray a little prejudice when he writes of looking across the table at her 'with her mouth open because of the British method of pronunciation', but his analysis of her methods of thought is at once penetrating and devastating. 'When she comes to the end of her own argument those who have not embraced her conclusions are incompetent, or addicted to half-measures or, last but not least, simply lacking in courage.'

I none the less find it surprising that in what was probably Giscard's last and deadly serious conversation with Jimmy Carter (for it concerned whether the United States would unleash nuclear warfare in order to save France from invasion) he was much struck by the fact that the US president wore long shoes with turned-up toes (winkle-pickers?). Even Giscard's foreign minister (François-Poncet), to whom presumably he was more used, excited favourable notice for his uncreased socks during an important meeting of disagreement with Giscard. I never realized quite how appropriate a 'please adjust your dress before arriving' notice would have been in the Elysée lobby.

The acuteness of observation does, however, produce some memorable descriptions. Brezhnev, arriving for Giscard's semi-illicit rendezvous (vis-à-vis his Western allies) with him in Warsaw in May 1980, walked with 'the swaying gait of a tired bear'. And moments of political decision are successfully mingled with irrelevant but convincing images. Thus, when he was deciding on his first Prime Minister: 'I wait a moment before letting in my next visitor. I go to the window. In sight are little groups waiting on the steps for the opening of the Musée du Louvre. Young women in bright-coloured skirts. A coach has pulled up, beige and white. It must come from The Netherlands. Tourists get heavily out, clinging to a glistening metal banister … My choice is definite. It will be Jacques Chirac.'

320

The fault of which some who had to deal with Giscard, and who admire many aspects of his constructive liberal statesmanship, would most accuse him was a certain false condescension. Does he dispel this in these memoirs? The answer must, I fear, be 'no', although he shows that it was balanced by many more attractive and less complacent characteristics. But it is still there. When he writes of the suicide of Robert Boulin, his minister of labour who was oppressed by a minor financial scandal arising out of his obtaining a free plot of land on the Côte d'Azur, Giscard was genuinely shocked by the tragedy. But it was a photograph of the villa '*sans grâce, sans charme*', which Boulin built on it that most stuck in his mind.

When he arrived in Venice for the 1980 summit he metaphorically patted Prime Minister Cossiga on the head: 'He was swimming in happiness ... it was the consummation of his political life' (Cossiga has since been president of the Italian Republic for seven years).

And when Giscard dined with the other heads of government in a great salon overhanging the Grand Canal, and was dazzled by the beauty of the surroundings, he was oppressed that no one else was appreciating the aesthetic feast. He may well have been right, but how did he know what was or was not going on in their minds? Perhaps that must wait for the sacred and profane memoirs of all of them. But of one thing we can be certain in advance: they will not be nearly as well written or elegantly self-revealing as are those of Giscard.

François Guizot

This miniature is based on a November 1990 European review *of* Guizot *by Gabriel de Broglie (Perrin).*

G uizot was the close contemporary of Palmerston and Lord John Russell and lived somewhat but not much longer than either of these octogenarians. Yet I find him more comparable with those Englishmen who were born half a generation or a little more after him, Gladstone, Newman, Matthew Arnold, even Tennyson. Guizot is almost a Victorian, very ungallic in some ways, with a career and a *mentalité* which at once illustrates the considerable similarities, shot through with profound differences, between the two leading countries of the nineteenth-century world.

François Guizot (although he was a man like Disraeli or Asquith who hardly needed or used a Christian name) was born in 1787, the son of a Protestant advocate living and practising in Nîmes. His Protestantism was important, not because he was primarily a *dévot* but because it deeply affected his cast of mind and character, rather as it had done with that twentieth-century Protestant French politician, Maurice Couve de Murville.

322

(Guizot's mind was, however, both more erudite and wide-ranging than Couve's.)

If this provenance and Guizot's close knowledge of English language and literature (with his future first wife he had translated the thirteen volumes of Gibbon's *Decline and Fall* by the time he was twenty-four) linked him with England, another part of his family background divided him sharply from the British experience. His father was guillotined in 1794, and his maternal grandfather, also part of the legal and Protestant establishment of Nîmes at best did nothing to save him and at worst was one of the instigators of the execution. So, mingled with the parchment- inspired respectability of legal life in a peculiarly urbane *cheflieu*, was an appallingly intimate experience of the unforgiving confrontationalism, with its periodical blood-lettings, which was a feature of French politics at least from the mid-seventeenth century Fronde until 1945, several hundred years after serious violence had disappeared from the English scene.

Guizot was certainly not a man of violence. He was a pacific minister of the regime which, of all those that ruled France in the nineteenth century, was the least concerned with 'la gloire'. Louis-Philippe, the bourgeois king who preferred an umbrella to a sword, was long and well served by Guizot, who reversed Thiers' policy of tweaking the tail of the British lion and produced the most famous summons to the arms of mammon that has ever been heard in the hemicycle of the Palais Bourbon. '*Messieurs,*' he told the assembled deputies of 1843, '*enrichissez-vous.*' Put in its context the remark was not nearly as materialistically self-seeking as it sounds, and Guizot never made much money for himself. Nevertheless, as a political leader he had more than a touch of Neville Chamberlain about him.

Yet outside politics there were sides to him that were well

beyond the life and style of the man of Munich from Birmingham. Guizot was a *savant,* a slightly reluctant figure of fashion, but the far-from-reluctant lover for twenty years of the exhibitionist Princesse de Lieven, and in general a writer of letters to women on a scale that fully rivalled Asquith. To combine this with a reputation for gravitas which put him closer to Gladstone and a literary output that exceeded that of any nineteenth-century politician of either side of the Channel made Guizot a very remarkable man. Hippolyte Taine, whose historical judgement is not negligible, placed him with Balzac, Stendhal, Sainte-Beuve and Renan as one of the 'five writers and thinkers who, since Montesquieu, have most added to the knowledge of human nature.' He was a member of the Académie Française for the massive span of forty years, and during this period, on top of his seven years as Louis-Philippe's first minister, he poured out his multi-volume historical works: six on the English Civil War, eight of his own memoirs, four of a history of France, another three of which were edited by his daughter after his death.

Guizot had two wives, the first twelve years older than himself, the second her niece. They were both dead, each time to his great dismay, by the time he was forty-five. Four years later, in the midst of other more exclusively epistolatory relationships, he began his very public and wildly unsuitable liaison with Dorothea de Lieven. It was unsuitable not least because he soon became a sober-sided minister of foreign affairs and she tried to be the greatest political intriguer in Europe. It was public in Paris, where he visited her house twice a day and even conducted diplomatic interviews there. But it was private, although hardly secret, in relation to his family. He spent a lot of time at a Normandy property called Val-Richer, which he acquired almost at the time he acquired her and which became almost synonymous with his name. She was only allowed to pay one morning call there. Nor was she allowed in London when he was ambassador here.

Altogether he was a strange and rewarding man, and it is not surprising that, right through to his death in 1874, he was the favourite port of call for British politicians passing through Paris. A visit to him was almost as obligatory for a would-be statesman of intellectual tastes as was a large luncheon at the Café Anglais for the Prince of Wales. And the fare that he provided, while not as rich, was more than adequately sustaining.

Nigel Lawson

This was a 1992 Sunday Telegraph *review of Nigel Lawson's ministerial memoirs* The View from No. 11 *(Bantam).*

This monstrous and self-obsessed book is only partially redeemed by the intelligence of the author and by his retention of a certain writing craft, which could not, however, be called art because of a lack of both overall proportion and of any positive stylistic qualities beyond that of lucidity. One may search in vain for (intentional) jokes, or for evocative writing, or for shafts of insight into the character of himself or others.

It is a long search, for we have over a thousand pages on Lord Lawson's ten ministerial years. There are eighty chapters, a number I have rarely seen exceeded in any book other than a Victorian 'three-decker' novel. And *The View from No. 11* does not have quite the narrative compulsion of, say, *Middlemarch* or *Can You Forgive Her?*

Memoirs or autobiographies are of course by their nature fairly solipsistic. But Nigel Lawson goes beyond the habitual bounds of egocentricity, as is illustrated in two ways. First, the photographs. In an autobiography, these necessarily include a good number of the author himself, but variety is normally sought by changing the background and the companions as much as possible. Lawson, *per contra,* specializes in close-ups of his own features. One page contains four different versions of the familiar countenance. I was reminded irresistibly of a long-defunct confectionary product known as Fry's Five Boys Chocolate Bars. Each wrapping was covered in five munching faces, all displaying varying aspects of self-satisfaction.

Second, it is a tremendous book for putting the blame on others. The third chapter on his Chancellorship is rather poignantly entitled 'A Job with Few Friends'. But if the number was small when he was doing his duty at the Exchequer it is difficult to believe that this book will not make it still more exiguous. Even allies get fairly dismissive treatment. At the beginning of the Thatcher Government, for instance, Lawson was Geoffrey Howe's Financial Secretary at the Treasury and in charge of the then panacea subject of monetary policy, although as the interplay between the stubbornly disloyal monetary aggregates of Mo, M1, M3, M4 and even M5 are developed, a lay reader could easily be forgiven for thinking that the narrator must have been at the Ministry of Transport. But it was to Chancellor Howe that Lawson was then responsible, and many opinionated minutes, all too frequently reproduced here, he fired off to him.

Except as a silent recipient of such effusions, however, Howe is not at this stage allowed a role beyond that of a sort of furry pet padding around in his Hush Puppies and greeting the initiatives of his brilliant lieutenant with a mixture of incomprehension and apprehension. Better in some ways a direct stiletto into the back, which is what, to take a few random examples, Peter Rees, his first Chief Secretary at the Treasury, Gordon Richardson, Governor of the Bank of England until 1983, and Arthur

Cockfield, Conservative tax expert until he became a Brussels Commissioner, all receive. Enemies within the government, such as Prior, Walker, Biffen, Gilmour, receive still shorter shrift, although they at least get the dagger in the front. And several of them will probably be more pleased with the book than will Lord Tebbit, who gets one of the few unalloyed tributes for his performance in the 1983 Parliament accompanied by the (to him) infuriating statement that he was a strong supporter of entry into the ERM in 1985.

Lawson's unconcealed lack of admiration for colleagues does, I suppose, make the long watches on the Medium Term Financial Strategy and exchange rate policy less tedious than they might otherwise be. But it does give an unappealing impression of everyone being out of step but Johnnie. And it is not made better by an excessive use of Christian names, which sometimes carries a flavour of *Girls' Own Paper* quarrels: 'John felt so strongly about it, however, that he wrote personally to Margaret setting out his objections to the MTFS which understandably annoyed Geoffrey when he got to hear of it.'

All previous skirmishes, however, are merely a run-up to the 1987–9 epic battle with 'Margaret'. This has almost an operatic quality about it, except that a wise intendant would have insisted on a much shorter overture. At first there was mutual admiration, and scenes with considerable duet potential. On the night of the 1985 Budget she unexpectedly rang the Number 11 doorbell and our hero who always slept naked (the 1100 pages allow room for such graphic detail) only had time to slip on trousers but no shirt or shoes before going down and holding a 'somewhat stilted chat' in the open doorway against the appropriate backdrop of the dreaded Foreign Office battlements. Yet even at such happy times there were rumbles of menace from the distance which hinted that all might not be well in the end.

Then comes the story of the mounting quarrel itself, beginning after the 1987 election and gathering momentum with the Prime Minister's open disapproval of the Chancellor's exchange rate policy, until two and a half years later it burst into resignation over the return to 10 Downing Street of Sir Alan Walters as her economic adviser. This is well and convincingly told except perhaps for Lawson's claim that Mrs Thatcher was seized with jealousy of him after his triumphs in the 1987 campaign.

His determination to shift, or at any rate spread, the blame for the bonanza which helped to make the subsequent slump deeper and longer than it need have been, is a good deal less convincing. The general tone is one of claiming that he did not cause the trouble, with an alternative plea that, if he did, there were plenty of others, commentators as well as ministers, urging him to go even further.

How will Lawson look in history as a Chancellor? My guess is: technically well equipped for the job (although to judge from the success of the non-economists Cripps and Butler and the relative failure of the economists Dalton and Maudling this is not crucial), durable (in a category comparable in this respect this century only with Lloyd George and Neville Chamberlain), confident, probably good to work for, but insensitive, brutally opinionated, and by believing that he had created a miracle whereas he had merely dashingly ridden a long upswing, heavily responsible for present discontents.

Is his vast budget of events accurate? Probably mostly so, although of his six references to me, two are directly and factually inaccurate and one inferentially so. But I daresay others are luckier.

Selwyn Lloyd

This essay is based on a 1989 Observer *review of D. R. Thorpe's* Selwyn Lloyd *(Cape).*

Selwyn Lloyd, born in 1904 and dying in 1978, was Foreign Secretary, Chancellor of the Exchequer and both leader and then Speaker of the House of Commons, without ever quite becoming more than a middle-rank politician. Nevertheless, he thoroughly deserved a good-quality biography, the more so as he was in my view an unusually nice although sad man, and he got exactly this from D. R. Thorpe. Mr Thorpe's book is tailor-made to fit Lloyd, and indeed sits on him more easily than any of his oddly stiff suits (abundantly illustrated within) ever seemed to do. These tailor-made qualities of the book are neatly summed up by a phrase from a review, quoted by Mr Thorpe, of Lloyd's own memoir of his five years in the Speaker's chair: 'modest, open-minded, friendly and honest'.

I use 'almost' because 'modest' understates Mr Thorpe's achievement in building a highly readable and rewarding new account of the politics of the 1950s and 1960s around Lloyd. This list omits, however, a certain nostalgic provincial piety which was a quality of the subject as it is of parts of the Thorpe book. The account of Lloyd's funeral in Wirral, with its description of the service and the principal participants, could almost be a '50 years ago' extract from the *Hoylake Gazette* (shades of the recurring 'Mr Hoylake Urban District Council' joke about Lloyd in the *Spectator* of thirty years ago, on which Bernard Levin made his reputation). But these sorts of detail fit the narrative and add to the interest, as well as illustrate what emerges as a fascinating sub-theme of the book, which is the uneasy interplay of Harold Macmillan's self-conscious metropolitan Edwardianism and Lloyd's instinctive respect for the golf courses and villas of 1930s Cheshire suburbia.

Macmillan, late in life, when reminded that Lloyd was from the Wirral murmured, 'up there ... juts out ... funny place to come from', and had not made things better by referring to him earlier as 'a little country notary'. Selwyn (rather like Austen Chamberlain he could be referred to by his Christian name without undue familiarity) probably minded the tone more than the substance, apart from treating Merseyside as a bucolic village, for he was eager to call his never-written autobiography 'A Middle-Class Lawyer from Liverpool'.

He was not a very notable lawyer – a reliable Northern Circuit junior before the war and a part-time silk earning barely £2000 a year from his practice after it – he was amongst Liverpool barristers not merely well behind great advocates like F. E. Smith and Hartley Shawcross but not quite up to Maxwell Fyfe. The one surprising thing that the Bar did for him, however, was to make him a determined opponent of capital punishment. On that he never subsequently wavered.

If he was a second-class lawyer he was undoubtedly a first-class soldier. He leapt into the Territorial Army just before the war began and bounded up in rank. By the end of 1939 he was through the Staff College and a brigade major. He never commanded troops, but he was a staff officer of the highest quality who ended the war as one of the select band of 'civilian' brigadiers. He loved the army because it filled his life, kept his endemic loneliness at bay, provided him with official accommodation, demanded the loyal and efficient discharge of higher orders, and rewarded him with the prestige of rapid promotion. Much of his remarkable political career he spent trying to get the same benefits out of political life, and succeeding for a high proportion of the time.

He began as Minister of State at the Foreign Office. *Esprit de l'escalier* made him subsequently believe that he said on appointment, 'I think there must be some mistake; I've never been to a foreign country, I don't speak any foreign languages, I don't like foreigners,' and that Churchill responded, 'Young man, these all seem to me to be positive advantages.'

Even if this had been entirely true, he would have been no worse than Edward Grey in these respects. After this start he not only served three reasonably successful years as Minister of State, but, after a fourteen-month sabbatical as Minister of Supply and then of Defence, came back to the Foreign Office to serve as Secretary of State for five and a half years, until very recently the longest continuous period for any Foreign Secretary since the equally insular Grey.

They both landed the country in disastrous wars. Grey's was won after four and a half years of slaughter. Lloyd's was lost after twenty-four hours of humiliating miscalculation and chicanery. But there the comparison stops, for Grey's foreign policy under an easy-going and domestically oriented Prime Minister was very much his own, whereas Lloyd's, under a fretful and externally obsessed one, was very much his master's. Mr Thorpe portrays him as being snatched away from negotiating a perfectly tolerable Suez settlement with the Egyptian Foreign Minister in New York, brought back overnight and even more jet-lagged because it was (just) the pre-jet age, half-charmed and half-brainwashed over lunch alone with Eden, and then rushed off to Paris for secret and committing talks with Prime Minister Guy Mollet and Foreign Minister Christian Pineau without any officials present. The verdict for which Mr Thorpe goes on Lloyd's role in the Suez affair is one of guilty but with heavily diminished responsibility because of a mind enfeebled by excessive loyalty and inadequate self-confidence. It can hardly be a ringing exculpation but I think he achieves it. In any event his Suez chapter is a very good one, fair, convincing and compelling.

Being willing to take punishment almost without limit (although certainly not without pain), Selwyn, 'the great survivor', overcame all this and had three and a half years as Macmillan's Foreign Secretary before being transferred from the one top departmental job to the other. Mr Thorpe conveys the impression that he was happier when he became Chancellor, preferring the 'candle-ends' of the Treasury to foreigners. It must be said, however, that, while he was an insensitive Chancellor, he was also an effectively innovative one. It is a general paradox of the Chancellor's position that his *ex-officio* dominance in the government is balanced by the fact that most of his work is building sandcastles that are predictably washed away by the high tide of his successor. Lloyd was unusual in leaving the semipermanent landmarks of the National Economic Development Office and Council (which survived until the magisterial Chancellorship of Mr Lamont made such cross-industry advice unnecessary) and the Regulator (by which indirect taxation could be easily varied between Budgets).

Then he was the leading and most shattered victim of Macmillan's 'day of the long knives'. Loss of office destroyed his life. He had nowhere to live and little to do. He was also very bitter about the injustice. But he kept his mouth shut, buckled down, became more relaxed and bonhomous, forged a lucky alliance with Alec Douglas Home, and was back in office as Leader of the House of Commons within fifteen months. It was a quick tit-for-tat with Harold Macmillan. In this post, which seemed to require most of the qualities he did not possess – delicacy of touch, wit, and detachment – he was a considerable success. It lasted only a year until the general election of 1964, but was the indispensable foundation of his 1970s Indian summer of five years as Speaker.

The last time I saw Lloyd, in July 1977 when I had recently become President of the European Commission, he told me that he was writing about Suez and I told him that my Secretary-General, who had been Guy Mollet's *directeur de cabinet* at the time, probably knew more about it than most people. He said, 'Then he may well know certain things which I do not, and which were kept secret, even from me, by Eden and Mollet.'

The Longfords

This essay is based on Observer *reviews of Elizabeth Longford's memoirs,* The Pebbled Shore *(Weidenfeld and Nicolson, 1986), and of Frank Longford's* History of the House of Lords *(Collins, 1988).*

The Pakenham/Longford clan constitute without question one of the most remarkable and prolific literary families in Britain. Apart from the parents, Frank and Elizabeth Longford, Thomas Pakenham has recently and deservedly won the W. H. Smith prize, Lady Antonia Fraser (Pinter) is English chairman of PEN as well as an author whose publications are always an event, and Lady Rachel Billington is a novelist of subtlety and perception.

This essay, however, is concerned only with the parents. Elizabeth Longford, to whom I would give the first place in the whole family, has had a literary career of unusual shape. Although she had done many other things, such as inspiring Maurice Bowra to a proposal of marriage, awakening her future husband like George IV arousing the spirit of Brighton in Rex Whistler's allegorical painting, having eight children, moving calmly from Unitarianism to disbelief to High Anglicanism to Roman Catholicism, three times becoming a Labour candidate and twice fighting an election, she had never written a book until she was fifty-three. And even then her first, *Jameson's Raid,* was not one of her best.

She has since become a most accomplished biographer, partly because she learnt one lesson from the only partial success of *Jameson's Raid,* which is that, as Mrs Beeton might say, in order to prepare a fine dish you must first catch a succulent bird. Her subsequent choice of subjects, sometimes strengthened by a delicate special connection, has been brilliant. *Victoria R.I.,* her first great success, was the first life of the matriarch of Europe's royal houses to be written by a wife and mother. Gynaecologically it comfortably outclassed Lytton Strachey.

Her next subject was the Duke of Wellington, whose wife was a Pakenham forebear. This she did in two volumes, the first mainly military, the second mainly political, and both handled with a rare blend of meticulousness and verve. She is not a stylist of note; she could not be parodied. But she has a strong narrative gift and an unusual capacity to combine respect for historical fact with what is almost a gossip columnist's instinct for what will interest her readers.

After Wellington, she turned to Byron and then to Wilfrid Scawen Blunt as well as to two or three further royal studies which were perhaps more commercial and less historical than *Victoria R.I.* These, however, do not come within the scope of the 1986 volume of her autobiography, which stops, quite sensibly (better perspective, hope of another instalment) but without much explanation over twenty-five years ago, when Lady Longford was sixty. These first six decades of her life contain quite enough action, variety, and above all names, to keep us going comfortably over 330 pages. She retains all her narrative sense, there is hardly a dull page, and the photographs, always extremely important in a volume of memoirs, are great fun.

What impression of her life and her qualities does the book leave? The latter are manifold, but pride of place, the book convinces me, must be given to prodigious energy behind a calm exterior. Elizabeth Harman, as she was born in 1906, was the daughter of a Harley Street eye-specialist who married the daughter of Joseph Chamberlain's younger brother. She never knew the founder of Chamberlain family fame, who was struck down by an incapacitating stroke a few weeks before her birth, but during her formative years first Austen and then Neville Chamberlain were major Conservative figures. She was not only impervious to their political influence but also to the social nexus of the Birmingham 'cousinage'. The only significant twitch upon the thread was about 1955 when she thought of writing a life of her great-uncle. But there were difficulties about the papers, and eventually only a tiny wing (*Jameson's Raid*) of the planned mansion was constructed. For the rest she was soon as socially upmarket of the Chamberlain connection as she was politically to its left.

Nor do I have the impression that her own parental home was a decisive influence upon her life. She did not rebel against it, but she fluttered away from it with all decent speed. Her principal destination was Oxford. She arrived there as a scholar of Lady Margaret Hall in the autumn of 1926, and proceeded to have a success which was the more remarkable because she broke away from her contemporaries rather than epitomized them. During their first three or four decades of life the Oxford

337

women's colleges had been substantially a blue-stocking world of their own, mostly filled with earnest young women reading English Literature or Modern Languages and mingling only marginally in the male activities of the University. Girls for Commem. Balls and other activities were much more likely to come from London than from St Hugh's or St Hilda's.

Elizabeth Harman changed all that. She became a welcomed invader of almost every field of male Oxford life. She even changed her subject to assist her penetration, deserting the safe Eng. Lit. in which she had achieved her scholarship for the more dangerous but masculine *Lit. Hum.* Her success was on a wide front: amorous (although chastely so, she is at pains to assure us); social (she was on close terms with almost everyone in the University who subsequently gained fame, and dined if not at Blenheim at least at the George Restaurant twice a week); journalistic (she wrote fluently and was one of the first women to be accorded the accolade of being an 'Isis Idol'); and, up to a point, academic. To her great disappointment she obtained only a second class, which was a considerable achievement after her late start on the classics. However, she received forty-eight letters of condolence on missing a first, which must surely be a record.

What faults can be found? The galaxy of names does occasionally become almost oppressive. And there is a small deficiency of critical judgement. Every goose turns out to be if not himself a full swan at least closely related to a particularly resplendent one. Even their Headington family doctor was Graham Greene's elder brother. Yet this is a dilemma for any autobiographer or diarist. It is difficult to make the bricks of interest without the straw of fame.

Frank Longford as a writer has been even more prolific than

his wife, and his eclecticism has been almost limitless. The full extent of this I realized only when looking at the 'books by the same author' list in one of his recent publications. Normally one's eye goes over such a list with hardly a flicker. But not on this occasion. It was a revelation. The full variety is an almost breathtaking tribute to sustained energy and dauntless self-confidence. The list is long (twenty-two books, one for every thirteen months since he resigned from ministerial office and began to write intensively at the age of sixty-two), but its composition is by a wide margin still more striking than its size.

Who else could have produced *Humility* in 1969, *Eamon de Valera* in 1970, *The Grain of Wheat* (a volume of autobiography), *Abraham Lincoln,* and *Jesus Christ* all in 1974, *Kennedy* in 1976, *Saint Francis of Assisi* in 1978, *Nixon* in 1980, *Ulster* in 1981, and *Pope John Paul II* in 1982? That year he supplemented his papal biography with *Diary of a Year* (his own) and then swept on through *Eleven at No. 10* (1984), studies of the Prime Ministers he had known, exactly the same number as did Gladstone, as it happens, *One Man's Faith* (also 1984), *The Search for Peace* (1985), *The Bishops* (1986), *Saints* (1987), to a gentle tribute to the Peers entitled *A History of the House of Lords* (1988), which can be regarded as completing a spiritual and temporal trilogy.

How does the quality of Lord Longford's work stand up to these prodigious tests to which he subjects his stamina? There is inevitably an element of Dr Johnson's famous comparison between women preaching and dogs 'walking on their hinder legs' about it. It could hardly be otherwise. The result is neither meticulous scholarship (it would not be appropriate, for instance, to compare his House of Lords book with Enoch Powell's *The*

House of Lords in the Middle Ages), nor a particularly polished pattern of writing. Subjects are often unceremoniously hauled in by the scruff of their necks and the simple device of beginning the sentence 'Incidentally ...'

There is indeed often an engaging inconsequentiality about the writing, and a certain lack of stringency in the structure is balanced by a similar avoidance of astringency in the comments about individuals. Compliments come naturally to Lord Longford. Almost every book cited is 'impressive', 'invaluable', 'brilliant' or 'penetrating' and almost every noble family justifies its nobility. There is, however, sometimes a hint of steel beneath the velvet. He can clothe a rebuke in a compliment with unique skill. When he writes of the Law Lords, 'We would be honoured if they mingled with us more freely outside the Chamber,' I take it that he means that he finds them a stand-offish lot.

Equally, I shall never forget the sharpest thing he ever said to me. Anthony Crosland and I had successfully opposed a pet scheme of his in a mid-1960s Cabinet meeting. When it was over he upbraided us in the middle of the road outside 10 Downing Street. I think he was quivering with (probably well-justified) rage, but what he actually said was, 'I will still write very favourably about you both in my autobiography, but not quite so favourably as I would have done until this morning.' This did not prevent what he subsequently wrote about me, mostly in his *Diary* of 1981, being thoroughly agreeable, for he is instinctively a generous man.

On another occasion he made a very successful joke against me in the House of Lords. He was describing the difficulties of resignation, which he had done in 1968, but said that there was the compensation of many people having been kind and sympathetic. Then, following a slight pause, he added: 'The noble Lord, Lord Jenkins of Hillhead, for instance, told me afterwards that he had very nearly written to me.' The laughter was convulsive. I joined in it but was, I suppose, mildly discomforted, the more so as the story was true, although omitting the fact that his resignation had been against my early public expenditure cuts as Chancellor, which made it difficult for me to find the right words to put on paper. However, I regarded the joke as well within the bounds of courtesy and even friendship and thought no more about it until I received an agonized letter from Frank Longford. He claimed he had hardly slept at all on the night afterwards, worrying that he had been offensive. He added, very engagingly, that he had succumbed to what had been a temptation throughout his life, that of desiring to amuse at almost any cost. He almost suggested that he might have to go on a pilgrimage of expiation. I wrote back reassuring him that he had not offended me. But a couple of weeks later when there was to be a spouse-comprising dinner given by my wife after a National Trust lecture by Elizabeth Longford, he wrote again to say that, following his offence, I would surely prefer that he did not come. Once more I wrote a letter of reassurance. A few months later he got up in the House of Lords and made the same joke again.

The trouble with most people of Longford's degree of generalized generosity is that the absence of a sharp edge of criticism makes their speeches and their writings (if they exist) dull. What makes Frank Longford wholly exceptional is that with him this is the reverse of the truth. Across the table, on his feet, or with his pen, he is one of the funniest men that I know. He is also an extremely clever man, although not at all in the 'too clever by half' category. He accompanies this by being uninhibited by the fear that people will laugh at him. He does not, perhaps, like being ignored, a fate which he has for many years avoided by a fairly wide margin, but he is quite indifferent to being mocked. This is an essential ingredient of his being a great Anglo/Irish eccentric, and relentless crusader for his chosen causes, as well as a most prolific author. It does not guarantee that the causes or the subjects will always be chosen with perfect discrimination, but they will certainly be pursued with a unique combination of courage, zest and wit.

François Mitterrand

This piece was a 1990 European *review of* Le Président, *by
Franz-Olivier Giesbert (Editions du Seuil).*

Franz-Olivier Giesbert, now editor-in-chief of *Le Figaro,* wrote
a life of François Mitterrand, the aspiring French politician,
in 1977. Now, thirteen years later, he has produced this second
book, *Le Président,* on Mitterrand the successful statesman, who
on grounds of impact on the political life of France and longevity
in office, must stand an unchallenged second among the four
presidents of the Fifth Republic.

Mitterrand presumably liked the first book, for he has collabo-
rated a good deal with the production of the second. This
suggests either a considerable tolerance on Mitterrand's part or
an indifference to whether he is portrayed as amiable (which
Giesbert certainly does not do), provided he is treated with a
reluctant respect and admiration as an extraordinary political
animal (which Giesbert equally certainly does do).

Giesbert is a highly successful journalist who, barely on the
threshold of middle age, has established a star's reputation, both
as a political writer and as an editor. Most good journalists write

343

books because they feel they should master a less ephemeral medium than the column or the report. But, only too often, they then proceed to nullify this purpose by choosing the most ephemeral subjects and treating them in the most ephemeral way. In Britain, Hugo Young's *One Of Us* (about Margaret Thatcher) and Anthony Howard's life of the former Conservative minister R. A. Butler are notable and rare exceptions.

Superficially Giesbert is in the mould rather than the exception. He likes writing books about events on which the dust has hardly settled: he likes reporting in direct speech conversations at which he was not present; and a certain addiction to reporters' clichés shines through the linguistic haze. People who are displeased even if unseen are too easily described as being 'rouge de colère'.

That almost exhausts the criticisms, for Giesbert writes with a compelling penetration. He takes one over the terrain of the Mitterrand years with the impartial but pitiless clarity of a powerful searchlight sweeping across a convoluted tract of countryside. The 'direct speech' technique may be presumptuous and unscholarly, but this is balanced by Giesbert's uncanny skill in avoiding false notes. His accounts carry a great ring of conviction. It is as difficult not to believe them as it is to stop reading his high-paced narrative.

His vignettes of Mitterrand's changing acolytes, allies and adversaries, Mauroy, Fabius, Rocard, Delors, Attali, and many others, are almost as good in a small way as the picture of the great spider at the centre of the web, silent, subtle, more predictable in method than in political position, which Giesbert cumulatively builds up. Essentially it is a portrait of ambiguity. All of his personality is founded upon it, according to Giesbert. 'This man, in fact, is never the one that one believes he is. He is at once better and worse.' 'François Mitterrand is never wholly himself nor wholly someone else.' The book's central message is that the President always takes great care to be elusive. His actions never follow his words. He is the greatest master of secrecy and dissimulation since Talleyrand.

So, Giesbert's compliments are distinctly barbed, even if apparently acceptable. To what extent are the barbs justified? I have never worked closely with Mitterrand. I ceased to be President of the European Community four months before he became President of the Republic. I was once summoned to have an hour's engaging conversation with him (in Buckingham Palace of all places, when he was in London on a state visit) during which I thought he exercised great charm.

But my major encounter with him was in Brussels eight years before that. As the challenger to the French government of the time he wished to pay a day-long visit to the Commission. That was a perfectly reasonable request. Mrs Thatcher, then leader of the Opposition, paid one at about the same time. So did future Chancellor Helmut Kohl. However, the Giscard Government became very edgy about it. I cannot quite think why for I doubt if being photographed with me in the Berlaymont was going to win many votes in Château-Chinon, or anywhere else for that matter.

This did not prevent it being one of the trickiest diplomatic days I have ever spent. In order to avoid great *'remous'* in Paris, I had to refrain from going down to meet him on the pavement or allowing him to meet an assembly of Commissioners in the Commission meeting room or proposing a formal toast at luncheon, all of which verged on being head of government treatment.

I thought Mitterrand behaved very well in the circumstances.

345

The neurosis was on the other side. However, this book combined with that recollection makes me realize that Elysée politics, both ways round, are a fairly rough affair, perhaps a little more so than in most other democratic countries.

I also recollect that at lunch that day Mitterrand told me that he thought he would probably be too old to fight the 1981 presidential election. In 1990, with two presidential victories behind him, that may I suppose be regarded as mild supporting evidence for Giesbert's dictum that '*Il ne fait jamais ce qu'il dit, il ne dit jamais ce qu'il fait*'.

Jawaharlal Nehru

This essay is based on a 1989 Observer *review of* Nehru *by M.J. Akbar (Viking).*

Jawaharlal Nehru, born in 1889, was Prime Minister for the first seventeen years of Indian independence. The quarter century since has produced six Prime Ministers, but three of them – Shastri, Morarji Desai and Charan Singh – were short-lived. Nehru's daughter filled the office for sixteen of these twenty-five years and his grandson then added another four. It is a dynastic record without parallel in any democracy.

Among the Viceroys there were two Elgins and two Hardinges, but no English (or Scottish) political family in India or Britain has maintained that degree of individual pre-eminence over three generations. The Nehru feat is the more remarkable because India is much the most disparate country of the three. What also seems to me to be remarkable is that Mrs Gandhi, who was an immensely filial daughter and a somewhat perfunctory wife, did not call herself, and hence her son, Nehru, particularly as the Gandhi has no connection with the Mahatma.

Was the Nehru family feat sufficiently remarkable to call in question India's democratic credentials? Only superficially so, I think. The intervals, and particularly the Desai intrusion into Mrs Gandhi's reign, are an answer to that. Indian governments pay the Raj the unfortunate compliment of inheriting from it too great a taste for the use of political imprisonment, but that apart there can be little doubt that by the tests of freedom of expression, freedom of political manoeuvre and freedom of electoral choice, India has astonished the world by showing that a country does not need to be rich to be a liberal democracy.

Nehru was the primary architect of this, which alone would make him one of the great men of the twentieth century. Beyond this pluralism, he gave India in the 1950s a major presence on the world scene – a presence greater than, even with its somewhat more solid economy, it has today. The non-aligned movement, of which, flanked by Tito and Nasser, Nehru was the clear leader, sometimes seemed 'holier-than-thou' and needed the resolution of Truman and Eisenhower for there to be something to be non-aligned between. But it gave to fissiparous India a valuable sense of the prestige of nationhood.

Nehru was accused of preaching conciliation abroad and practising ruthlessness at home. But his implacability was largely confined to anything touching the fragmentation of the country which had already lost Pakistan. He liked to think of himself as a Gandhian with Abraham Lincoln's problems. No doubt there were elements of vanity and double standards in the balance sheet. But the achievement and the sweep of his perceptions were by any standards formidable.

In addition he encapsulated three different and even contradictory strands of India's relationship with Britain and the West. For his first twenty-five years Nehru lived the slightly parasitical life of a rich Westernized Indian. His father, Motilal Nehru, later

348

a notable Nationalist leader but at this stage an immensely successful, high-living advocate, a sort of F. E. Smith without the swashbuckling, appears in the early part of the book as a more interesting character than Jawaharlal Nehru was himself.

Jawaharlal emerges as a fairly dim Harrow schoolboy, Trinity College, Cambridge, chemistry undergraduate, and Inner Temple pupil barrister. He rather wanted to get away from Indians and recalled disdainfully (of his compatriots) E. M. Forster's remark that the reason the races could not meet was that the Indians bored the English. If they did I do not think that Nehru was at this stage an exception. He was a silk-shirted hedonist admiring but not really penetrating English life.

Back in India after seven years away he began to undergo a remarkable and forceful metamorphosis. He became Gandhi's disciple and heir, he converted his devoted father (who threw away – or at any rate suspended use of – his champagne cellar and Western clothes), and together they began lives of alternating agitation and gaol. In Motilal's case this ended with his death in 1931, but in Jawaharlal's case it continued until he was released from his last spell in a Raj prison on 15 June 1945.

Of the preceding twenty-three years he had spent almost nine of them incarcerated. There is a too comfortable impression in Britain today that for someone of Nehru's stature these imprisonments were the equivalent of a reading and writing rest cure on the island in the lake of Udaipur; and that any boredom was made tolerable by the prospect on release of the adulation of the crowds and a no-hard-feelings singing of 'Forty Years On' with the provincial governor. Only the adulation of the crowds had reality. For the rest the long gaol sojourns were as depressing as they were unhealthy.

Within fifteen months of the last one, however, Nehru was

Prime Minister; within two years he was apparently the lover of the Vicereine (which might be regarded as a more seductive embrace than Harrow songs, although Akbar seemed commendably uninterested in this relationship); and within ten he was putting on a remarkably good show as the patronizer of the leaders of the Western world.

He became the arbitrator of the future of the Commonwealth. Churchill, who twenty-five years before had called Gandhi a seditious Middle Temple lawyer posing as a half-naked fakir, took to telling Nehru in private letters that he was 'the Light of Asia'. And Eisenhower, who had allowed Dulles for most of the 1950s to preach against India's immoral neutralism, ended the decade by coming on a state visit to Delhi and paying a notable tribute.

Mr Akbar therefore has a splendid subject, and publishing a quarter of a century after Nehru's death was a good vantage-point, provided he could avoid being oppressed by the bulk of S. Gopal's authoritative three-volume 1976 biography. Does he succeed? I cannot quite decide. He is a notable journalist, and he writes compellingly with vividness and passion. But he writes journalist's history.

Maybe in substance he does achieve proportion and perspective: I certainly feel that I understand the balance of Nehru's life better for having read him. But he never achieves a reflective style. He is a natural polemicist (and – an anti-partition Muslim himself – he has a polemical sub-theme, which is to put all the blame for dismemberment on Jinnah), so that even when he strives for balance his method is to refute one polemical passage with another polemical passage the other way.

His book also demonstrates the width of the gap between the Indian and the British literary traditions. There is some odd

English. Governments are constantly 'protesting' activities of 'the hostiles' with weapons nefariously 'gifted'. And in the passages dealing with anything British, the solecisms are thick upon the ground. Mountbatten is a sufficiently central character that it is a pity for Akbar to inform us that he was always known as Dicky and not 'Dickie', as he himself invariably wrote it. And there are many others of a similar degree of unimportance. Furthermore, I have never read a book which so cried out for pictures, and which has none. I longed, for instance, to be able to look at one of Motilal Nehru – which is a tribute to the strength of the narrative. Indeed there are times when Akbar himself seems to be referring to and describing his own non-existent illustrations. Were they in the Indian edition, but could not be afforded in the enterprise culture of modern Britain?

Cecil Parkinson

This is based on a 1992 Observer *review of Lord Parkinson's memoirs,* Right at the Centre *(Weidenfeld and Nicolson).*

This book is to me a disappointment. I thought it might provide a companion volume to the rich delights of the memoirs with which Lord Young of Graffham marked the completion of the economic miracle of the 1980s and his own decline into silence. However, Lord Parkinson is a much better politician than was Lord Young, and is not similarly addicted to strangulated jargon. As a result this is quite a good although intensely political book, with nothing much in it for those who are not enthralled by how Michael Portillo became 'a deservedly popular minister' or how 'Eric Ward, our excellent Central Office agent in Yorkshire' rearranged the order of a meeting so that Parkinson could hasten back down the motorway 'with headlights on at full speed' (but it was all legal, for the boys in blue were part of the plot) to be at Margaret Thatcher's side within two hours.

There is, as might be expected, a great deal of Lady Thatcher in the book, and indeed Parkinson straightforwardly sums up his life as having been 'a Thatcherite ministerial career'. He begins with fifty pages on her downfall, which moves him, with the literary assistance of Lord McAlpine, into the poetry of a Chinese proverb about 'dragons in shallow waters being the sport of shrimps'.

Then we have forty pages that cover everything from the author's birth in 1931 to his entry into active Conservative politics a third of a century later. He began in the small railway junction town of Carnforth (where Gladstone was anxious to discover the politics of the stationmaster after the Queen's famous *en clair* telegram on the murder of Gordon – 'these news are too dreadful' – had passed through that functionary's hands). Parkinson does not tell us about this, being more concerned in those days with his membership of the Labour League of Youth than with high Victorian politics. He writes frankly and well about this period, although he allows his parents to remain very shadowy figures.

In 1952, having just attended as a Bevanite supporter the most blood-letting of all Labour Party Conferences at Morecambe, he went to Cambridge, and during three years in that university underwent an unexplained transformation from slightly truculent left-winger to excessively clean-cut runner and glee-singer who was happy to become a management trainee with the Metal Box Company. From there he elided into being a City accountant, a member of the Hertfordshire bourgeoisie, and a natural and neighbourly Conservative activist.

The rest of the book, except for a rather dignified six pages ('manly' is the faintly mocking adjective which I cannot get out of my mind) about his parental and matrimonial troubles, is all politics, and politics seen very much from the level of the plain and not from the high peaks of questioning thought.

353

It is autobiography by manifesto, with party conferences (not the fratricide of Morecambe, which is left far behind, but the black ties of the Conservative agents' dinner and the gratifying embarrassment of the standing ovations) erected into stations of the cross. It was Blackpool that made him in 1981 when he had become party chairman, but it was also Blackpool that was the scene of his breaking in 1983, when he honourably and quickly decided that he should not go on as a liability to Mrs Thatcher. And 1990 at Brighton – 'my final speech to a party conference' – was sufficiently *l'ultima lacrima* that it required extensive quotation, rarely a good recipe for memoirs.

The interesting question that remains is what was it that turned Cecil Parkinson, the railwayman's left-wing son from Lancashire, into the most perfectly attuned to the Home Counties machine politics of the Conservative Party of any of his contemporaries. He notes with faint worry that Willie Whitelaw, whom he half admires, hated being chairman of the party, whereas he loved it. (Rab Butler also disliked it, but he is a bit outside Parkinson's historical sweep.) And it must be stressed that Parkinson did not, in my view, love the Conservative Party because he could not find anything else to love or any other role to perform successfully. The evidence from this book as from elsewhere suggests that he was a competent departmental minister, a bit dogged by dogma, but not more.

Parkinson's nearest rival for Conservative Associations' favourite of the decade was, I suppose, the man whom he constantly proclaims as his friend, Norman Tebbit. Yet Tebbit, more abrasive, more original and, in a curious way, more intellectual than Parkinson, is not really the man for leafy suburban garden fêtes in the way that is Parkinson. Tebbit is to be wheeled out occasionally for big and rough jobs, but not to be wasted. He is of course Essex man in a way that Parkinson is not. But while Essex man may be alleged to have provided the marginal votes of Thatcherism it is Hertfordshire man who has the more central position on the M25 and is cosier for the chairmen, the treasurers and the ladies' sections.

Politics have moved on, and Cecil Parkinson has not been so narrowly confined that he cannot enjoy the Bahamas, golf and skiing. Nevertheless, his book reminds me of a forty-year-old story of a politically obsessed Labour MP who on a delegation visit to Switzerland was shown a breathtaking view of the Matterhorn and said, 'Ee, I wouldn't like to go canvassing up there.'

Parkinson's canvassing days and indeed his conferencing roller coaster days of triumph and setback are as much over as are mine. But I think he will have a niche in history that will have nothing to do with his troubles. He may well look in retrospect as quintessential a figure of the 1980s as was, say, George Brown of the 1960s or Selwyn Lloyd of the 1950s.

Enoch Powell

The lives of Enoch Powell by Patrick Cosgrave (The Bodley Head), reviewed by me in the Observer *in April 1989.*

The central thesis of a 1989 biography of Enoch Powell is that he alone and single-handed determined the results of two general elections: by his last-minute endorsement of Conservatism in 1970 he created the Heath Government, and by his anti-European 'vote Labour' speech in the February 1974 campaign he snatched away the power that he had reluctantly given and allowed Wilson his 'tit-for-tat with Teddy Heath'.

Hyperbole apart, this is an odd claim in a hagiographic biography, for these were the two most perverse and deleterious election results in recent British history. In 1970 Labour deserved to win and it would have been better both for its future as a party of government and for British interests in Europe had it done so. In 1974, by contrast, Labour did not deserve to win, Harold Wilson had little idea what to do with his victory once he had achieved it, and the course was set for both the weak leadership and the trade union excesses of the late 1970s which between them destroyed one of the two best instruments of left-of-centre government in the world (the other was the Brandt/Schmidt SPD) since Roosevelt's Democratic Party.

All this can of course be given some teleological justification by saying that it was a necessary vale of sorrows on the way to the sunny uplands of Thatcherism. But this will not wholly do, for Mr Powell is by no means a strict enough Thatcherite, and I am not sure that Mr Cosgrave is either.

However, Enoch Powell's role as an architect of misfortune is not nearly as strong as Cosgrave presents it, not because the misfortunes did not occur, but because he was far less in control than this implies. His key 1970 speech did not take place until thirty-six hours before the poll, and it was for him in unusually convoluted terms. It requires a great deal of faith in the immanent power of every word of the hero to believe that these late words bestowed victory on Mr Heath. I think two jumbo jets in the May trade figures had more to do with it. And the most that Powell did was to cease during that campaign to be quite as much of a nuisance to Heath as he had been during the latter's not very skilful five years as leader of the opposition.

In 1974 Powell's 'vote Labour' appeal was at least delivered so as to leave a little more time for it to sink in, and there was certainly something very odd that happened at the end of the campaign to Conservative expectations, particularly in the West Midlands. But there was a mismatch between Powell's power and his objective. His power sprang from the populist nature of his views on immigration. But he could not in his right mind have wished to shift votes to Labour on that issue. Heath might be bad from this point of view, but Wilson was worse. What made him want to move votes was the European issue, where his conviction was passionate but based on abstract

357

and highly intellectualized views about sovereignty and the nature of national identity.

Inevitably there was some difficulty about using the shovel for a task different from the purpose for which it had been made. In any event he was markedly unsuccessful a year later in persuading Tories to vote 'no' in the European referendum. I find it difficult to believe that they had found it easier a year earlier to accept his still more jolting advice to vote Labour on the issue.

The paradox of Cosgrave's book is that he is better on Enoch Powell as an extraordinary and interesting man than he is upon him as a politician. It is a paradox because the author is a devout political follower who is prepared to defend even the most perverse of his subject's swoops as being yet another example of his 'logic and honour', while he appears to find some of his personal idiosyncrasies as mysterious as do others.

Even so, the book is not at all bad politically until it comes to the last hundred pages, when for some inexplicable reason (unless it be the dead hand of Ulster) it goes to pieces. It then becomes inaccurate (a whole constitutional theory is created upon Barbara Castle's attempt to reform industrial relations in 1967, a year in which she was still Minister of Transport, and even the month of the European referendum is wrongly stated), without sense of proportion (there are pages on an allegedly plot-sustaining academic interview given by some obscure official in the Northern Ireland Office), inconsequential, and cloying. 'Look upon him. Learn from him. You will not see his like again,' as the concluding passage of the book is the language of monuments, not of rational biography of someone who happily is still alive.

Three-quarters of the book, however, is much better than this. It is very well written in a measured yet gripping tone with a perfectly acceptable degree of partisanship which avoids both shrillness and the need to decry the hero's opponents. Occasionally a fairly breathtaking statement is slipped in, as when he says that there have been only two occasions when politicians have spoken with a full moral authority this century: the first was Churchill in 1940 and the second was Powell in 1970, this second authority stemming, as far as I can follow the argument, from the popular response to the Birmingham 'River Tiber foaming with much blood' speech in 1968. This is odd, for while there are some things in this book and outside it that have made me think more highly of Enoch Powell than I did twenty years ago, that speech still seems to me a tawdry affair, stuffed with cheap sentiment and demagogic intent.

Yet, as Powell has always been such a contradictory figure, that has not been incompatible with fastidious scholarship and noble actions. The meticulousness of his scholarship, the range of his knowledge, and the (maybe somewhat mechanical) quality of his linguistic skill all leave me gasping with a mixture of admiration and intimidation. So do his self-sufficiency and harsh self-discipline. When Powell went to Trinity College, Cambridge, in 1930 he worked, mostly shut up in his rooms, from 5.30 in the morning until 9.30 at night, and refused an invitation to dine from the Master's wife on the ground that he was too busy. He took an hour off for a walk each day, but did it unvaryingly to the station and back because that was the right distance.

In personal relations I find him as unpredictable as did Lady Thomson of Trinity (for it was the great J. J. Thomson, the discoverer of the electron and the presiding genius who made the Cavendish Laboratory the world centre of experimental physics, who was then Master). I assume Powell has mostly deeply disapproved of me. But when I published a rather light biographical essay on Baldwin, he wrote a review that was not only very friendly but also the most perceptive of what I was trying to do. Equally at the Cambridge Union in 1984, after I had been ill for a couple of months, he suddenly launched into a public tribute that was way beyond the call of politeness. I was rather moved and thought it an appropriate peg on which to improve relations, for we had previously stalked past each other without acknowledgement in the corridors of the House of Commons. On the next occasion I made to speak. He stalked even more rigidly than usual.

Andrei Sakharov

This is based on a 1990 Observer *review of Sakharov's*
Memoirs *(Hutchinson).*

Imet Sakharov only once, in June 1989, six months before his
death. He came to the Oxford Encaenia to receive an honorary degree. I did not alas sit next to him at the luncheon. I did,
however, drive him home in the evening, but by then he had
become too tired to manage much English and we did not have
an interpreter. I regretted at the time that I did not have more
talk with him. Now, having read his *Memoirs,* I do so a great deal
more. Although inelegantly constructed and sometimes written
like a catalogue, parts of this massive autobiography give
Sakharov a greater vividness for me than either his fame or his
presence did fifteen months ago.

The early part of the book, broadly the first eighteen chapters (out of fifty), which takes us through the first four decades
of his life in the Russia of Stalin and Khrushchev, is the best.
This was all before the death of his first wife and his second
marriage to the formidable but adored Elena Bonner, before
any significant break between him and the Soviet establishment,

and before his world fame as a dissident and protector of dissidents. It is essentially the story of Sakharov's childhood and education as a core product of the liberal intelligentsia which somehow persisted, sometimes hazardously but also often patriotically and respectfully, in Stalinist Russia, and then of his crucial and undismayed contribution to the making of the Soviet H-bomb.

Sakharov came of a background as intellectually rarefied and well educated as Keynes or a member of the great Cambridge scientific cousinage. There is indeed a remarkable symmetry between the relationship of his intellect to that of his father, a physicist and talented amateur pianist who was the author of a successful scientific text book, and that of Maynard Keynes with his father, John Neville Keynes, who was Registrary of the University of Cambridge and nearly became Professor of Political Economy at Oxford. Sakharov had a less physically urbane early life than did Keynes (Russia in 1941–5 in particular was a rougher place than Edwardian Cambridge) but he was just as immersed in Pushkin and Tolstoy as Keynes came to be in Bloomsbury.

Sakharov then spent twenty years (from 1948–68) making thermonuclear weapons. During this period he had few doubts about the work. At first he might have wished to assist Soviet nuclear superiority. In 1953, when Stalin died, he wrote: 'I am under the influence of a great man's death. I am thinking of his humanity.' Then he developed a more sophisticated theory of nuclear balance. He believed in MAD (mutual assured destruction) and very sensibly became an opponent of anything that made it more difficult to achieve, from anti-ballistic missiles to SDI. But it was on the nuclear test issue that he began his break with the military-industrial complex, which perhaps even more

362

in the Soviet Union than in America melded seamlessly into political power.

For some time Sakharov made his protests on a very privileged network. He had been admitted to the Academy of Sciences, membership of which was highly restricted and which conferred specific and desirable benefits, at the exceptionally young age of thirty-three. He was three times decorated as a Hero of the Soviet Union, which must surely have been at least the equivalent of an OM, if not of a KG as well. And when he wanted to complain he often did it direct to Beria, Malenkov or Khrushchev, sometimes just by ringing them up.

It is indeed the case that while refuseniks or dissidents had to take terrible risks they were also, if grand enough, able to avail themselves of a surprisingly high proportion of the privileges of a plural society. Thus Sakharov for a long time after his suspension from 'the installation' (the equivalent of Harwell or Aldermaston) was able as an academician to summon a car and driver from the official pool. He was also able even when attending trials as a gesture of support for the defendant to flash his Hero of Socialist Labour card (until it was taken away from him in 1980) and get a priority seat on aeroplanes. And even during his occasionally persecuted exile in Gorky from 1980 to 1986 his wife was for the most part allowed to go by train to Moscow and hold press conferences.

One form that the persecution took was the purloining on two occasions of part of the manuscript of his memoirs. He had twice to reconstruct them from memory. That makes it the more remarkable that the first part is the better, for it was presumably that part that was twice stolen. No doubt his memory unassisted by notes was better for his early years. But there is also the indisputable fact that most sections touching the Elena Bonner years are written more defensively, more flatly, more dutifully. In the mid-eighties in particular she was subjected by the Soviet propaganda machine to calumnies in which she was portrayed as a fiendish puppet mistress. I discount that, but it is nevertheless the fact that she was not good for the liveliness of Sakharov's literary style – her own writing on the Gorky years was, I believe, much better.

This book ends with Sakharov's release from the Gorky exile. For six and a half years he had been deprived of a telephone but late one evening one was suddenly installed in his apartment there. He was warned to expect a call the next morning. When it came through it was Gorbachev himself who told him that he was free to return to Moscow and 'go back to his patriotic work'. Most people would have dissolved in a mixture of deference and gratitude. Instead Sakharov began to argue about other detainees and eventually hung up on Gorbachev in a huff.

That unselfish self-righteousness is no doubt what made him a great man. His was the voice that could not keep quiet. It was the more remarkable because he was always at least half a supporter of a reformed Soviet system, who disapproved of Solzhenitsyn's flip into a detached blanket hostility. Sakharov nearly killed himself by hunger strikes to get his step-daughter-in-law permission to go and live in Massachusetts. It was the last thing he would have wanted for himself.

Herbert Samuel

An Observer *review of a 'political life' of Samuel by Bernard Wasserstein, published in 1992 (OUP).*

Herbert Samuel was an able and diligent man of high public spirit who lived for a very long time, occupied a wide variety of public positions between 1905 and 1955, although not the ones he most coveted, was a slight disappointment in most of them, often made false judgements, most notably over Hitler, which was surprising for a leading member of the old Anglo-Jewish community, yet accumulated over the decades a considerable reputation for sagacity and integrity. He was made an OM at eighty-eight, a rare honour for any non-Prime Ministerial politician, and he died at ninety-two. 'He was vewy nearly a great man,' said Bobbety (5th Marquis of) Salisbury, who had as much difficulty with his 'r's as do one or two other politicians.

Samuel published his own discreet *Memoirs* in 1945, and in 1957 John Bowle, a schoolmaster who had had an adventurous career at both Westminster and Eton, wrote a friendly 'living' biography. This was an odd matching of writer and subject, for

Samuel, who was intensely puritanical on anything to do with sex, which made his two brief tenures of the Home Office Liberal with only a capital 'L,' was a dedicated scourge of homosexuals.

Despite these publications there was a gap waiting to be filled and Professor Wasserstein, who is British by upbringing but is now Dean of Arts and Sciences at Brandeis University, does so definitively. He is fully aware of the plodding and unspontaneous aspects of Samuel, and indeed draws devastating attention to the limitations this set to his friendships and his popularity. Yet, although thoroughly comprehending the boring side of Samuel, Wasserstein never himself seems to be bored by it. If he were an undisciplined writer this might have been a recipe for disaster, but as he is the reverse and has managed to fit the whole ninety-two years into a neat 170,000 words, it works out very well.

In addition, Professor Wasserstein, while not a pedantic writer, is an extremely accurate one. Almost his only solecism, let alone significant error of fact, is inserting two or three redundant hyphens in Lady Violet Bonham Carter. This latter tiny mistake has, however, a certain symbolic quality, for during the first half of his career Samuel probably admired the father of Violet Asquith (as she was then) more than anyone else, yet was totally excluded from his intimate circle, whereas his first cousin, the more worldly Edwin Montagu, in spite of going on to commit the double apostasy of marrying Venetia Stanley and serving under Lloyd George, was very much part of it. In correspondence with that lady Asquith habitually referred to Montagu as 'the Assyrian' and to Samuel as 'the infant Samuel'. Both were mocking, but there was no doubt which was the more dismissive.

Nor did Asquith greatly admire Samuel's public ability. In a

Cabinet order of quality that he drew up for private amusement in 1915 he placed him eleventh out of the sixteen he categorized, with below him only a 'tail' of five equal lasts between whom he could not be bothered to differentiate. But this was nothing compared with the dislike Samuel aroused in Lloyd George (which it must be said was mutual, although ingested by Samuel and extruded by Lloyd George). With almost schoolboy petulance (at the age of seventy-five) Lloyd George referred to him as 'the politician he hated most', and this was not the anger of a moment or provoked by Samuel's pro-Munich stance, for six years earlier he had spoken in a public speech of 'the flaccid oleaginous Whiggery of Samuel', and four years before that he had written of him as 'underhanded and grasping'.

There was obviously some special irritant quality about a Liberal politician who was so coolly treated by Asquith when he was in his forties and so excoriated by Lloyd George when he was in his sixties. Yet he did not really deserve either treatment. Lloyd George's strictures in particular were very wide of the mark. Samuel was not 'underhanded', but naïve and over-trusting, although often insensitive to his audience or his interlocutor. He would not have dreamt of behaving as Lloyd George did with the manipulation of his notorious private political fund. Nor was he grasping. He never sought personal fortune (he had quite a lot of money to begin with, but that is by no means necessarily a prophylactic against greed, and it began to run thin during World War II), and he was the one minister involved in the Marconi scandal (because he was Postmaster-General; the others were Lloyd George himself, Lord Reading and the Master of Elibank) whose behaviour was spotless. His weakness was that he liked high public appointments, but, with one possible exception (when he was not successful), there is no evidence that he

367

behaved badly in order to get them. The trouble was more that he behaved with technical efficiency but unimaginative insensitivity when he had got them. The possible exception was that his fruitless desire in the late 1930s to be a very elderly Viceroy of India may have predisposed him towards Neville Chamberlain and Munich.

Nor was Samuel really a Whig, oleaginous or otherwise, in so far as that prismatic political description, giving out different lights in different directions, has any precise meaning. Certainly it is impossible to imagine any public figure of this century who was less like Charles James Fox. Economically he was more a Cobdenite, although with a strong social reform overlay and also a non-Cobdenite attachment to imperial causes. He was close to the Webbs as a young man and remained in some sort of contact with them throughout their lives. Wasserstein, rather dismissing Samuel's wife, thought that Beatrice Webb was the woman who understood him best. What is certain is that he was the one person whose high seriousness even she found excessive. And her late (1939) judgement on him was *good but mediocre, devoid of distinction, except perhaps in industry, kindliness and sanity*'. While they do not make for excitement, they were not a bad trio of qualities.

Jean-Jacques Servan-Schreiber

This is based on a 1991 European *review of the first volume of M. Servan-Schreiber's memoirs,* Passions *(Fixot).*

Jean-Jacques Servan-Schreiber, now approaching seventy, has been for me an immanent but personally unknown figure near the centre of the French stage for most of the one and a half decades of the Fourth Republic and the three and a half decades of the Fifth. He has operated at the junction between journalism and politics, striking the attitudes of a 'Young Turk', and giving them conviction by appearing always to have the energy, style and certainties of a young man. Just as some people have gone through decades without appearing to change much – Jean Monnet and William Rees-Mogg are two disparate examples –because they were born middle-aged, so Servan-Schreiber has accomplished the more difficult feat of being perpetually a rather young thirty-five.

Growing old is therefore probably a more disagreeable experience for him than for most. However, this does not show in his writing, which retains all the virtues of vigour and some of the faults of immaturity. Sometimes he reminds me of the later

369

Hemingway. Virility is important, but at least it is not measured in the consumption of dry Martinis. Servan-Schreiber is not a reflective writer. *'A la une'* (on page one) is a favourite phrase of his, and it seems to me that he still sees life very much in *'à la une'* terms. Events and relationships are epitomized in snatches of conversation, which over a gap of forty years or more are always rendered in the most precise and dramatic of direct speech, with Servan-Schreiber himself present at a remarkable number of the turning points of recent history, and often delivering the punch-line himself.

Even allowing for some *'esprit de l'escalier'*, however, the first forty years of Servan-Schreiber's life, which is all that is chronicled in this first volume of memoirs, were fairly remarkable. He was the son of a well-known editor of the economic daily *Les Echos,* who was himself the son of a former private secretary to Bismarck, who had renounced Prussianism and emigrated to Paris on the eve of the Franco-Prussian war, and of a mother who was certainly more beautiful, with looks more spirited, and whom he describes as *'la femme de ma vie'*. At the age of thirteen he had an eyeball-to-eyeball encounter with Hitler (because he had not given the Nazi salute) on a bridge in Munich, and at the age of sixteen he and his father accompanied the French government so closely on their flight from Paris to Tours to Bordeaux that he gives the impression of being on bedroom-visiting terms with Paul Reynaud and Madame de Portes.

After a couple of years under Vichy in Grenoble, studying for his entrance to the Ecole Polytechnic, being seduced or 'initiated' as he prefers to put it by his thirty-five-year-old landlady and listening to the BBC, he departs via Spain to join the Free French in North Africa and to be sent to train as a fighter pilot in Alabama. Passing through Washington on his way to the

Southern base, he picked up the pieces from an historic row between de Gaulle and General Marshall. He qualified too late for combat in the air, but he manages to invest his training period with more drama than most people could get out of several campaigns. It culminated with his being offered a captaincy and the command of two squadrons in the American Air Force and immediate US citizenship. He refused *'pour la France'* but with a sense of self-sacrifice as strong as the emotion of disappointment with which he says the offering colonel received his reply.

From this account of Servan-Schreiber's first twenty-one years certain reflections flow. First, he cannot see a drama without imagining himself at the centre of it. He even writes about Roosevelt's death as though he personally brought the news from Warm Springs to the White House. Second, America made a tremendous impact upon him. When he was offered a choice of there or England as a training ground he says almost as a manifesto rather than a bare statement of fact: *'J'ai choisi les Etats-Unis.'* And he was long subsequently, and particularly during the Kennedy years, the man who tried to bring the clean-cut vigour of the New Frontier into the stale corridors of the Palais Bourbon. This had the effect of directing his Anglo-Saxon interest almost entirely away from Britain. When he was a BBC listener he had an uncritical admiration for Churchill, of whose determination to sink the *Bismarck* he writes a somewhat imaginative account, but thereafter shifts his gaze westward to where he thought the land was bright, and does not I think mention another Englishman in his remaining 340 pages.

Third, he insists on writing about his relations with women (in spite of putting her first he has not been too much of a mother's boy to avoid them) with the cool precision and the faint suggestion that he was doing each one a favour that he applied to

Madame Marcelle, the determined (but beautiful) Grenoble housewife. Even Françoise Girued, who was also his distinguished collaborator in the outstanding success of *L'Express,* the quality weekly he launched in 1953, is subjected to this treatment. This was none the less his finest hour. Apart from assembling an outstanding team of contributors which included François Mauriac and Sartre, as well as an in-house core of Girued, himself and Jean Daniel, he also associated Mendès-France, Mitterrand and Gaston Defferre with the paper. Its founding cause was the end of the war in Indo-China, which Mendès-France achieved with the help of Mitterrand as a Minister of the Interior at once subtle and determined. Its subsequent cause was the ending of the war in Algeria, which put Mitterrand on the other side and dragged on for another seven years, including a six-month period when Servan-Schreiber was re-embodied into the army and sent to take part in the *'sale guerre'* on the edge of the desert. During these years he did not have to imagine his conversations or delude himself that he was at the centre of the stage. He really was there for once, and this shows in the quality of the narrative, which is, however, always easy to read because of both its pace and the simple directness of the French.

John Simon

This miniature is based on a 1992 review of Simon: A
Political Biography *by David Dutton (Aurum Press).*

S imon has been the biggest remaining gap in political biography of the first half of this century since 1977 when David
Marquand handsomely filled the Ramsay MacDonald cavity.
Simon was a pervasive if not exactly great figure of his day, and
his day was a long one. He first held office under Asquith and he
was still there on VE Day.

He was the only man in British political history apart from
Rab Butler and James Callaghan to have been Foreign Secretary,
Home Secretary (twice in Simon's case) and Chancellor of the
Exchequer. Palmerston would have made a quartet had he not
refused the Exchequer when he was almost a boy, or at least so
early in his career that he was still in 10 Downing Street nearly
fifty years after he had declined to go to Number 11. After
holding these three great offices of state, Callaghan became
Prime Minister while Simon was thought lucky to be kept on by
Churchill as a very disregarded Lord Chancellor who was never
allowed to show his face in the councils of the war.

The difference in their fates may be thought to illustrate the advantage of character (or, as some might put it, bearing) over intellect in politics.

Simon had a fine if sterile legal mind. All references to his success at the bar always stress the 'quality' of his practice, which I think can be interpreted to mean that he was best at the lucid exposition before a high-ranking judge (juries were much less his *forte*) of the complicated commercial affairs of those who could afford very large fees. His appearance was impressive and of an episcopal cast, which made him a worthy companion of Archbishop Lang of Canterbury in the common rooms of All Souls.

His personality was chilling but not impressively so, for he was ingratiating and unctuous, seeking a fellowship which nearly always eluded him. Asquith, when Simon was his thirty-eight-year-old Solicitor-General, christened him 'the Impeccable', and after a few chance social encounters with him complained that 'the Impeccable' was becoming 'the Inevitable'. Nearly thirty years later Hugh Dalton (who in fact shared some of Simon's characteristics including the look of a worldly prelate and an unfortunate tendency to call people by the wrong Christian names, but redeemed it by a rumbustious earthiness which Simon lacked) referred to him as 'the snakiest of the lot'. Kingley Martin wrote an unforgettable sentence beginning 'Many of those who have shivered as he took their arm ...'. The 1930s Cabinet shivered when he invited his colleagues to call him 'Jack' and only Jimmy Thomas managed to do so. And Neville Chamberlain, not noted for warmth except to his sisters, complained that Simon 'hasn't a friend even in his own party'.

Between leaving the Woolsack in 1945 and his death in 1954

Simon spent many of his weekends at All Souls, of which college G. D. H. Cole, who combined being a too-prolific Left Book Club author of the 1930s with social fastidiousness, was then a professorial fellow. After one such weekend Simon encountered Cole on the platform of Oxford station and greeted him with excessive bonhomie. As the train came in, Cole, anxious to escape, said, 'I must get along to my third-class compartment' (it was before the days of standard class). Simon, eager not to be frustrated in his search for ecumenical companionship, said, 'But I travel third myself,' and loped after him. When the ticket collector came round they both, with varying degrees of embarrassment, produced first-class tickets.

Simon's twenty-year performance as a minister was very uneven. He was indecisive and often lacked both courage and conviction. He was an advanced Liberal in his younger days; and as Attorney-General (in the Cabinet) hovered on the brink of resignation against Britain's involvement in the 1914 war. A year and a half later, having become a very young Home Secretary, he did resign, against the government's move towards conscription. But somehow his withdrawal, although it put him out of office between the ages of forty-two and fifty-eight, managed to look calculating rather than self-sacrificial.

During these occluded middle-aged years he moved steadily to the right; delivered a celebrated denunciation of the General Strike as illegal, which finally separated him from Lloyd George (with whom there had long been mutual antipathy and who contributed to the large corpus of anti-Simon invective the memorable thought that while 'greater men' had previously crossed the floor of the House of Commons they 'did not leave behind them the slime of hypocrisy'); presided over the ineffective Indian Statutory Commission of 1927–30, which was chiefly notable for having Major Attlee, the future arbiter of the destinies of the sub-continent, amongst its quieter members; and, intermittently, earned still larger fees at the bar than even Rufus Isaacs or Edward Carson, Marshall Hall or Patrick Hastings had done or were doing.

Once he was back in office following the formation of the National Government in 1931 he was, like Charles II, although he did not have much else in common with that 'merry monarch', determined not to depart again on his travels. He had nearly fourteen continuous years in office, fluctuatingly esteemed by his colleagues, often dissatisfied with his performance and his life, but always limpet-like. He was worst as Foreign Secretary (until 1935), better as Home Secretary (1935–7), at first most influential as Chancellor of the Exchequer (1937–40) but looking increasingly hidebound as defence needs overwhelmed orthodox finance. As Lord Chancellor (1940–5) he was a distinguished judge and looked good upon the Woolsack, but was kept at such arm's length by Churchill that he would not even put him in the normal-sized Cabinet of his 'caretaker government' of May/July 1945 (the War Cabinet had been much smaller). It was an unprecedented slight for a Lord Chancellor to be reduced, as though he were a Minister of Pensions or of Overseas Development, to be a minister of Cabinet rank (that is not ranking to be in the Cabinet) as it is euphemistically and misleadingly described.

It was all too bad to be true, and there is an underlying feeling that Simon must have been better than this. He was dedicated to public service, devoted to his mother, and generous, not exactly in temperament, but in the donations and subventions that he quietly made and the help that he frequently gave to people who could be of no use to him. He would have greatly liked to be a popular and loved figure.

In 1992 we had a very good *political* biography, as the author himself described it, from David Dutton. He put all amateurs of twentieth-century political history in his debt by tackling a difficult even if nearly virgin subject and by telling us ten times as much about Simon as that statesman did in his own volume of prim and passionless memoirs.

G. M. Trevelyan

This is based on a 1992 Observer *review of* G. M. Trevelyan:
A Life in History *by David Cannadine (HarperCollins).*

George Macaulay Trevelyan was the most widely read historian of the first half of this century. His first book came out
in 1899, his last (of serious import) in 1944. But there was no
question of his giving up because of fading response. This last
volume *(English Social History)* sold 100,000 copies in its first year
and 500,000 in its first six. Nor was this a flash in the pan. His
British History in the Nineteenth Century (1922) had sold 68,000 and
his *History of England* (1926) 200,000. He and the publishing
house Longmans, Green kept each other rich. No writer of
history had sold like it since Thomas Babington Macaulay.
Macaulay was Trevelyan's great uncle and the provider of his
second name. So it was all tightly knit, particularly as Trevelyan's
father was George Otto Trevelyan, who served in all Gladstone's
governments and wrote a *History of the American Revolution* as well
as the main biography of Macaulay.

All three, who between them spanned the years from 1800 to
1962, were regarded as quintessential 'Whig historians'. What

exactly this meant is far from clear. 'Whig', even in England, let alone if the American connotation is added to it, always has been a fairly imprecise word, giving out different beams of meaning according to the context in which it was used and the angle from which it was viewed. In all three cases, however, it meant that they regarded the Glorious Revolution as one of the best things ever to have happened in English history. G. M. Trevelyan, whether by design or coincidence, even had 1688 as his Cambridge telephone number.

In Macaulay's case in addition it meant that he was infused by a liberal optimism which made him see history as the unfolding of a story of almost continuous improvement, and was saved from blandness only by the resonance of his style and a determination to see that the 'Tory dogs always got the worst of it'. In G. M. Trevelyan's case it meant that he started off from an attitude at least as partisan and rather more radical than that of his great-uncle. His early books on English history could see no good in Tories from Bolingbroke to Wellington and his three volumes on Garibaldi were not merely anti-Bourbon and anti-Papist but anti any form of religion as well. But he was always a somewhat 'pi' and even priggish radical. Although he respected Keynes's intellect, he disliked Bloomsbury in general and Lytton Strachey in particular, disapproving of the irreverence of *Eminent Victorians*.

Bertrand Russell's life he found a little rackety for his taste, and also thought him a weak walker, for when they once went on a West Country tour together Russell stipulated that they should do no more than twenty-five miles a day, which Trevelyan accepted until the last day when he insisted on going off on his own for a serious walk. (Professor Cannadine also tells us that when going on his honeymoon Trevelyan insisted on getting out of the train at Truro and walking the last forty miles to the Lizard. This story is however vitiated by the fact that the distance from Truro to the Lizard is under *thirty* miles; the Russell one is better authenticated.)

With Russell, however, after an intermediate coolness there was a later reconciliation (which death if nothing else precluded in Strachey's case) and Trevelyan was moved and satisfied by Russell's BBC eightieth birthday tribute to him. With Beatrice Webb he achieved the remarkable feat of making her half mock him for his over-planned self-discipline. Meeting him when he was nineteen, she wrote: 'He is bringing himself up to be a great man, is precise and methodical in all his ways, ascetic and regular in his habits, eating according to rule, "exercising" according to rule, going to bed according to rule, and neither smoking, tea or coffee drinking, nor touching alcohol.'

This somewhat self-regarding youth of 1895 turned into George Trevelyan the radical of 1900–14. By 1925, however, he had become a quiet Conservative, well attuned to the age of Baldwin, whom he greatly admired, because he thought him country loving, the 'kindest of Prime Ministers' and not at all a cad, unlike Lloyd George, F. E. Smith, Beaverbrook, and probably Churchill as well. Trevelyan, in the 1930s, although greatly disliking the dictators, became a rather depressed supporter of appeasement. Once Baldwin had gone John Simon and Walter Runciman became his favourite ministers. He lost his early optimism as well as his early radicalism, believed that most things in the world were getting worse, and that the best thing was resignedly to make them do so as slowly as possible. This did, however, make him a dedicated and effective supporter of the National Trust.

In the pre-war decade, however, his main role was to be the

chronicler to whom the nation confided its past. As Cannadine puts it: 'He was Britain's unofficial Historian Laureate, the Hereditary Keeper of the Nation's Collective Memory, combining – in terms of a later generation of practitioners – the popular appeal of Sir Arthur Bryant, Sir John Plumb, A. J. P. Taylor and Dame Veronica Wedgwood with the Establishment connections of Lord Blake, Lord Briggs, Lord Bullock and Professor Owen Chad-wick.' In 1935 he wrote the Jubilee speech which King George V delivered in Westminster Hall. In 1937 he became a member of the Order of Merit. In 1940 Churchill, forgiving of his affection for Baldwin, his respect for Neville Chamberlain and his acceptance of appeasement, made him Master of that greater Trinity in the Fens. It was an appropriate appointment, for he was a quintessential Cambridge figure, and Trinity College, then even more than now, was the quintessence of that university. His combination of unworldliness, frenetic walking, blandness of style and disapproval of cruel wit in others, would have been difficult to imagine in an Oxford context.

Trevelyan's reputation as an historian barely survived his death in 1962. He is now amongst the great unread, widely regarded by the professionals of a later generation as a pontificating old windbag, as short on cutting-edge as on reliable facts. Professor Cannadine has done a brilliant job of rehabilitation, the more impressive because it is surprising (to me at least) that he should have wanted to do so. He is in general irreverent and might easily have been expected to mock Trevelyan. The fact that he does not do so in no way prevents him being taut and entertaining.

Lord Young of Graffham

A 1990 Spectator *review of The* Enterprise Years *by Lord Young (Headline).*

David Young (or 'Lord' Young as he apparently wishes to be known to his intimates in the literary world) has been Mrs Thatcher's substitute for Churchill's (or 'Winston' as she respectfully prefers to call him) Lord Woolton. They both came to politics from a business background, although both admitted to a brief flirtation with socialism in their youth. They both entered the House of Lords to become ministers. And they were both attracted by the chairmanship of the Conservative Party, but the department store manager from Liverpool was one of the most successful occupants of that great office of state, whereas the property developer from Finchley found his way firmly blocked by Willie Whitelaw acting like a constable blocking the gentlemen's entrance into the pavilion.

The differences between Fred, 1st Earl of Woolton, and David, Lord Young of Graffham, were, however, about as great as those between 'Winston' and the Iron Lady. 'Uncle Fred' had a wonderful even if sometimes unctuous political touch, whereas

'Uncle David' (as he was not widely known in the House of Lords) had practically none, except for a certain ability to choose between competing firms of advertising agents. If Disraeli's fame is summed up by 'peace with honour', Asquith's by 'effortless superiority' and Churchill's by 'blood, sweat and tears', so Lord Young's must rest on his immortal phrase delivered in the darkest days of the 1987 election: 'If these are the ads she wants, then these are the ads she gets.'

Since hearing that throbbing aria Mr Norman Tebbit has never been quite the same man. He recognized that his days as *maître en titre* were effectively over. For the most part, Mr Tebbit has taken his rejection with a stiff upper lip, although enlisting with Lord Whitelaw as a rather improbable joint guardian of the gentlemen's entrance. He endured in silence the publication barely three months after the 1987 events of a short book by Rodney Tyler which seemed to draw heavily on Lord Young's diary, and which indeed put into circulation the little phrase about the advertisements. It was only when Mr Tebbit felt that his noble supplanter had let down the Faerie Queene that he spoke out, although he has compensated for his three years of restraint by the force, not to say the viciousness, with which he has eventually done so.

I find it difficult to decide where I stand in this Young-Tebbit clash. It rather reminds me of my feeling about whether it is better that the Fayed Brothers or Tiny Rowland should own Harrods. But it is impossible not to sympathize with Mrs Thatcher's persistent bad luck with favourites. It is easy to understand that she wanted a principal boy with more spring in his legs than Geoffrey Howe and more romantic-looking than Nigel Lawson. Tebbit ('the assassin', as he is apparently known to his admirers) has an air perhaps a little too menacing to play in

383

anything except *Treasure Island,* but Lord Young (the minister who brought her 'achievements rather than problems') was surely cut out for a real *Jack and the Beanstalk* role. Alas, it turned out that even he was more interested in getting to the top of the beanstalk (and in indiscreetly revealing what she said to him on the way up) than in cutting it down in her service. So she was left with only Mr Cecil Parkinson to rely on. And he, like Mr Norman Fowler, Mr Peter Walker *et al.,* may soon begin to find the call of spending more time with his family too strong to resist.

Lord Young's book has some virtues as well as faults. He emerges from it as a more and not less attractive character than I had thought him. He writes well about his family background, of his pietistic feeling as a member of an immigrant group, and of pride in his material success without in any way wishing to slough off this background. He is moving on his relations with his equally talented brother, the former chairman of the BBC, who died in 1986. He is also true to his subtitle, 'A Businessman in the Cabinet'. He may have been thrusting, but to an unusual extent he was interested in the details, often the tedious details, of administering his departments rather than in the higher politics that swirled around the Cabinet table.

This has its disadvantages as well as its advantages. It produces some dull narrative and some odd English. This latter misfortune is partly the result of a stylistic trick of using adjectives as nouns and nouns as adjectives. But it also comes from an addiction to opaque jargon. Although as a minister Lord Young was inordinately interested in presentation and treated his public relations adviser as at least as important as his permanent secretary, I find it difficult to believe that, because of their language, all of his announcements had as much impact as he could have hoped. I am still puzzling over one which he describes as 'probably as far-reaching as any that I made during my time in Government'. 'We announced', he writes, 'the additional spectrum for the existing cellular telephone service that would serve to relieve congestion within the M25.' After reading that four times I sympathize with Lord Young's feelings of 'culture shock' which he, again four times, says he experienced on moving to a new job.

He is also cavalier with his spelling of proper names, as indeed he is from time to time with syntax. The British Ambassador in Washington was not called Ackland. Lord Grimond does not spell his Christian name Joe, and the exact whereabouts of that great Brussels building, the Balleymont, escapes me.

Harold Wilson

This was a 1992 Observer *review of* Harold Wilson *by Ben Pimlott (HarperCollins).*

Pimlott's Life of Hugh Dalton, published in 1985, was the most relentlessly penetrating political biography that I can recall. It was in no way a hatchet job. It just turned on the X-ray machine and watched with clinical detachment both the healthy and diseased tissue which was exposed.

It rightly made Pimlott's reputation. Although he has produced no intermediate full-length biography his subsequent editing of Dalton's diaries, his various essays and reviews, together with the knowledge that he was working on this major study of Harold Wilson, have given him the status of the foremost Labour biographer. The expectation produced the same frisson of malicious excitement and more charitable apprehension that the news of Francis Bacon being called in to paint a portrait of a vulnerable chairman might, ten years ago, have aroused amongst the directors of a cautious and conventional company.

I therefore approached this book with two questions equally in my mind. First, would it show Pimlott's reputation to be too high; and second, would it show Wilson's to have long been too low? On the former point I was quickly reassured. For its first 280 pages (out of 730) I thought this an almost perfectly structured biography. This does not mean that it then (1963, when Wilson became leader of the Labour Party following Gaitskell's death) goes to pieces. On the contrary, it continues to be fascinating and penetrating in its account of Wilson's two premierships and of the dispiriting four years that separated them. But there are to my mind (and judging by very high standards) certain faults of construction which appear from this point forward.

Mr Pimlott writes up some issues to an extent that puts them out of proportion. It is not sensible at this stage to give us a 6000-word essay on the details of the Profumo case. This fault reflects itself more seriously in the long penultimate chapter. This is devoted to Wilson's entanglement with the Security Services and to an analysis of whether this was a factor in his resignation, whether there was anything in the ludicrous allegation that he was a Soviet agent, and what on earth provoked him to blow off to two unknown journalists who produced a sensational book called *The Pencourt File* and then either to regret what he had done or to lose all interest in the issue. The analysis is done with skill and judgement, but it is none the less an unfortunate wadge to be sitting so near to the end of the book and risks making Pimlott look on a par with the purveyors of sensational investigation, which he most certainly is not.

There are also a few signs of haste towards the end, although some of the unimportant errors of fact come earlier. The few that exist are curiously gratuitous. Very close to a subtle and convincing description of Wilson's approach to economic planning and the creation of the ill-fated Department of Economic Affairs, Pimlott suddenly informs us (for the second time) that

387

the St Ermin's Hotel (an old battleground in Labour history) is 'off the Strand'. It is not. It is behind St James's Park tube station. It does not matter where it is. However, unnecessary facts, which can have their interest, ought not to be brought in unless you know them. It is as though a great pianist, having gone faultlessly through a most difficult *scherzo,* suddenly struck a simple chord bang wrong.

These are all fairly minor faults. Pimlott's reputation survives intact, and is even enhanced. What about Lord Wilson's? Pimlott's verdict on him seems to me to be less clear than mine on Pimlott. At the end of the book I was far from certain what he believed, and what he wanted us to believe, about that sure-footed climber to the top of the greasy pole who dominated British politics between Macmillan and Thatcher, and who both won more victories for the Labour Party than any other leader and sowed the seeds of its decline into a party as weak on elect-ability as on a consistent direction of policy.

I do not regard this ambiguity as a biographical fault. It stems from the fact that Pimlott is more anxious to explain than to denounce or to justify. He unravels the complex issues of law and fact like an advocate before a sophisticated supreme tribunal rather than a police court lawyer going for a quick verdict. Thus there is a masterly description of the mixture of scholastic assur-ance (although within a narrow range of intellectual interest) and social wariness (although cosseted by a small close-knit family of similar tastes and outlook) with which Wilson's educational career advanced. At his various schools there was a story element of 'please, teacher, I know the answer' rather than of the mould-ing of his mind by easy companionships. At Oxford he flowered into an outstanding academic performer but not into an outstand-ing University figure. His exact contemporary, Edward Heath, who came from equally quiet beginnings and was less clever, was incomparably better known. Wilson allowed most aspects of Oxford life of the 1930s, from the Union or the Labour Club to excitement with the left-wing poets, or even exploring the then remote continent of Europe, to pass him by. However, he liked his 'other Oxford', became a fellow on graduating, was married in his BA gown and in the chapel of Mansfield, the nonconformist college, and would have made his wife happier by settling for life in the city of dreaming spires. Furthermore, Pimlott informs us, he was disappointed when, in 1977, University College (where his fellowship had been) preferred his solicitor, Lord Goodman, to himself as Master.

This admirably captures the half insider/half outsider position that characterized Wilson's relationship not only with Oxford but with the upper civil service, the Bevanite group, and indeed the British public. Pimlott is anxious to be fair to Wilson, and pays appropriate tribute to his nerve, his kindness, his good manners to colleagues (and to people generally), and to his willingness to undergo personal humiliation in order to hold his party together as an effective instrument of democratic government.

Yet you can almost hear Pimlott changing gear before his favourable passages. None the less I hope and believe that his book will mark an important stage in the recovery of Wilson's reputation which is already taking place. If I were a dealer in Prime Ministerial shares I would at present buy Wilsons as eagerly as I would sell Majors, although it is of course the case that there is room for a very sharp recovery in Wilsons before they begin to approach par.

The other thought with which I am left is that subjects who are alive, even if as quietly so as Lord Wilson alas is today, impose certain elusive but real limitations upon their biographers. Ben Pimlott has written a very good biography, but he has not written a definitive one. Philip Ziegler, whose more private-paper-assisted study is due out next year, need not fear that there is nothing more left to say. But even he will be writing with his subject in the wings. There is a lot to be said for allowing the doors of history to slam shut before the biographer gets to work. Widows are difficult enough, as several hopeful chroniclers have found, without having to cope with the living presence, immanent even if not interfering.

A NOTE ON THE AUTHOR

Elected to Parliament as a Labour member in 1948, Roy Jenkins (B: 1920) served in several major posts in Harold Wilson's First Government and as Home Secretary from 1965–1967. In 1987, Jenkins was elected to succeed Harold Macmillan as Chancellor of the University of Oxford following the latter's death, a position he held until his own death in 2003. Jenkins grew to political maturity during the twilight of a great age of British parliamentary democracy. As much as Churchill, though in quite a different way, Jenkins was from the cradle a creature of the system that nurtured Palmerston and Disraeli, Gladstone, Asquith and Lloyd George.